STUDIES IN PACIFIC HISTORY

In recent years scholars have begun to conceptualize the history of the Pacific Ocean as a subset of world history. This question is taken up in the introductory chapter of this volume, which sets out four periods of modern Pacific history: a silver period, 1570s-1750; a period of early integration, 1750–1850; a gold period, 1850-c.1900; and a period of imperial strategies after the gold rushes. The next chapter looks at the fur trade of the Pacific coast of America, and its dependence on markets in China and Russia, followed by a set which focuses on the era of the gold rushes in California, Australia, and New Zealand, when the pace of Pacific integration grew rapidly and new markets opened across the ocean. The last chapters examine aspects of the subsequent evolution of the Pacific Ocean into an 'American lake', looking in particular at the interlocking of politics and migration.

This volume carries forward study of the 'Pacific Centuries', promoting the conceptualization of the Pacific Ocean as a coherent unit of analysis, and providing further important steps toward provision of the multi-century framework that is required for proper understanding of today's 'Pacific Century'.

Studies in Pacific History
Economics, Politics, and Migration

Edited by

DENNIS O. FLYNN, ARTURO GIRÁLDEZ
University of the Pacific
and
JAMES SOBREDO
California State University, Sacramento

Routledge
Taylor & Francis Group
LONDON AND NEW YORK

First published 2002 by Ashgate Publishing

Reissued 2018 by Routledge
2 Park Square, Milton Park, Abingdon, Oxon OX14 4RN
711 Third Avenue, New York, NY 10017, USA

Routledge is an imprint of the Taylor & Francis Group, an informa business

A Library of Congress record exists under LC control number: 2001099633

ISBN 13: 978-1-138-73037-3 (hbk)
ISBN 13: 978-1-138-73034-2 (pbk)
ISBN 13: 978-1-315-18823-2 (ebk)

Contents

List of Figures, Maps, and Tables

Acknowledgments

Materials contained in this volume were presented in preliminary form at the third Pacific Centuries conference held at the University of the Pacific in Stockton, California in April 1998. This conference was co-organized with the California History Institute and the John Muir Center for Regional Studies, both of which are headquartered at the University of the Pacific. Special thanks to Professor Ron Limbaugh, Director of the John Muir Center at that time, and Pearl Piper, who handled a multitude of conference tasks with energy and grace. UOP's Eberhardt School of Business contributed a comfortable venue for conference sessions, thanks to ESB Dean Mark Plovnick. Robert Coburn, Professor of UOP's Conservatory of Music, organized a splendid "Concert Celebration of Music and Dance from Across the Pacific Region." Sharlene Messer and Heath Wheeler, able undergraduate research assistants, worked on this volume's production. Finally, the 1998 conference occurred because of a generous grant from the office of Dr Philip Gilbertson, Provost of the University of the Pacific, in collaboration with Robert Benedetti, Dean of the College of the Pacific.

We wish to thank Dr John Smedley, publisher, and Celia Hoare, Editor, of Ashgate Publishing, for provision of a forum for sharing thoughts about historical interconnections within and across one-third of the earth's surface.

1

In Search of Periodization for Pacific History: An Introduction

Dennis O. Flynn, Arturo Giráldez, and James Sobredo

Overview

In an opening plenary address at the initial 1994 'Pacific Centuries' conference at the University of the Pacific, K.N. Chaudhuri expressed skepticism that anyone had devoted serious attention to defining 'the Pacific' as a coherent unit of analysis. Aware of the legitimacy of this criticism, we nonetheless proceeded through two subsequent Pacific Centuries conferences in 1996 (Melbourne) and 1998 (Stockton) with faith that a clearer conceptual framework would emerge in due time.[1] Contributions by researchers since the first Pacific Centuries conference seven years ago, including the new essays of this volume, permit us to offer: (1) a clearer conceptualization of the Pacific as a unit of analysis, and (2) an attempt at periodization of Pacific history from the sixteenth through the nineteenth centuries.

The Pacific Ocean occupies one-third of the surface area of the planet, is larger than all earthly landmasses together, and is equal in area to the remaining oceans/seas combined. The Pacific is twice as large as the Atlantic Ocean and contains more than double the water (because of greater depth). Much economic and social coherence around the Pacific region stems ultimately from geological history. Colliding plates created the volcanic 'Ring of Fire' that encircles the world's greatest ocean. Subduction zones along the American (i.e. eastern) edge of the Pacific produced rugged, volcanic mountains that span the length of the Americas. Earthquakes and volcanic activity are characteristic of these mountain ranges, as well as of the islands and archipelagoes of the Pacific. It may be more accurate to describe the Pacific as an 'Ocean of Fire' rather than a 'Ring of Fire'. Since the oceanic islands are all volcanic, today's emphasis on the 'Rim' – and de-emphasis of Pacific islands – indeed makes little sense in terms of geology or history. The mid-twentieth-century 'War in the Pacific', for example, mainly involved battles over control of crucial islands. Control of island ports and island resources are fundamental to understanding the history of the Pacific from the beginning.

Plate tectonics and the Ocean of Fire may initially seem tangential topics for the study of history, but we believe that consideration of geologic/geographic conditions is essential to a more complete understanding of the history of the Pacific. Conceptualization of long-term history necessitates discussion of human opportunities and constraints, both of which are largely determined, in turn, by the natural environment. Specifically, we have in mind tectonic forces that endowed smoldering mountains around the Pacific's edge with vast holdings of metals. Indeed, nothing influenced trade relations around the Pacific Ocean more – from the mid-sixteenth century to the mid-nineteenth century – than the production and shipment of metals.

The silver period

From the mid-sixteenth century to the mid-eighteenth century, the exchange of Peruvian and Mexican silver for Chinese exports (especially silks and porcelains) dominated the trans-Pacific commercial world.[2] Tectonic forces – on the Americas side of the Pacific – made possible discovery of unprecedented silver deposits in the Andes and in Mexico beginning in the 1540s. Japanese silver production – on the Asian side of the Pacific – was also immense in the sixteenth and seventeenth centuries (perhaps half as large as total Spanish American output). Virtually all Japanese silver was exported to China. China was simultaneously the end market for the bulk of the silver emanating from American mines. China became the dominant 'suction pump' for world silver production because the price of silver in China was double its price in the rest of the sixteenth century world. Unsurprisingly, merchants worldwide recognized that it was profitable to buy silver cheaply in Japan, Spanish America, and Europe and sell it at lofty prices in markets connected to China. This protracted phenomenon signaled one of world history's most spectacular cases of arbitrage trade, buying a product cheaply in one sub-market and selling it dearly in another.

We know why the value of silver had escalated so dramatically in China. Collapse of China's paper-money system in the fifteenth century, combined with subsequent conversion of China's tax system to a silver basis, resulted in a protracted 'silverization' of Chinese society.[3] Given that China contained a quarter of world population at the time (not to mention Chinese tributary states that were also wedded to silver), demand-side dynamics emanating from within China caused Chinese silver prices to rise dramatically. Europeans played the role of middlemen on the global silver stage; they were important intermediaries between American and Japanese mines (on the production side) and the Chinese marketplace (the end-market). It is worth emphasizing that an overwhelming preponderance of world silver production occurred around the Ocean of Fire. On the supply side, geological conditions predetermined the locations of silver-rich American and Japanese mines. On the demand side, dynamics emerging from China's silverization guaranteed that the earth's most populous country would become the world's main silver client all the way into the early twentieth century.

Two general themes arise from analysis of the 'silver period' just discussed. First, Pacific Basin geography is unique. An important aspect of this uniqueness has been mentioned: tectonic activity led to unusual concentrations of metals around the perimeter of the Pacific, the rim of an Ocean of Fire. Other aspects of Pacific geography assured that certain nodal points would become crucial for both Pacific and world history. The American side of the Pacific contains few natural harbors. The excellent bay at Acapulco, however, was strategically located and therefore served as a crucial trade link along the eastern shores of the Pacific. Favorable ocean currents and trade winds permitted Acapulco's rise as the main American entrepôt linking Mexican/Peruvian silver to crucial markets on the Asian side of the Pacific.[4] Manila Bay furnished an equally crucial harbor/entrepôt on the Asian side of the Pacific. As is true of airports today, it was useless in times past to possess the right to embark from one port in the absence of secure landing rights at the destination port. Yet, no European state possessed sufficient military power to control a mainland Asian state up through the middle of the eighteenth century. European interlopers were either: (a) convenient collaborators who were tolerated on Asian home soil (e.g. the Portuguese and Dutch in Nagasaki and the Portuguese in Macao); or (b) they were compelled to seek defensible ports among thousands of islands in archipelagoes off the Asian mainland (e.g. the Portuguese in Goa, the Portuguese and Dutch in Malacca, and so on). Spain had the good fortune to gain control of one of Asia's best natural harbors, Manila Bay. The Spanish Crown did its best to monopolize trade between Acapulco and Manila (although smuggling was rampant), while profiting mightily in the process, but Chinese merchants dominated the trade leg between Manila and the Asian mainland. Indeed, Chinese merchants outnumbered Spaniards in the city of Manila by a wide margin. Geography on the Asian side of the Pacific was once again crucial, in other words, including the location and configuration of archipelagoes. Mutually beneficial collaboration between Spanish and Chinese trading interests (eruptions of confrontation and bloodshed in Manila notwithstanding) evolved in the context of unique geographic formations, as well as convenient access to the world's biggest markets.

While Spain was remarkably successful in controlling most of the Atlantic silver trade, crucial ocean trade routes that connected Europe and Asia had previously fallen under the control of the Portuguese and the Dutch. Spain dominated the Atlantic leg of silver's journey to China, in other words, but was shut out of the Europe-to-Asia leg of the global silver trade. Thus, the Acapulco–Manila trade route via the Pacific represented perhaps Spain's only hope of interfacing directly with Chinese merchants. Manila became the linchpin of Pacific trade; and her galleons yielded immense profits for the Spanish Crown in the process.[5]

During the mid-sixteenth to mid-eighteenth century 'silver period', it is in a sense true that the Acapulco–Manila galleons linkage of the Americas with Asia was narrow and limited. Immense profits from silver and silk commerce indeed riveted the attention of Spanish, Chinese and other merchant interests. But the vast

Pacific beyond this crucial thread of trade was considered mostly irrelevant by superpowers focused on trade profits. It is important to recognize, on the other hand, that trans-Pacific trade also introduced biological/ecological exchanges of immense importance to Pacific and world history. John McNeill calls this environmental connection a 'Magellan Exchange' counterpart to Alfred Crosby's much-discussed 'Columbian Exchange' across the Atlantic Ocean.[6] Not only did AfroEurAsian diseases eventually devastate Pacific Island populations in percentages reminiscent of the well-known demographic collapse of Native Americans, but many American plants also reached Asia (and Pacific Islands) aboard the very Acapulco–Manila galleons that carried silver through the Philippines. These galleons represented an important vector through which the American sweet potato, peanut, corn, tobacco and other flora were introduced into China. American food crops, in turn, contributed to a substantial increase in Chinese population during the eighteenth century.[7] Reverberations throughout world markets in response to China's eighteenth-century population growth must certainly have been huge, yet we have been able to find little discussion of this complex and important topic.[8]

Before leaving discussion of the Pacific's 'silver period', a significant non-precious metal deserves brief mention. Tectonic dynamics also generated tremendous copper mines around the Pacific. At a time when Japanese silver mines were playing out in the latter half of the seventeenth century, Japan became the world's largest source of copper (producing twice as much as did Sweden in the late-seventeenth century).[9] Most Japanese copper was exported to Asian markets, especially China, but significant quantities of copper were also exported to Europe. We have found no evidence to suggest that significant Japanese copper exports across the Pacific to the Americas during Japanese copper's heyday, but this mining boom is an important subject of Pacific history nonetheless. Chile became a major copper producer along the eastern edge of the Pacific Ocean of Fire much later on, but integration of the Chilean copper story into a multi-century fabric of Pacific history will have to await the efforts of scholars with specialized knowledge of this topic.

Exploration and early integration of the South and North Pacific with 'the Rim' c.1750–c.1850

Between the end of the 'silver period' in the mid-eighteenth century and initiation of a 'gold period' in the mid-nineteenth century, intensified exploration combined with new commercial opportunities to yield further integration of the Pacific region. As early as 1669, an age of exploration began with Dampier's voyage contributing Australia to the global map. Voyages by Bouganville and Cook a century later added Tahiti, Samoa, eastern Australia, New Zealand, and Hawaii to the list of 'new worlds' to be explored by Europeans. These Pacific lands became more fully integrated with continental societies as new technologies and business opportunities evolved. Sometimes the consequences were devastating in environmental terms. For example, attractive sandalwood prices in China induced the King of Hawaii to set island forests ablaze in order to detect the distinctive odor of sandalwood; this was evidently the least expensive way to determine the whereabouts of this valuable product.[10]

Sheep were introduced in Australia when this made sense for the textile industry. And plantations likewise emerged on islands around the Pacific when conditions were favorable for continental markets for sugar, tobacco, and other tropical products. Plantations around the Pacific mainly employed native or Asian wage laborers. Pacific plantation history therefore followed paths distinct in many ways from Atlantic plantations based on African slave labor. Having said this, it nonetheless seems peculiar to us that precious little scholarly attention has been paid to the African Diaspora in the Pacific.[11] Africans were dispersed widely throughout the Pacific since the sixteenth century – in Mexico City, Manila, Nagasaki, Batavia, Beijing, and so on – yet blacks of the Pacific are routinely excluded from discourse on the African Diaspora. But this is the sort of neglect that renders Pacific Centuries a vibrant research area with numerous opportunities.

Once the main thrust of the 'silver period' ended around 1750, the Chinese marketplace continued to dominate Pacific trade and imperial policies after that date.[12] Jim Hardee's article on the trade in California animal skins will be discussed more completely in a moment, but his label 'soft gold' for animal skins is both interesting and an appropriate subject for this volume. Like gold and silver, animal skins can be considered natural resources that could be (and were) depleted when heavily exploited. And like silver (but unlike gold), Hardee informs us that China was a principle market for animal skins harvested along America's Pacific coast. Indeed, the northward spread of Spanish missions up California's coast was a response to southward expansions by non-Spanish fur traders, especially Russians. A general conclusion arising from the work of Hardee and others is that the histories of peoples around and within the Pacific involved long-distance links for centuries. Much of what passes for local history cannot, in fact, be properly understood without consideration of global connections. Indeed, the main unifying theme to have emerged from the first three Pacific Centuries conferences is that China dominated the demand-side of numerous Pacific market products over several centuries (e.g. silver, sandalwood, sea cucumbers, mercury, and so on).[13]

The gold period

Following the main 'silver period' and an interim period of exploration and 'soft gold' animal skins, another precious metal – gold – ushered in the next major phase in Pacific history. The 'gold period' began with California discoveries in

1848, followed shortly thereafter by discoveries in Australia and New Zealand. Half of the articles in this volume involve – either directly or indirectly – these nineteenth century gold rushes.

Individual articles in this volume

Silver Period 1571–c.1750

None of the articles in the present volume deal with the silver period as described above, although contributions to previous Pacific Centuries volumes do discuss the birth and evolution of trans-Pacific relations up to 1750.[14]

The exploration and early integration period c.1750–c.1850

"Soft Gold: Animal Skins and the Early Economy of California," by Jim Hardee, contradicts the myth that pre-gold-rush hunters and trappers along the American coast were autarkic characters operating locally in isolated environments. Pre-gold-rush trade in animal skins along the California coast was in fact firmly linked to intercontinental markets connected via the Pacific Ocean.

Abundant sea otter pelts enticed Russian ships to travel farther and farther along the Aleutian chain and down toward California. But this Russian maritime expansion was also a response to vigorous demand for sea otter furs within Russia; Siberian merchants had long monopolized this trade by sending regular caravans across the Gobi desert to the Russian border. Merchants were well aware of Chinese demand as well, since sea otter prices in Canton had risen to $80 and $100 per pelt during the last quarter of the eighteenth century, bringing "vast changes to the economy of the Pacific Rim" (p. 1). Indeed, spectacular skin prices simultaneously attracted the intense interest of English, French, Spanish, and American merchants and authorities. Soon after British Captain James Hanna shipped sea otter skins directly to Canton in the 1780s – via the Hawaiian Islands – the old caravan trade routes were abandoned. Russian and American collaborators established hunting bases along the coast, consciously avoiding Spanish population centers that spread up the coast to block them. Collections of otter skins peaked at perhaps 8,000 to 17,000 annually between 1804 and 1812, leading to depleted sea otter populations in California around 1815. American beaver trappers invaded coastal waters during the 1820s in any case, and by 1835 the sea otter trade had virtually ceased.

Prior to the close of the eighteenth century, however, cattle raising had become the chief source of food, occupation, trade, and wealth in California. Between 1822 and 1834, Catholic missions were the source of most California hides (from their combined herd of perhaps 500,000 cattle). New Englanders derived considerable advantage from the hide and tallow trade, according to Hardee, and "California furnished enough leather to give Connecticut and Massachusetts a monopoly on the early boot and shoe industry in the USA" (p. 12).

Beaver trappers next invaded California's interior waters. California was a relatively minor source of beaver pelts, but these trappers opened important overland routes to the Pacific coast. For example, regular commerce was opened between Los Angeles and St. Louis via Santa Fe, New Mexico. Mexican goods were brought from Santa Fe to the coast, including Mexican silver destined for China. On the return journey Asian silks, spices, and other products flowed eastward overland from the Pacific. Hardee's work is important because central aspects of California history are framed in terms of global markets, as opposed to the conventional practice of depicting these issues as local phenomena. California was connected to Pacific markets long before its famous Gold Rush.

The gold period c. second-half of the nineteenth century

"San Francisco's Pacific Exports, 1850–1898" by David J. St. Clair provides export data for the port of San Francisco during the second half of the nineteenth century. California mines produced over $300 million worth of gold from 1854 through 1859, about 80 per cent of which was exported to eastern US destinations (England received the remaining 20 per cent). Practically all California gold was exported eastward, while silver flowed westward to the Pacific. Its famous gold rush notwithstanding, California was itself on a *de facto* silver money standard. Since Nevada's Comstock mines did not begin silver production until 1859, Mexican pesos were imported into California while gold was simultaneously exported during the 1850s. Mexican pesos fed California's monetary appetite for silver, but they were also re-exported to China in volume (via San Francisco). True, silver comprised only 5.4 per cent of combined California gold and silver exports during the 1854–63 gold boom, but it is important to note that the white metal flowed westward to China (in the opposite direction of gold flows). Even when Comstock silver production heated up later on (1882–98), re-exported Mexican silver dollars comprised over half of the silver exported into the Pacific via San Francisco.

After 1870, non-metal exports from California were dominated by wheat, followed by flour, wool, and quicksilver. Exports of wheat to Great Britain surged, while flour was exported mainly to China. Over 80 per cent of California's mercury production (sometimes comprising two-thirds of world production) was exported to China and Mexico. Notwithstanding these trends, California's trade with Hawaii, Latin America, and British Columbia was often even greater than its trade with China in the late nineteenth century. Except for gold and wheat exports, according to St. Clair, the California economy was linked closely to Pacific forces: "Indeed, aside from the huge wheat trade with England, San Francisco [non-gold] exports are best characterized as the exports of a diverse set of products all around the Pacific" (p. 38).

"Powerhouse Economies of the Pacific: A Comparative Study of Gold and Wheat in nineteenth Century Victoria and California," by Warwick Frost, compares the great gold rushes of California (1848 onwards) and Victoria (1851 onwards) as well as their attendant booms in wheat production. Both areas were pastoral prior to the discoveries of gold, but Victoria was far more developed initially. Melbourne, the capital city of Victoria, for example, boasted a population of 23,000 at the time of Australian gold discoveries; San Francisco contained perhaps 500 inhabitants. Vigorous wool exports explain early dynamism in Victoria. Indeed, Victoria's population was 40 per cent larger than that of all of California by 1860, and even in 1870 Victoria's population exceeded that of California by 150,000 inhabitants. California became slightly more populous by 1880 and 1890, then surged to a 25 per cent advantage by 1900. Even with the tremendous population boom of San Francisco during the second half of the nineteenth century, Melbourne's population (494,000) was still larger than that of San Francisco (439,000) by the turn of the century in 1900.

There was tremendous urban growth in Victoria's gold towns, while California's urban growth was concentrated in non-gold towns. At its peak, California's Grass Valley was only 15 per cent the size of Victoria's Ballarat, while Nevada City never surpassed 8 per cent of Ballarat's size. Even the capital of California, Sacramento, contained only half the population of Ballarat by 1880. One explanation for this phenomenon is simply that Australian gold deposits lasted longer than did their California counterparts. Ballarat and Bendigo were also surrounded by extensive agricultural hinterlands, while the foothills of the Sierra Nevada mountains were limited in terms of agricultural potential.

Both California and Victoria were major areas of wheat production during the second half of the nineteenth century (indeed, California wheat was exported to Australia during the early stages of the latter's gold rush). Wheat production collapsed in both areas at the turn of the century, however, as California's wheat production fell 85% between 1896 and 1909, while Central Victoria's wheat production shrank by 88% between 1876 and 1894. Frost argues that falling wheat prices (a popular explanation for declining production) cannot in fact explain the acreage decrease in either location. Indeed, during the first decade of the twentieth century wheat acreage dropped in California despite a rise in wheat prices there. Another explanation for decline is soil exhaustion, but Frost finds little evidence to support this contention either. Rather, he finds convincing evidence that suggests that rising prices for non-wheat crops offer the best explanation for the switch away from wheat production in both Victoria and Central California. Studies of comparable areas around the Pacific can shed light on many developments that remain obscure when they are viewed (incorrectly) as isolated phenomena.

"New Zealand and the Gold Rushes of the Mid-Nineteenth Century," by Kenneth E. Jackson, reminds us that New Zealand experienced a gold rush (in 1861) that began in earnest one decade after its Australian counterpart (1851). New Zealand had been both positively and negatively impacted by the Australian boom of the 1850s. On the positive side, New Zealanders exported products into the trans-Tasman economy, but there was also a negative resource movement effect in the sense that population was lost to Australia. Australia's gold boom attracted grain imports both from New Zealand and California (California's own gold rush boom notwithstanding).

The Australian discoveries of 1851 no doubt prompted a search for gold in New Zealand. Indeed, government inducements were offered to anyone who could locate a substantial gold deposit in New Zealand and the big payoff began in 1861. Jackson utilizes a three-sector model to analyze the impact of gold discoveries on New Zealand: gold represents the booming tradable sector, while wool is the lagging tradable sector, and services the non-tradable sector. As expected, a resource movement into the booming gold sector within New Zealand did indeed put a cost squeeze on the other sectors, especially the other tradable – wool – during the early 1860s. Wool exports accounted for over 50 per cent of total exports in 1855, but mineral exports shot past 70 per cent of total exports in the early 1860s. In the longer term, however, rapid immigration into New Zealand from Australia seems to have offset domestic labor shortages, and increased spending by the expanding population tended to dominate the resource movement effects, especially for the service sector. Wool producers did suffer, but they were also able to switch to meat production. The Australian gold rush led to immigration rather than rising standards of living, and the same mechanism seems to have held for New Zealand. The domestic manufacturing sector expanded after the decline of gold, but large employment opportunities awaited the advent of refrigeration in the 1890s, when primary processing rather than manufacturing led the way. Jackson concludes that there "are similar mechanisms at work in the New Zealand, Californian and Australian cases, but the speed, strength of the impact and the eventual outcomes are all different in terms of the detail. By considering the interaction between them it can be seen that there was a Pacific rim economy effect as well as their own internal impacts, and that this effect was not confined to the population shifts between them" (p. 70).

In "Gold Rush California Bound: New Evidence from French Passenger Lists," Annick Foucrier provides quantitative evidence concerning the 'forgotten migrants' of the Gold Rush – the French. French passenger lists and passports in French county archives furnish a rich sample of 1,722 passengers sailing for California aboard 32 different ships between September 14, 1849 and April 9, 1852. The average age of male passengers was 31.70 years, while the average age of women migrants was 29.15 years; half of the women over 20 were married, while women in general comprised 8.6 per cent of all migrants (a relatively high figure compared with other nationalities). The lure of gold was a powerful attraction indeed, but Foucrier also points out that the "amazing variety of trades involved attests to the power of the general economic crisis in France at the time" (p. 83). Most of these migrants proceeded first to the mines, but soon thereafter returned to San Francisco where they tried to practice their professions as bakers, butchers, cooks, tailors or hatters. Others became laundry workers, a needed profession at the time.

That portion of the English-language literature that does not neglect French migrants entirely tends to focus on the arrival of paupers, the *Lingots*, but Foucrier points out that only perhaps 3,000 people belonged to this category, out of 25,000 to 30,000 French people who migrated to California during this period. Recent French authors also frequently mischaracterize French migrants, including what Foucrier labels "inconsistent fantasies" involving the assertion that Napoleon placed Parisian prostitutes on California-bound ships in order to rid the French capital of them. Foucrier's archival information shows that, on the contrary, artisans, merchants, and gentlemen were over-represented among migrants, and most of them were literate. French male migrants to California were wealthier than their fellow migrants to other parts of the United States, probably because travel to the west coast was more expensive. Ten per cent of the female migrants from France were actresses, and they were considerably more educated than female immigrants to the US generally. Foucrier's data indicate that "[c]ontrary to the mythical and popular image of the French in the Gold Rush, adventurers, soldiers of fortune, and prostitutes – although high in profile – actually comprised a very small minority" (p. 85). French immigrants were relatively successful in California, and the impact of gold remittances back to France is a topic that deserves future scholarly attention.

The time frame of "The Rim of Fire: Pacific Rim Cities and the Problem of Fires," by Lionel Frost, extends before and after nineteenth-century gold rushes around the Pacific, but it primarily focuses on population booms during the second half of the nineteenth century. Asia contained virtually all the major cities on the Pacific Rim at the dawn of the nineteenth century. And there was a new burst of population growth in Asian behemoth-cities during the second half of the nineteenth century as well (with the Chinese city of Hankow reaching 1 million inhabitants by 1890 and Shanghai 3 million by 1930), but smaller dynamos were emerging in the Americas and Australia simultaneously. During the 1850s alone the population of US Pacific states rose from 106,000 to 444,000, and the colony of Victoria, Australia rose from 76,000 to 540,000. (Noting that in 1858, however, Chinese comprised 40,000 out of 140,000 inhabitants of Victoria's goldfields.) Intense urbanization around the Pacific during the second half of the nineteenth century created tremendous challenges in terms of providing suitable infrastructure, including aspects related to fire control.

Frost documents fire hazards around the Pacific. As new residents flooded into cities constructed of combustible materials, and containing flammable liquid and solid items, fires devastated Pacific Rim cities with regularity. In Frost's words, most of these cities "were highly combustible lumps of capital" (p. 93). Over 800 major fires have been recorded in Edo (Tokyo) since 1602, while over 200 important fires plagued Hankow in 1880 alone. All of the cities at or near gold fields around the Pacific suffered fires repeatedly – including Sacramento, San Francisco, Melbourne, Ballarat, Seattle, and so on – but all of these paled in comparison with Asian fires, such as those that killed 140,000 people in Tokyo and Yokohama in 1923 as a result of the Great Kanto Earthquake.

Some urban areas seemed to devise successful strategies to deal with age-old problems surrounding the threat of fire. Urban fires continued to plague some areas, while other places managed to largely escape fire as a continuous threat. And Lionel Frost offers a number of tantalizing explanatory glimpses. Leaders in all urban areas confronted a Prisoner's Dilemma in terms of fire-retardation policies: it made sense for each owner to build his/her structure of cheap, flammable materials because frequent fires caused him/her to rebuild frequently. Why not invest as little as possible in one's structure itself, while protecting liquid assets in fire-proof containers in order to pay the cost of rebuilding after the next fire? Indeed, people followed this strategy all over the Pacific. As time passed, however, newer cities in Australia and the Americas developed far more successful anti-fire strategies than did their Asian counterparts. Why? Aside from policies such as the mandating of wider streets (that provided fire breaks), sub-urbanization ameliorated many problems. Even when suburban structures contained flammables, space between buildings reduced the threat of a conflagration. The building of suburbs required substantial expenditures on social infrastructure, on the other hand, and a sufficient financial base must exist in order for taxpayer capacity to permit implementation of a suburb-building strategy. Immigrants to all of the gold rush areas were relatively affluent, according to Lionel Frost, otherwise transportation costs from such formidable distances around the world would have been impossible. (Note that Foucrier also stressed this requirement of a certain level of affluence among French immigrants to California during its gold rush.) In contrast, ancient and huge Asian cities had long been inundated with poor immigrants traveling by foot. These cities were so much larger that implementation of sub-urbanization policies would seem to have been more formidable in any case. Comparisons among locations around the vast Pacific portend much benefit for the field of urban history, according to Frost, and extension of his analysis of fire policy to the cities of Latin America and Pacific islands would assuredly yield additional, worthwhile insights.

Imperial strategies after the gold period

The US Pacific coast differs from its Atlantic coast counterpart in that the Pacific contains few natural harbors in comparison with the abundance of harbors along the Atlantic coast. San Diego is the southernmost Pacific port. Moving northward we encounter the largest of them all, Los Angeles/Long Beach, before reaching San Francisco/Oakland, Portland, Seattle, and finally Anchorage. Thus, the American Pacific contains only seven major ports north of Mexico (when Vancouver, BC is thrown into the mix). It is worth noting that practically all the US West Coast population either surrounds those seven ports, or lives in urban areas connected by water, roads, or rails to those seven Pacific ports. For many purposes, it makes more sense to categorize international trade in 'Pacific' versus 'Atlantic' terms, than to aggregate trade from both coasts into a 'US trade' concept. Korean and Japanese steel coils, for example, compete vigorously with steel coils produced on/near the US Pacific coast, whereas steel coils produced in Pennsylvania compete with European counterparts that are connected via the Atlantic Ocean. In other words, it makes sense to speak of a Pacific market for steel coils today, as distinct from an Atlantic market for steel coils, because cheap water transportation unites markets that share the same ocean, especially when considering bulky items such as steel coils. Ocean ports play exceedingly important economic and social roles at the dawn of the twenty-first century. As we cast our gaze backward over trade history, cost advantages of water transportation over land transportation seem to have been, if anything, more pronounced the further one projects backward into times past. Many important innovations in land transportation – the US transcontinental railroad, for example – were indeed significant in linking previously remote areas to preexisting, vibrant oceanic transportation networks.

Connections to Pacific ports were crucially important for Utah coal from the late-nineteenth century to the middle of the twentieth century, as demonstrated by Nancy J. Taniguchi in "World War I, the American Interior, and Pacific Markets: A Look at Distant Markets." At its commercial inception in the 1880s, Utah coal had been tied to a large market network, albeit one oriented eastward via railroads connecting to mines and silver-lead smelters in Colorado. Indeed, railroads themselves developed Central Utah coal mines for the express purpose of vertically integrating their business operations. All Western trains used coal for fuel, so access to abundant supplies of this crucial, relatively low-value substance was crucial to the survival and success of railroads. After Alexander Graham Bell transmitted speech through copper wire in 1876 and New York City began to electrify street lights via copper wires in 1882, the richest deposit of copper sulfide ever was discovered at Butte, Montana in late 1882. The Anaconda smelter was completed in 1884, and Anaconda immediately contracted with eastern Utah's largest coal producer to provide 150–200 tons of coke per day, seven days a week. A second massive copper discovery near Salt Lake City occurred at the end of the century. As the United States electrified in the late nineteenth and early twentieth centuries, demand for both copper and coal soared. The expanding sugar refining industry in Utah and Idaho also ran on coal as well. Utah coal abandoned its eastward-only orientation.

There was a sharp business downturn during the Panic of 1907, but President Theodore Roosevelt soon sent his Great White Fleet cruising throughout the Pacific in 1908. This fleet's fuel demand helped revive the Utah coal industry. By 1910 the Western Pacific railroad reached Oakland, California, furnishing Utah coal fields a direct route to the Pacific coast. Completion of the Panama Canal in 1914 provided even further impetus to Pacific demand for Utah coal. Woodrow Wilson meantime signed the Underwood–Simmons Tariff in late 1913, however, and this bill removed monopolistic protections for US coal producers. British Columbian coal poured into Pacific markets as a result, and Utah coal production fell 20 per cent by May 1914. Protections for other US industries vanished simultaneously. Utah sugar faced competition from Philippine sugar, for example, and Utah sugar was a major purchaser of Utah coal. The wartime British Parliament declared copper a contraband trade item in November 1914; Utah copper production declined sharply, which again generated a negative impact on Utah coal. European copper production was no longer available to the US marketplace, however, and US wartime demand in the Pacific rose dramatically. Utah copper production soon surged dramatically and Utah's excellent coke coal became essential for iron and steel production required by US war industries. Utah sugar competed desperately for coal as well. Coal prices soared some fourfold in 1917. A new United States Fuel Administration grouped Utah together with other Rocky Mountain states into a single Pacific coast zone; Wyoming coal was sent eastward, separating it from Utah's coal market for the first time in history. When peace broke out in late 1918, the Utah coal industry went into a tailspin. The depression in Utah coal was partially mitigated by shipments of its product via Pacific ports to South America and Japan after World War I, but the Great Depression deflated the market tremendously. When other industries switched from coal to gas or diesel, and when cooking began to switch to electricity, the coal industry depression continued. Good times awaited surging demand by Utah and California steel producers during World War II. After World War II, Utah coal mines became captive to US companies along the Pacific Coast. The Japanese Itochu Corporation purchased three Utah coal mines in 1996, whose production it shipped from a new Los Angeles Export Terminal. Utah coal's firm entrenchment with Pacific markets is not as recent as most would suspect. Is its history of Pacific linkages unique? Taniguchi offer an understandable plea: "Studies of other locales and industries are needed to compare the depth and breadth of commercial influence tied to our western seas" (p. 122).

Katharine Bjork's "Race and the Right Kind of Island: Immigration Policy in Hawaii and Cuba under US Auspices, 1899–1912" explores debates concerning immigration to Cuba and Hawaii in the aftermath of the Cuban-Spanish-American War and Hawaii's annexation to the US in 1898, particularly issues having to do with race and citizenship under US auspices. Cuba and Hawaii faced similar questions relating to immigration and labor policies because both were dominated by plantation agriculture. Debates over the future of these two semi-autonomous, sugar-based plantation societies were polarized around two racialized alternatives for labor immigration, "bracero" versus "citizen" models.

About 125,000 Chinese contract laborers migrated to Cuba between 1847 and 1874, but both state and planter interests in Cuba were later united in their preference for white immigrants (particularly settlers from the Iberian peninsula and the Canary Islands) between the Spanish-American War and World War I. The idea was that the white elite could thereby protect itself from being overrun by a black population. Black, non-Spanish speaking laborers were finally imported nonetheless, but only because Cuba's sugar industry grew faster than could the influx of white labor immigrants. Notwithstanding US law to the contrary, restrictions on the immigration of contract laborers were lifted entirely in 1900 when Cuba's labor pool was inadequate. Colonial industrial needs triumphed over American principles that were no longer deemed applicable to this peripheral area.

In the Hawaiian case, European immigration – especially Southern European 'citizens' – were likewise perceived by the US government (and Teddy Roosevelt in particular) as a superior alternative to 'oriental' labor. This advocacy of 'citizen labor' in Hawaii was, however, inconsistent with Hawaiian planters' desire to continue 'oriental' labor migration under contract. Labor migration under contract had, in fact, served as the primary mechanism for assuring sufficient tractable labor for the plantations of Hawaii and Cuba from the end of slavery, but since 1885 US law had prohibited immigration of laborers under contract. Thus, closer ties to the United States suggested new sources of immigration (former slaves from the US South and Puerto Ricans, for example), yet US immigration laws also excluded traditional sources of 'oriental' labor supplies. The Hawaii Sugar Planters' Association (HSPA) encouraged fragmentation of the workforce along ethnic lines and paid differential wage rates for the same work. Divisions actually had more to do with class relations than with race or color definitions, since Hawaiians tended to be grouped with 'whites'. In both Hawaii and Cuba, the extension of US immigration laws necessitated new strategies for meeting the 'labor problem'. Race provided colonizers with a convenient language for categorizing and managing colonial projects, from organizing labor migration to dealing psychologically with the novel challenges of colonial administration.

James Sobredo's essay, "The 1934 Tydings–McDuffie Act and Filipino Exclusion: Social, Political, and Economic Context Revisited," addresses the immigration and exclusion of Filipino Americans. The Philippines became a colony of the United States at the conclusion of the 1898 Spanish-American War, an event that also symbolized the emergence of the United States as a world superpower. Historically, citizens of conquered territories became subjects of the conquering nation. Citizenship was synonymous with subject status, but in this case the United States Supreme Court made a distinction between citizens and subjects. In Gonzalez vs. Williams in 1904, the Court provided legal justification for American imperialism by stating that the constitution allows for the acquisition of conquered territories and colonies outside of the contiguous United States. Filipinos would not, however, be granted citizenship rights. The Court ruled that they were political "wards" of the United States and would have the legal status of "nationals."

It is within this political and legal context that Filipinos immigrated to the United States, following in the footsteps of Chinese, Indian, Korean and Japanese immigrants from Asia. Asians provided the agricultural economies of Hawaii and California with a cheap and reliable source of labor, but during economic downturns Filipinos became scapegoats, as had previous Asian immigrants. Sobredo argues that it was not economic and political factors alone that led to the passage of the Tydings–McDuffie Act. Race relations also played a crucial role in the passage of this legislation, which granted the Philippines independence and simultaneously stopped Filipino immigration.

In "Communists, Christians, and Japanese Imperial Subjects: Okanawan Immigrants within the Japanese Diaspora, 1899 to 1941," Edith Kaneshiro re-examines the experiences of Okinawan immigrants beyond Hawaii and South America. Contrasts between Okinawan immigrants in southern California and Okinawan immigrants in Mindanao (the Philippines) prior to the outbreak of war between the US and Japan in 1941 are the focus of her study. Recent research has challenged the conventional depiction of poverty and backwardness in Okinawa as a force pushing migrants out; rather, emigration occurred in the wealthier regions of the island. Indeed, since contract labor laws were gradually abolished in the western hemisphere, only those Okinawans who could afford to travel as free migrants voyaged to Hawaii and North America. Transoceanic voyages may have been three times more expensive for Asian immigrants crossing the Pacific than was passage for European counterparts crossing the Atlantic.

For many decades exchanges between British merchants and China were organized through the Canton system, but with Britain riding the wave of Industrial Revolution during the nineteenth century, the Canton system came to end with the Opium Wars in 1839–42. Five ports were forced open to trade and Hong Kong fell under the control of the British Crown. New steamships and guns produced by English industry were decisive in overthrowing the Canton trade system. With this background in mind, Frank H.H. King's "Hong Kong: Constitutional Development and Corporate Culture" tries to answer the following question. How could Hong Kong be British for 150 years, yet lack a constitution with traditional British constitutional voting rights until immediately prior to its 1997 incorporation by China?

Professor King divides British colonies into three categories: (a) colonies of settlement, (b) colonies on trust, and (c) 'special purpose' territories. Territories falling under the first two categories did achieve democracy in one form or another, but Hong Kong's status as a 'special purpose' territory led to an absence of democratic developments. The first Sino-British war resulted in British occupation of Chusan and Hong Kong. The British abandoned Chusan precisely because it contained a sizable Chinese community. Hong Kong became a military base occupied, not for the purpose of colonization, but explicitly for diplomatic, commercial, and military purposes. There was never a social contract; a governor was responsible only to London. The Chinese population became the main group in time, but this had nothing to do with the purpose of Hong Kong from the beginning. It was for the British merchants – and their protection – that the territory was established. A small group of elite merchants advised the governor.

British firms hired and trained employees in Britain; juniors continued with the same firm until retirement. Social life in the Colony reflected separation among different levels within companies and among different ethnic groups. The closed business culture existed in order to control managers and employees who otherwise could be influenced by powers outside of the firm. Matrimony with foreigners was discouraged. Members of a business usually belonged to the same sports club. (The opium trade – the India link – played a crucial role in the Colony's commerce. Discussing the possibility of extinction of the opium habit among the Chinese, in 1907 the British Finance Minister in Calcutta estimated a loss of revenue in India of 3.66 million British pounds per year.[15]) Only by the mid-1960s had the corporate culture changed sufficiently for Portuguese and Chinese to replace expatriate British managers. At the same time, local companies began to participate in the global marketplace in less circumscribed ways. Many began to view Hong Kong as a "free and international city," but colonial powers felt otherwise. Hong Kong was viewed as a trade and financial entrepôt, as always, and the influence of China was to be minimized. Only after 1970 was constitutional reform argued. Hong Kong returned to Chinese sovereignty without a democratic government in 1997, a final outcome of the Opium Wars.

While Hong Kong was a strategic possession for the economic fortunes of the British Empire, China was also an essential component of the strategy of United States Pacific policy in terms of the annexation of Guam, Wake Island, and the Philippines after the Treaty of Paris in 1899. In "The Philippine Annexation: An Experiment of Profound Interest," Arthur P. Dudden studies the occupation of the Philippines archipelago.

The United States had become a formidable industrial economy during the second half of the nineteenth century and began to exercise its might internationally via the Monroe Doctrine. The US Pacific strategy began with American hegemony in Hawaii – stepping stone for the California Gold Rush – in the 1840s. American merchants became more active in the Pacific during the 1850s and 1860s. Commodore Perry entered Edo (Tokyo) Bay in 1853. He amazed the Japanese the following year by displaying an electric telegraph and a tiny locomotive steam engine in Yokohama, portending a powerful, steam-based American Navy. By 1898, Hawaii had become part of the Union. The granting of a base in Samoa in 1878 to the US Navy led to the annexation of eastern Samoa in 1899. The United States formulated the Open Door Policy for China in 1900 and joined an international expedition against the Boxer Rebellion.

It was the occupation of the Philippines that marked the first American war in Asia. Filipino patriots were defeated by July 1902, having lost 20,000 Filipino warriors "while an estimated 600,000 noncombatant Filipino civilians, men, women, and children, perished" (pp. 209–10). Education became a priority. American-style public schooling was introduced and the University of the Philippines opened in 1908. The US Congress passed the Philippine Organic Act in 1902. Two Filipino resident commissioners were elected to the House of Representatives in Washington, DC. The US Supreme Court determined that Philippine citizens were US nationals, but without the rights of American citizenship. The Autonomy Act of 1916 "greatly enlarged Philippine powers of home rule, and promised independence as soon as a stable government could be established" (p. 213). Professor Dudden states that from this 1916 document:

> there arose between American authorities and the Filipinos a fascinating, yet paradoxical, system of collaborative colonialism exercised through the politics of mutual manipulation ... Filipino leaders acquiesced in the promise of eventual independence, yet inside themselves grew ever more reluctant to allow the United States to withdraw altogether (p. 213).

Tensions between Filipino and American economic interests increased under Roosevelt's New Deal. Tobacco and sugar interests "joined the party's core anti-imperialists, to press for freeing the Philippine islands as soon as possible" (p. 214). Philippine isolationists, fearing imperialist Japanese strategies in Asia, added support for independence. The Tydings–McDuffie Act of 1934 granted independence in ten years. Manuel Quezon was elected the first President in 1935. Then, World War II dramatically altered original political intentions. The Philippines became an independent nation after the Japanese defeat in July of 1945, but Dudden claims that the economic situation has not changed. In economic terms, the Monroe Doctrine persists.

The atomic explosions in Hiroshima and Nagasaki at the end of World War II initiated a legacy of continuous atomic research on a grand scale. These new armaments possessed the capacity to spread destruction beyond anything in human experience and created a new phase of hostility among superpowers emerging from the war. "Cold War Casualties: The Impact of American Nuclear Testing Policies in the Pacific, 1954," by Martha Smith-Norris, studies the consequences of this arms race for populations in the Pacific Ocean: "On March 1, 1954, the United States detonated a devastating 15-megaton thermonuclear weapon at its grounds on the Bikini Atoll in the Marshall Islands ... the explosion vaporized the test island, leaving a huge crater in the lagoon floor. The blast then pushed outward, stripping the nearby islands of all vegetation" (p. 219). A crew of Japanese fishermen and perhaps thousands of others were seriously harmed by this test.

Europe was the first priority for American Cold War strategy, but the Pacific was also an important component. In 1949 Douglas McArthur said that the "Pacific has become an Anglo-Saxon lake and [our] defense runs through the chain of islands fringing the coast of Asia" (p. 220). Given the fact that health concerns precluded thermonuclear testing in the continental USA, Pacific archipelagoes appeared convenient grounds. The BRAVO incident is a case where world dynamics are essential to local history, and global strategies are molded by local events. The incident involved the people of the Marshall Islands, Japanese fishermen from the *Fukuryu Maru No. 5*, and by extension their governments and the US administration. The Marshall Islands had been a Trust Territory of the US since a 1947 accord with the United Nations: "the American government had agreed, among other things, to 'protect' the lands, resources, and health of the inhabitants" (p. 226).

After the March 1, 1954 explosion, the US Atomic Energy Commission advised the withholding of all information regarding fallout in the region. The Japanese government informed Americans of radiation exposure of the crew of the *Fukuryu Maru No. 5* fishing boat. Besides compensation for the families involved, Japanese leaders asked for a suspension of testing in the Pacific, at least during fishing season. The United States refused on security grounds.

The Marshallese population was not evacuated for more than two days after the blast, despite reports of fallout within 7 hours: "Many of the children played in the white dust and 'ate it', thinking that it looked like snow" (p. 224). In response to Marshallese protests to the United Nations, "the U.S. embassy in Tokyo warned the State Department that the 'language and form of the petition might indicate a communist inspiration'" (p. 227). In a joint statement, the Atomic Energy Commission and the Department of Defense stated that there was "no medical reason to expect any permanent after-effects on the general health [of the inhabitants] due to fallout" (p. 228).

Reports reached the American government in late 1954 concerning the existence of about 54 million pounds of contaminated tuna aboard Japanese vessels fishing in areas far away from Bikini. High levels of radioactivity were also detected in rainwater and vegetables in different parts of Japan. Eighty-two Marshallese previously exposed to the fallout were returned to Rongelap Island, along with another 100 Marshallese who had not been previously exposed: "The AEC considered this latter group to be an 'ideal comparison population' for medical studies since it was composed of people who were genetically related to the Rongelapese but not present at the time of the explosion on March 1, 1954" (p. 231). Medical reports soon indicated high rates of cancer and other health problems among the Marshall Islanders. Despite these findings, these people were not evacuated from Bikini for another ten years. As late as 1994, the Mayor of Rongelap inquired: "How much local food can we eat? Should our children be allowed to play in the sand? How many times a day should we wash their hands? How do we keep their hands out of their mouths? Is it safe for a baby to drink its mother's milk?" (p. 234).

US Congressional hearing documents from 1994 indicate that the Atomic Energy Commission and Department of Defense "knew at least twelve hours in advance of BRAVO that the wind direction was changing in an unfavorable easterly direction (towards Rongelap) but proceeded with the explosion anyway" (p. 228). Twenty-six American servicemen were evacuated after the explosion, but the indigenous people remained in the area for two more days. It was admitted in the 1994 hearing that perhaps thousands of indigenous people were affected instead of the hundreds previously acknowledged by the Atomic Energy Commission.

Conclusion

This is the third book in a series of "Pacific Centuries" conference volumes. Taken together, they suggest a preliminary synthetic overview of Pacific history since the sixteenth century. The founding of the city of Manila by Spaniards in 1571 no doubt represented the birth of continuous and significant 'Pacific Rim' trade. No "silver period" [1571–c.1750] in Pacific history could have existed in the absence of demand-side dynamics emanating from China throughout this period. Moreover, the silver-laden Acapulco–Manila galleons also provided an important vector for the introduction of American foodstuffs to the Asian mainland and Pacific islands. The resulting demographic surge within China in particular created reverberations throughout the commercial world from the eighteenth century onward.

The century prior to the California/Australia/New Zealand gold rushes can be considered a period of "exploration and early integration" of the Pacific Basin. Europeans explored Australia, New Zealand, and many islands of the Pacific. Newly explored areas supplied raw materials for continental markets, dominant among which was the Chinese marketplace. Animal skins collected in California by supposedly autarkic individuals were, in fact, destined for Asian marketplaces. Sometimes deleterious environmental impacts within the Pacific were devastating.

Plantations around the Pacific mainly employed native or Asian wage laborers, in contrast to African slave labor characteristic of Atlantic plantation economies. An African diaspora throughout the Pacific has now entered its sixth century, but world history's collective ignorance of this fact is symptomatic of the tremendous opportunities awaiting scholarly investigation of Pacific history.

This volume's essays tend to concentrate on the Pacific's "gold period" during the last half of the nineteenth century. Economic/demographic surges that resulted from these great gold discoveries (as well as silver discoveries in Nevada) helped reshape societies linked by the Pacific Ocean. Agricultural expansion both facilitated, and was stimulated by, urbanization around the Pacific. But urbanization in then-remote gold rush regions of the Pacific involved relatively affluent immigrants, compared with poor immigrants traveling by foot to vast cities on the Asian mainland. Differing urban infrastuctures therefore evolved along distinct trajectories that would partially determine the shapes of cities indefinitely.

Imperial strategies after the gold rushes adapted to technological innovation. The Industrial Revolution had a tremendous impact upon maritime warfare and commerce, of course, as powers struggled for access to raw materials and end-markets. Railroad expansion intensified the connection of interior regions with continental ports, while steamship technologies revolutionized intercontinental commerce. The United States became an industrial power and simultaneously dominant in the Pacific Ocean. Hawaii was annexed by the United States in 1898. Spain simultaneously ceded control of the Philippines to the US and eastern Samoa was annexed in 1899. Not coincidentally, the US's Open Door Policy for China was formulated in 1900. Great Britain's control of Hong Kong and other jurisdictions in the western Pacific was formidable, but two world wars in the twentieth century left no doubt that the Pacific had become an American Lake. America's post-World War II policies in the Pacific have sometimes been neither benign nor forthright. It has taken nearly a half-century to learn more fully the extent of official concealment of damage from nuclear tests in the Pacific, especially the disgraceful legacy of the Bravo incident of 1954 in the Marshall Islands.

While a 'Spanish Lake' between the mid-sixteenth and mid-eighteenth centuries, the world's greatest ocean was exploited with remarkable success by Iberians (and the Dutch, in addition to merchants from China and elsewhere) who controlled key ports and therefore access to major market areas. From the mid-eighteenth through much of the nineteenth century, numerous nations vied for control of sections of the Pacific. Gold rushes subsequently stimulated commercial connections. And industrialization in select jurisdictions narrowed the range of contenders for supremacy in Pacific waters. The Pacific had certainly become an 'American Lake' after World War II, and American commerce and power remains a dominant force in the Pacific today. But the rise of Asian economic powers during the second half of the twentieth century, and the reemergence of China in particular, make it difficult at this time to detect the structure or timing of the next important period in the history of the Pacific. Changing concentrations of economic, demographic, and military power will probably interact with ecological factors to produce a new era. At least, such has been the case during five previous Pacific Centuries.

Notes

1 S.M. Miller, A.J.H. Latham, and D.O. Flynn (eds), *Studies in the Economic History of the Pacific Rim*, London: Routledge, 1998; D.O. Flynn, L. Frost, and A.J.H. Latham (eds.), *Pacific Centuries: Pacific and Pacific Rim history since the sixteenth century*, London: Routledge, 1999; and this volume.

2 Two distinct 'cycles of silver' heavily influenced both Pacific and world history. The 'Japan/Potosi Cycle' lasted from the 1540s to the 1640s, while the 'Mexican Silver Cycles' lasted from approximately 1700 to 1750. Discussion of these two cycles can be found in D.O. Flynn and Arturo Giráldez, "Cycles of Silver: Global economic unity through the mid-eighteenth century," *Journal of World History* (Fall 2002, forthcoming).

3 For a classic treatment of Chinese monetary history, including the silverization of China, see Richard von Glahn, *Fountain of Fortune: Money and monetary policy in China 1000–1700*, Berkeley: University of California Press, 1996.

4 For discussion of the magnitude of the Pacific galleon trade, see D.O. Flynn and Arturo Giráldez, "Arbitrage, China and World Trade in the Early Modern Period," *Journal of the Economic and Social History of the Orient*, 38, No. 4, (1995), pp. 429–48. These authors support the earlier contentions of Chuan Hang-Sheng, "Trade Between China, the Philippines and the Americas During the Sixteenth and Seventeenth Centuries," *Proceedings of the International Conference of Sinology: Section on history and archeology*, Taipei: Academia Sinica, 1981, pp. 849–54.

5 D.O. Flynn and Arturo Giráldez, "Spanish Profitability in the Pacific: The Philippines in the sixteenth and seventeenth centuries," in Flynn, Frost, and Latham (eds), *Pacific Centuries*.

6 John McNeill, "From Magellan to MITI: Pacific Rim Economies and Pacific Island Ecologies Since 1521," in Miller, Latham, and Flynn, *Studies in the Economic History of the Pacific Rim*, pp. 73–4.

7 The same holds true for non-Chinese locations: "A new root crop of ultimately South American origin, the sweet potato, reached New Guinea, probably by way of the Philippines, where it had been introduced by Spaniards ... The result of the sweet potato's arrival was a highland population explosion", Jared Diamond, *Guns, Germs, and Steel. The Fates of Human Societies*, New York and London: W.W. Norton & Company, 1999, p. 149.

8 See Flynn and Giráldez, "Cycles of Silver," for discussion restricted to the interplay between the world silver market and eighteenth-century Chinese population growth.

9 Kristof Glamann, "The Dutch East India Company's Trade in Japanese Copper, 1645–1736," *Scandinavian Economic History Review*, Lund, 1953, pp. 41–79.

10 McNeill, "From Magellan to MITI," p. 78.

11 Papers were presented at "Session 3b: Africans in the Pacific" at the 3rd Pacific Centuries Conference (University of the Pacific, Stockton, California), April 24–26, 1998, but we have been unable to locate a single published article (in any language) devoted to the history of Africans in the Pacific region.

12 It is important to note that huge volumes of silver continued to flow to China after 1750, but by 1750 the market price of silver had declined to production costs in America. Mexican mines still generated 'normal profits', but the extraordinary profits of the first half of the eighteenth century had been squeezed out (Flynn and Giráldez, "Cycles of Sivler").

13 See e.g. McNeil, "From Magellan to MITI," and David J. St. Clair, "California Quicksilver in the Pacific Rim Economy, 1850–1890," in Miller, Latham and Flynn, *Studies in the Economic History of the Pacific Rim*, pp. 210–13.

14 See note 1 above.

15 Cited in Henry Higgs (ed.), *Palgrave's Dictionary of Political Economy*, vol. III, London: Macmillan and Co., 1926, p. 705.

2

Soft Gold: Animal Skins and the Early Economy of California

Jim Hardee

Imagine, if you will, standing on the icy deck of a three-masted sailing ship, splashing through the curling waves as it steers up the western coast of North America. Recent winter storms have shattered the mizzenmast, rot has been discovered in the foremast, and the upper works are leaking, badly in need of fresh caulk. The captain, James Cook, desperately seeks a sheltered inlet in which to mend his ailing vessel. In what is today known as Nootka Sound, in late March of 1778, Her Majesty's Ship, the *Resolution*, dropped anchor to make repairs.[1]

Standing at the rail, shivering in the cold, you watch fellow sailors on shore bartering with the natives. The Indians have many furs to trade: bear, wolf, fox, deer, and others. For a couple of knives, a chisel, a few pieces of iron or tin, some nails and a handful of buttons (trade goods worth only a few dollars), the seamen negotiate for pelts of luxuriously black, glossy fur. Six of the finest skins cost only a dozen large, green, glass beads.[2]

Eventually, the *Resolution* sails on to Canton, China. There, you discover the value of these dark, thickly furred pelts. Although worn bare in places and infested with lice and other vermin, they sell for nearly one hundred dollars a piece to Chinese merchants, who are anxious to own them at any price. The crew nearly mutinies trying to convince the captain to return to the Pacific Northwest to make their fortune in the soft gold of the sea otter.[3]

News of the value to be gained from this soft gold spread throughout the world, bringing vast changes to the economy of the Pacific Rim in an era of essentially exclusionary mercantilism. Russia already knew of the Chinese demand for these furs and had been actively collecting otter pelts for some years. Vitus Bering, in search of the Northwest Passage, had shipwrecked on the island that still bears his name. In 1742 his men found their way home – to a man stricken with scurvy, gaunt from starvation, and wrapped in a wealth of furs, including those of the sea otter.[4]

After hearing the tales of Bering's crew, Russian fur hunters hurriedly put to sea in crude galleys made with green timbers lashed with leather thongs. In 1745 the first company returned, their fortunes made, confirming the richness of the region. Each season Russian ships traveled farther and farther along the Aleutian chain in search of fur grounds. Their crude vessels got bigger and better built in order to withstand the longer voyages. In 20 years' time Russian fur men had sailed the length of the Aleutian Islands to the mainland of the North American continent.[5]

After the return of the *Resolution* Europe also learned of the riches up for grabs in the Pacific. England, France, and particularly Spain were more than interested in Russian activities. Madrid sent orders to colonize California without delay to halt further Russian advancement on the mainland. Spaniards were sent to establish a colony at Nootka Sound and the mission chain was pushed northward as far as Sonoma.[6]

Chinese economic policy during this period was effectively exclusionary also. The government allowed foreign merchants to import trade goods at only two sites: a fortress about two hundred miles south of Russia's southernmost Siberian village and the seaport at Canton. For a long time, Siberian merchants had a virtual monopoly on the fur market, sending regular caravans across the Gobi Desert to the borders of Russia; but in the 1780s Captain James Hanna brought a cargo into Canton, including 560 sea otter skins, and changed the way business was done.[7]

Sea otter fur was sought after by Asians for both practical and ornamental purposes. Of great warmth because of its denseness and of exceeding beauty, it became the royal fur of China. Ladies in high social standing wore otter capes and sashes or belts constructed of this luxurious fur. Otter skin robes were the order of the day for the Chinese Mandarins. Tails were also valued for caps, mittens and smaller trim. By 1790 a sea otter hide in the Chinese market brought from $80 to $120.[8]

The Chinese were willing to pay high prices for otter pelts, no matter who brought them. It was easier to buy them in Canton than to travel all the way to some distant Siberian outpost. As other British traders followed Hanna's lead, old trade routes were abandoned in favor of the sea-lanes from the northwest coast of North America, via the Hawaiian Islands, directly to Canton.

This sea otter trade was the first, and by far the most profitable, commercial interest to draw United States merchants into Pacific waters. American products and American citizens entering California coastal ports during the Mexican period, in many respects, determined the ultimate political destiny of that segment of the Pacific Rim, in addition to significantly influencing the commercial outlook of the region.[9]

The presence of sea otters in California waters had been known for some time. Father Sigismundo Taraval recorded sightings of the creature at Cerros Island as early as 1733, but Spain initially failed to recognize the value of the commodity lying at its own doorstep. In 1774 to protect and expand her northern frontier, Spain sent out mariners to not only explore but also to investigate the activities of the Russians. During these voyages, incidental bartering with local natives brought sea otter pelts back to Spanish ports. Abalone shells, unassumingly displayed on board their ships, were avidly sought by Indians who frequently traded an otter skin for one or two of these shells.[10]

Spaniards in both Upper and Lower California soon began collecting otter skins from the natives. While not great in numbers, otter pelts started finding their way on board the annual Manila galleons, bringing Spain small profits from Asian traders.[11]

Two species of sea otter inhabit the coastal waters of the Pacific. The northern variety is called *Enhydra Lutris Lutris*, while the southern group is known as *Enhydra Lutris Nereis*. Sea otter habitat ranged along an arc formed by the shores and islands of the North Pacific Ocean. From the Northern Sea of Japan, otter grounds proceeded northeastward, past Kamchatka, to the Aleutian Island chain. Following the curve of North America, the sea otter was common southward to about the middle of Lower California. There was a partial break in this arc between the Straits of Juan de Fuca off the coast of Washington State and the northern California coast near Trinidad. The geographical differences in that section of coastline could explain the fewer animals in that area. In this region, the rocky coastline commonly frequented by otters is replaced by a straighter shore of sand dunes and cliffs. This gap also appears to form a natural division between the two species of sea otter.

William Sturgis, a veteran sea otter hunter, said there were only two objects in the world describing the elegance of the otter's fur – a beautiful lady and a lovely infant. The largest hides were as much as 90 inches long and 36 inches wide consisting of unusually fine, soft and dense underfur, about three-fourths of an inch in length. The base of the roots is a lustrous white or silver color, darkening at the ends to a black in the finer skins and various shades of brown in the more common pelts. Pelt quality remains virtually consistent despite the season although winter hides were marginally better for their dark color. Thus, hunting for sea otters was done in all seasons. California skins were generally inferior to those taken in the northern regions, being predominantly brown in color.[12]

Sea otters were predominately hunted rather than trapped. Russians hired Aleut natives experienced in hunting this creature. Aleutian methods of pursuing otters were used along the California coast throughout the Spanish period. Small canoes, called *baidarkas* by the Russians and *kayaks* by the natives, scoured the coast for miles. Arrows or darts with bone points were fitted into a fluted board sling by a line of whale sinew. When the arrow lodged in its prey, the otter was greatly slowed by the drag created by this shaft.

The moment an otter was sighted nosing its head above the surface of the water, a silent signal was given. The first hunter to spot the animal raised a paddle above his head. Other hunters tried to surround the otter, rowing swiftly to circle it with a cordon of *kayaks*. The wary otter dived almost instantly. Hunters would maneuver their crafts to cover the area where they expected the creature to reappear. The hunter nearest the spot where the otter resurfaced would cry out, forcing it into another dive before it could take a complete breath. At the same time, if he were close enough, an arrow would be fired. Taking up his place at the new spot identifying where the otter had dived, he elevated his paddle while his comrades repositioned themselves. The chase continued in this fashion until the exhausted and wounded otter was finally dispatched or it escaped, which was frequently the case. The hunter who first wounded the animal or the one whose arrow was nearest the head held claim to the kill, depending on tribal custom.

Motivated by two main considerations, the Spanish government eventually organized a plan to procure this soft gold. Firstly, their American miners were greatly hindered by insufficient and irregular supplies of quicksilver or mercury, necessary for the refining process. China had large quantities of this needed element, and the medium of exchange most wanted by the Chinese was plentiful in the waters off the coast of California. Secondly, Vicente Vasadre y Vega, noting the encroachment of both Russians and English into the otter fields of the North Pacific in greater and greater numbers, advocated a California–China trade policy that could potentially alleviate this problem. On June 2, 1785, the king of Spain ordered the plan be commenced.[13]

The plan called for Vasadre to be the ultimate recipient of all the otter skins taken in California. No one would be allowed to trade with any other person, Spaniard or foreigner. Christian Indians would bring their catch to the mission padres in exchange for cloth or other Mexican articles. Soldiers and inhabitants of the pueblos who purchased skins from unconverted natives would turn them over to the presidio immediately. Furs accumulating at the missions and the military forts would then be collected by Vasadre himself.

Vasadre's initial collection was creditable enough, gaining him over one thousand skins by November; however, the gathering of furs was hampered by several factors. The Indians living in California had never been stimulated to hunt for sea otter. Mild climates did not require the natives to hunt the creature for furs to keep warm; thus hunters were not skilled as were their northern relations along the coast of Washington. There was also a lack of suitable articles to entice the natives to pursue the animal. A general lack of understanding as to how this new venture would benefit the missions' charges kept the padres from getting solidly behind the program. Additionally, soldiers were leaving the service to get skins and using violent, unfair methods in dealing with the Indians.[14]

To complicate matters further, Spain's primary trading company in Asia, the Philippine Company, had virtually halted all attempts to trade into Canton. Even with changes advised by Vasadre, economically the next two years were not much better. By the time Vasadre's venture ended four years later, something less than 10,000 otter skins had been shipped to Asia at a value of $3,120,000 or about $321 each.[15]

Nevertheless, Spain had been fully alerted to the significance of the sea otter trade, and the Spanish/Mexican policy served to establish a degree of protection for the coast of California from Baja to the Oregon border. Indians learned the value of the pelts, and now sent them to the missions and ports with some regularity.

As the end of the eighteenth century drew to a close, vessels were swarming into the North Pacific. Most were Yankee merchant ships since English traders were controlled by the British East India Company, which held a virtual monopoly on all British trade in Asia's South Pacific regions. For the most part, the British withdrew from the California otter grounds. The Russian American Company, on the other hand, extended its activities, especially after the founding of its colony at Sitka, Alaska, in 1799. The competition between American and Russian vessels began to stiffen.[16]

Northern coastal Indian tribes were becoming increasingly hostile because of adverse trade conditions resulting from fraudulent and often violent dealings with unscrupulous white men. Enterprising Yankee captains decided to try the southern fields along the Spanish coast of California. They were surprised to find a high mercantile wall erected against foreign interlopers. Behind this exclusionary wall were people with the same interests that had attracted the New England traders. Competition between the otter men and the protectors of Spain's mercantile system heated up.

Illegal trade in contraband otter furs was the name of the game. Smuggling and lying to officials became everyday occurrences. Spanish officials soon learned to take precautionary measures when a strange vessel came into harbor. Help was generally provided to a ship in need because of maritime law, but foreigners were rather limited in further actions. Authorities sometimes made ships remain at anchor a league out from the harbor, forcing the crew to make repeated trips in their smaller rowboats to get supplies on board. These smaller skiffs, however, often managed to carry on some trade while on shore. In 1800 the *Enterprise* put in at the bays of Todos Santos, San Quentiñ and San Jose del Cabo, successively, only to repeat at each place its demand for supplies – a slow and difficult way to collect otter pelts.[17]

Each year the Spanish commercial system tightened. As the military stepped up its oversight of smuggling attempts, Boston merchants found themselves in quite a predicament. After trying every expedient, Captain Joseph O'Cain hit on an idea that turned out to be quite profitable. Knowing the fur trade could not effectively continue by bartering and smuggling, O'Cain realized if his crew could hunt the otter personally, they could obtain more hides and still keep clear of the populated centers watched so closely by law enforcement. The drawback was that he did not have the equipment nor experienced hunters among his crew. O'Cain sought assistance from the Russians farther north.

Negotiations with Alexander Baranov drew O'Cain into a successful enterprise. The Russians supplied the hunters and their *baidarkas*, while O'Cain gave equal shares of the take to his new partner. A line of hunting bases was established along the coast, all of which essentially avoided Spanish population centers. Bodega Bay, Drake's Bay, the Farallon Islands, the Santa Barbara Channel Islands, to name a few, were such points from which sea otters and seals were stalked in all directions.

Collaboration became the key method of gathering these precious hides from 1803 until about 1812. Without that partnership, the Americans could not have afforded to stay in the field.[18]

For the Russians the contract system was a means of hunting along the California coast at a time when they lacked adequate transportation. For them, the finding of new otter grounds was paramount to staying in business as well. The contract also kept the Americans from having the exclusive run of these new fields.

By 1812 the Russians were launching their own independent hunting excursions along the California coast. The Americans, now drawn into the War of 1812 with Great Britain, brought most of their trips across the Pacific to a screeching halt because of patrolling English men-of-war and a blockade at the Canton harbor.[19]

With the outbreak of Mexico's revolt from Spanish rule in 1810, supplies getting into California had become irregular. Missionaries, as well as other groups, began to push for a dependable method of gaining clothing, staples, and sundry supplies. California was fast becoming a product-hungry land, rich soil for an increase in contraband trade. During the years 1812 to 1826, Boston ships became wandering trade centers and expert smugglers. The captains made personal contacts on shore where they found willing Californians often disposed to break the law.[20]

Following the Revolution, newly independent Mexico cast off Spain's ruinous mercantile policies and opened a liberal commercial system; and for the first time, foreign vessels could trade legally in California for otter skins. The Mexican government began its own attempts at gathering hides as well and with Russian presence at Fort Ross on the northern California coast, began negotiations.

A contract system with the Russians was negotiated starting on December 1, 1823. Luis Antonio Argüello, acting governor of Mexican California, purchased an 83-ton schooner, the *Rover*, from Captain John Rogers Cooper in June of that year. He then sought otter skins from the Russians for cargo. The contract allowed Kiril Khlebnikov and his Aleutian hunters four months to hunt sea otters and other marine animals anywhere from San Francisco to San Diego. The take was divided equally between them. The Russians were to sell their share to the Mexican government at a set price. The Russians were also responsible for the expenses of both hunters and equipment, while the Mexicans supplied provisions for the crews.[21]

Khlebnikov felt he had profited from what he described as "the confused condition of the California government," which might have been so for the first shipment was reasonably profitable. On the return of the *Rover* from its second trip to Canton, however, a change in governor created many difficulties for the ship's captain and direct participation in the otter trade by the Mexican government ended.[22]

During the 1820s, another group of Americans entered the region – the beaver trappers. Many were lured to the coast by reports of wealth to be gained in fur from the sea. The first beaver trapper-turned-otter hunter, Isaac Galbraith, arrived in California with the overland party of Jedediah Smith in 1827. Galbraith used

William Goodwin Dana's license to engage in hunting otter. Galbraith rankled at the thought of doing all the work and only getting half of the rewards, but such was the condition of hunting under someone else's legal authority. The leader of another trapping party, James Ohio Pattie, used his rifle to kill otters while waiting for a boat to take him south in the spring of 1830. He made $300 from the 16 hides he gathered in ten days along the coast near Monterey.[23]

William Wolfskill's party yielded several men who took to the otter fields. George Yount had little more than seen the ocean for the first time in his life when he began chasing sea otters. Wolfskill himself tried to enter the trade under the license issued him in Santa Fe to trap *nutria*. In New Mexico *nutria* might have meant beaver, but in California, it meant otter.[24]

Other beaver trappers who resorted to hunting otters include Ewing Young, Job Dye, Isaac J. Sparks, and George Nidever. The overland trapper may not have introduced the idea of using guns to shoot otters, but they certainly made it the method of choice. The first specific reference to using firearms is a statement by George Nidever in 1836, "They generally used buckshot, their arms being the old English musket."[25]

From 1804 to 1812, annual collection of otter skins ranged from about 8,000 to over 17,000 hides, although the highest recorded figure for any specific year is 1811, when 9,356 skins are known to have been obtained. Existing otter hunting records are very incomplete, and estimates of numbers harvested are difficult to ascertain. Because of various political and economic conditions, hunting records probably do not correspond to actual otter skins traded.[26]

For about two decades after the end of the contract system with Russian and American traders, the greatest amount of hunting seems to have been done in predominantly Russian regions, between Point Reyes and Trinidad Bay. Russians at Fort Ross were estimated to be obtaining about 2,000 otters every year, mostly taken north of the Golden Gate.

California sea otter harvests began declining around 1815. The day of the sea otter as an important factor in California economic history was essentially over around 1820. By 1835 exports of sea otter skins had faded to virtually nothing. Other markets were entered; and collection of otter hides, on a much smaller scale, became more of a sideline business.

The void was filled by other entrepreneurial merchants who provided California with yet another form of soft gold to mine, one which was a far greater source of revenue during the Mexican period. For nearly a quarter of a century, the extensive export of cow hides, horns, and tallow kept Californians supplied with commodities from foreign lands.

The natural conditions in California were remarkably compatible for raising cattle. Before the close of the eighteenth century, this industry formed the chief source of wealth, trade, food and occupation in California. Beef, in one form or another, was an essential article in the region's diet. Tallow supplied fat for cooking and grease for the manufacture of soap and candles. Rawhide was the "baling wire, fix-all" of these early days.

Cattle were butchered for food as needed. The *matanza*, or roundup, and wholesale slaughtering was carried out at certain specified times of the year, becoming a festival for local citizens. Only a small part of the meat from each animal was saved. These better cuts were often cut into thin strips and dried in the sun to become *carne seca*, the universally used meat in the local menu. The rest went to feed the half-tamed dogs of the ranches, vultures, and multitude of coyotes found in the surrounding hills.[27]

The fat of slaughtered animals was rendered in large kettles and poured into rawhide bags called *botas*, the largest of which could hold nearly a thousand pounds. Tallow was sold by the *arroba*, a standard Mexican weight equal to about twenty-five pounds.

Money was little known and seldom carried. Almost all business transactions were carried on by barter. Cowhides, or "California bank notes," as they were often called along the coast, fluctuated in value from one to three dollars a piece during this period. Except for a few simple household crafts, Californians had few manufacturers of any kind and, consequently, depended upon foreign ships to supply nearly everything they required. A trading vessel contained a fascinating array which might include dry goods, liquors, cigars, raisins, sugar, spices, silks, hardware, cutlery, guns, powder, shoes, pins, calicoes, stockings, combs, shawls, furniture, an occasional billiard table or piano – almost anything imaginable.[28]

From 1822 until 1834, most of the hides were supplied by the missions, several of which counted their cattle by the tens of thousands. All told, these mission herds numbered nearly half a million animals in 1834. When secularization took place, privately owned ranches became the chief source of supply. Some of the missions still continued to furnish a considerable number of hides each year.

Jedediah Smith's clerk, Harrison Rogers, recounts "upwards of 30,000 head of cattle" at Mission San Gabriel upon the party's arrival in 1826. He continues, "they slaughter at this place from 2 to 3000 head of cattle at a time; the Mission lives on the profits." Rogers was also impressed with the soap works at the mission. He wrote in his daybook, "The soap factory consists of four large cisterns, or boilers, that will hold from 2000 to 2500 gallons each; the cistern is built in the shape of an sugar loaf made of brick, stone and lime; there is a large iron pot or kittle, fixed in the bottom where the fire strikes to set them boiling, the mouth of the cisterns and the edge of the potts are lined around with sheat iron 8 or 10 inches wide, the potts or kittles, will hold from 200 to 250 gallons each, and a great many small ones fixed in a like manner."[29]

Englishmen William P. Hartnell and Hugh McCulloch initiated the export of this hide and tallow soft gold. They arrived in Monterey in 1822 and went directly before Governor Pablo Vicente de Solá and the mission prefect, Mariano Payeras, to propose the formation of a contract with the missions for hides and tallow. Consent was readily obtained from both. Payeras wrote enthusiastically to the mission fathers, pointing out the advantage of the proposed agreement and urging them to enter the contract. Solá wrote that it was an "opportunity for which they had been waiting;" and if the inhabitants of the province did not take advantage of it, and, in his words, "leave off their character of slackness and abandon," they deserved to be treated as vagrants were treated in Mexico.[30]

Entrance into the contract was purely voluntary, but acceptance obligated the parties to a three-year term beginning in January 1823. Ships were to be sent to all the harbors and bays of the California coast from San Francisco to San Diego. Although hides for British markets and tallow for South America were the principal objects of trade, several other commodities were specified as of secondary interest – chiefly soap, horse hair, horn, hemp, beef in brine, *manteca* (suet), *aguardiente*, and wheat. The agreed price for hides was one *peso* and for tallow, two *pesos* per *arroba*.

This unprecedented event was pulled off with relative ease. The entrance into the California market of a foreign business house had been facilitated through a mission contract approved by both governor and prefect. The establishment of McCulloch, Hartnell and Company was further secured by official permits. Additionally, early in 1823 the governor granted a petition asking for permission to build warehouses at Monterey and San Pedro.

McCulloch and Hartnell began personal solicitations of the missions. In the north Hartnell persuaded all the missions, except San Francisco, to enter the contract. McCulloch encountered problems among the missions of the south but managed to get several signatures on the bottom line.

A month after contract negotiations began, William A. Gale, a Boston merchant active in the sea otter trade, sailed into Monterey Bay. Gale had similar intentions of entering the hide and tallow business. As Gale traveled from mission to mission, he found himself preceded by Hartnell and all the year's production already under contract. The mission fathers welcomed the chance to trade their surplus hides and tallow for mission supplies. The English firm had a market but discovered the mission required a distinct type of goods. Furthermore, the widely scattered missions presented a problem in distribution. Building the trade was not an easy task.

Arriving on the coast, a trading vessel first put into the port of Monterey, site of the only Mexican customs house. Every vessel trading in California was supposed to enter its cargo here. Duties levied on the goods were nominally high, a single vessel paying from $5,000 to $25,000 on its cargo. Costs of duties were shifted from the New England merchant to the Californian in higher prices. Once the ship entered its cargo with customs, it was free to trade along the entire coast until its cargo was exhausted, which often required from a year and a half to three years.[31]

Meanwhile, the ship's goods might get replenished clandestinely from the cargoes of other vessels that had not yet received a trading license. Records of provisions for the ship's crew were often inflated because no duty was charged on goods used to sustain sailors during the voyage. This surplus was then sold, tariff-free. Manifests were also made out for the Columbia River or for any other market besides California. Sometimes, a small portion of goods was sold to a Mexican resident; then the entire ship was placed under Mexican colors. Such evasion of tariff charges was supplemented by bribery of customhouse officials or through outright smuggling.

While the ship dealt with customs, flyers announcing the arrival of the brig, along with a list of the goods on board, were dispatched to the northern and southern ends of the mission chain. The newly arrived vessel then sailed southward, stopping at specified hide collection points. The supercargo, or ship owner's agent, arranged with the missions and ranches for the purchase and delivery of the hides to the nearest seaport. Traveling overland on horseback ahead of the ship, he passed from mission to mission and from ranch to ranch, a welcome guest as well as commercial agent.

Hides were transported to the seacoast on pack-mules or clumsy, oxen-drawn carts. Once at the beach, the hides were dumped unceremoniously on the ground. Cart drivers squatted beside the cart to wait while the sailors readied a return load of merchandise. The hides were carried by the ship's crew on their heads, through the surf, over stones slippery with sea moss, to the long-boats that would transport the hides out to the ship.

William Henry Dana, in his book *Two Years Before the Mast*, describes learning to "toss" a hide while working at San Diego. "Throwing the hides upon the pole was the most difficult work," according to Dana, "and required a sleight of hand which was only to be got by long practice. As I was known for a hide-curer, this post was assigned to me, and I continued at it for six or eight days, tossing, in that time, from eight to ten thousand hides, until my wrists became so lame that I gave in, and was transferred to the gang that was employed in filling the boats, where I remained for the rest of the time."[32]

The doubled, dried skin of a steer was an awkward bundle; and they sometimes caught the wind like a sail. Dana was once blown over on the beach by a mere breeze while hoisting a hide upon his head. Rowing out to the mother ship, sometimes anchored two or three miles offshore, was the final test of strength after a long, hard day of tossing hides. The work was arduous and severe, but no other method was available since there were no piers or docks yet built along the coast. In the eyes of the sailor, San Pedro, with its steep landing, sticky clay soil and long stretch of kelp-covered rocks over which the hides had to be carried, was probably the worst of the ports. Despite these hardships, more hides were taken on here than at any other landing.[33]

To complete a cargo for shipment east, 20,000 to 40,000 hides were needed. These were gathered in various ports, chief of which were San Diego, San Juan Capistrano, San Pedro, Santa Barbara, San Luis Obispo, and Monterey. William Dane Phelps gives a good idea of the magnitude of the task in taking on hide cargoes from such scattered collection points. Phelps reported, "We were seven times at San Francisco, thirteen at Monterey, three at Santa Cruz, four at St Louis, seventeen at Santa Barbara, seventeen at San Pedro, five at Refugio, and returned to our depots ten times, frequently anchoring at various other points along shore." The depot to which Phelps refers was San Diego.[34]

At San Diego, the hides were soaked in brine, scraped, dried, and beaten with flails to rid them of dust. Then, they were stored in large warehouses to await shipment around the Horn. Buyers complained that California hides were stretched too much in width. They explained, "It is not the size of the hide that is looked to but its weight and the smaller compass this is in so much the better."[35]

Dried and cleaned, the hides were folded lengthwise, hair to the inside. Stacked in piles, their own weight, along with frequent turning, completed the drying process and also eventually pressed the hides flat. Initially, some hides were shipped salted, with the hair folded outside. This method damaged the hair from contact with the salt, resulting in lower prices because skin dealers judged the quality and soundness of the hide by its hair. Curing in a salt brine was also tried. While the hides arrived in premier condition compared to dry hides, the additional weight in shipping was a major drawback. Dry shipping thus became the preferred technique.

For shipment, salted hides were laid in the bottom of the hold as far up as the keelson to serve as ballast. Dried hides were piled into the hold and lime was strewn over them. Once the hold was filled to within a few feet of the beams, the process of "steeving" began. Beginning in the aft of the ship, a "book" of from 25 to 50 hides was inserted by a mechanism of ropes, pulleys, and weights. With this method, a hundred to a hundred and fifty more hides were forced in. When the last hide was stowed, the bulkheads were put up and the hatches caulked down.[36]

Although the mission fathers remained more or less faithful to the terms of the contract, difficulties did arise. Large quantities of mixed tallow and "*gras*," an edible fat, were discovered in the cargoes of earlier ships. McCulloch advised Hartnell, "although they are Christians in that quarter … look sharp after them – several have got very bad tallow."[37]

With the regular appearance of American traders along the coast in competition with the English, cash offers and higher prices not only bought up every hide direct from the cattle owners outside the contract, but also caused discontent among those within the contract. Hartnell received frequent complaints from the mission fathers regarding the high prices of English goods in comparison with cheaper offers from Boston merchants.

For the next two decades, Yankee goods were the style and Yankee traders always welcome. Bryant and Sturgis, the firm for whom William Gale worked, did a thriving business. The total number of hides for Bryant, Sturgis and Company from 1822 to 1842 approximated 500,000. Of that total, almost four-fifths were exported in the ten-year period, 1830 to 1840.[38]

New Englanders derived considerable advantage from the hide and tallow trade. In the eastern United States, California hides fetched $11 to $13 a piece in 1832. They furnished enough leather to give Connecticut and Massachusetts a monopoly on the early boot and shoe industry in the United States. These hides also provided a channel through which surplus products of New England factories found a steady, though somewhat restricted, foreign trade on the west coast.[39]

By 1828, when Hartnell, McCulloch and Company dissolved, California was vastly different, commercially speaking, from what it had been in 1822 when their contract was first suggested to the governor. A demand and dependence on the yearly arrival of foreign goods had been created. The missions were scenes of industrial activity. Neophytes at every mission were occupied with the annual slaughtering, melting tallow, transporting hides to the collection depots, and other related chores. Trade had become a major part of mission life as the padres made out their annual list of needed supplies.The hide and tallow trade created far more direct contact with the local people than had the sea otter trade. This commercial intercourse also brought many Americans into the province as permanent residents. Many of them took out naturalization papers, became large landholders, and married women from prominent California families.

The gold rush brought a virtual end to the trade's dominance as an economic factor. After 1848 the arduous life of the hide and tallow trade was quickly abandoned for the supposedly easier life and fast track to wealth found in mining.

While the hide and tallow trade geared up, an adventurous young beaver trapper named Jedediah Smith appeared in California, searching for his own version of soft gold.[40] Other mountaineers from the Rockies soon followed. From 1826 through the early 1840s, as many as two dozen trapping parties plied their craft in California's interior waters. As the overall fur trade of North America goes, California was a minor source of beaver pelts, but the search for this flat-tailed creature opened the trails soon to be followed by pioneers on the Oregon Trail and the Forty-Niners of the gold rush. Many of these trappers stayed after the beaver market plummeted, positioning themselves as surrogate parents in the birth of a new state.

Beaver was found throughout California. Three sub-species of *Castor canadensis* have been identified. The Golden beaver occupies the greater Central Valley, comprised of the drainages of the San Joaquin and Sacramento Rivers. This long-toothed species was never known to exist at altitudes above 1,000 feet. The Shasta beaver is limited to the drainages of the Klamath and Pit Rivers in the extreme northern part of the State. The Sonoran beaver lives mainly in the lower Colorado River and its tributaries. Historically, the Golden beaver was trapped in the largest quantities.[41]

As an economic factor, beaver brigades had little direct impact on the commerce of Mexican California. Some brigades purchased a few supplies from the missions or traded occasionally with Indians. For the most part, however, trapping parties entered the state, trapped the beaver, and left, a predominantly one-way exchange. Some trappers had greater involvement in the local economic and political scene. One such example is John Augustus Sutter. While building his empire in the early years of his residency in the state, Sutter relied on trapping beaver pelts to help finance New Helvetia.

The Hudson's Bay Company sent its first trapping brigade through California as early as 1826 when Peter Skene Ogden cut the top of the state during his third Snake Country expedition. HBC interest increased dramatically, however, after Jedediah Smith showed up at Fort Vancouver following the massacre of most of his men on the Umpqua River in southern Oregon. The Americans had spent some time trapping the interior waters of California and were headed for the HBC outpost when attacked by Indians shortly after entering what is now Oregon. Once at the fort, Smith extolled the richness of California beaver fields causing Hudson's Bay trapping parties to be sent out almost immediately. HBC Governor George Simpson attempted to halt American encroachment onto what he deemed British trapping grounds by declaring an exploitive trapping policy that would turn the entire region south of the Columbia River into a fur desert. This policy was pursued with vigor by such brigade captains as Ogden, Alexander McLeod, Michel LaFramboise, and John Work. In 1841 the Hudson's Bay went so far as to open a company store in San Francisco, which operated until the 1845 suicide of its manager, William Rae.

The extensive trapping by Hudson's Bay brigades quickly depleted the beaver in the state. The sea otter had been hunted for several years prior to the Americans arrival by land, and little of that trade was left for the mountain men. Consequently, for the beaver trappers arriving after about 1832, there was not enough peltry to make a profit. Unable to make a living trapping, they turned to other opportunities.

As the principal work of the overland fur trappers came to a close, many of those remaining on the West Coast turned settler or tradesman. Most had marketable skills prior to entering the fur trade, such as blacksmithing, carpentry, or milling. Others turned to ranching or farming. Horse stealing, too, was particularly easy. With the continual upheaval in the Mexican government, there was little organized effort to pursue horse thieves.

A significant result of the beaver brigades coming into California during this period was the inauguration of regular commerce between Los Angeles and St Louis, via Santa Fe, New Mexico. This route was initiated following the expedition of William Wolfskill, Ewing Young and David Jackson in the early 1830s. This trade, conducted by pack train, carried Mexican goods from Santa Fe – such as woolen products, blankets, and silver – along with American wares from St Louis into California. On the return journey, traders brought back chiefly Chinese products – silk, spices and the like – obtained from trading vessels on the coasts, but also California horses and mules bound for American markets.

Foreign population in Mexican California increased dramatically as a result of the beaver men. Many fur trappers fell under the spell of the province, making it their permanent home. These Americans rivaled those who came by sea in number. They settled in various regions, but were especially numerous in and about Los Angeles. Many of these men – William Wolfskill, J.J. Warner, Isaac Williams, William Workman, Jacob P. Leese – to name only a few, were men of excellent character and faithfully served the interests of their adopted country.

The bulk of these men, however, were of a more reckless character. Instinctively daring, contemptuous of Mexican control, and always heavily armed, these trappers were a source of fear and annoyance to California officials. In the numerous revolts amongst Mexican leadership, the beaver trapper was often a key factor for the winning side.

The search for this soft gold further served to familiarize settlers of the western states with the easy conditions of life in California and to acquaint them with the undeveloped resources of the Pacific slope. Reports and tales brought back by returning trappers quickly found their way into local newspapers raising a fever of interest in California, which spread along the American frontier.

Beaver trappers, having opened overland routes to the Pacific coast, became guides for immigrant parties using maps held mostly in their heads. They made it possible for government survey parties, such as that of John Fremont, to cross the Sierras successfully. Joseph Walker, Kit Carson, James Bridger, and many other less familiar names, learned the passes over the mountains that protected the eastern boundary of California while engaged in trapping beaver.

Besides being the first American to find his way into California by an overland route, Jedediah Smith made the first west to east crossing of the Sierra Nevada and the first overland entry into Oregon by following the Pacific coastline. Joseph Walker discovered Walker Pass and later guided the Chiles–Walker party to California. James Ohio Pattie, though trapping relatively few beaver, played a role in the political life of the region and wrote a book that helped attract Americans to the west.

As great as these contributions were, Smith, Walker, and Pattie had far less effect on the economic growth of the state than did trappers like William Wolfskill or George Yount. While operating a shingle-splitting business, Yount became friends with General Mariano Vallejo, which helped Yount secure a large land grant near modern Napa. The town of Yountville was named after him. On this ranch, Yount built the first flourmill in California.[42] His farm became known for its strawberries, grains, honey, and livestock.

Wolfskill settled in the Los Angeles area in the mid-1830s. He converted a two-acre, weed-covered field into an orange grove. This grove was so successful and was expanded so greatly, that by 1863, half of the state's orange trees were in his grove. Wolfskill's vineyards did just as well, making him one of the first to produce wine on a private, commercial basis. In 1859, he produced 50,000 gallons of wine. He also cultivated peaches, almonds, lemons, and walnuts.[43]

Trade in soft gold was a major enterprise that formed the economic basis for the acquisition of California by the United States. It was soft gold which brought the first New Englanders into the Pacific and to California. After the opening of California ports during the Mexican period, sea otters were the chief economic incentive for the many Americans occupied in the California–Hawaii–Canton trade triangle.

With the beginning of the hide and tallow trade, missions found a ready outlet for the products of their labor and a source of revenue with which to keep them well supplied with foreign goods. This venture led to further slackening of trade restrictions and a more liberal approach to commerce.

In the late 1820s mountain men pushed westward beyond the bounds of their own country and into Mexican California. Fortunately for men like Jedediah Smith and James Ohio Pattie, early trade in sea otter and cowhides put in place a resident American population willing to bail them out of diplomatic difficulties.

The search for soft gold monopolized the economy of the American Pacific until that remarkable find of a different gold at Sutter's Mill in 1848. United States diplomacy, prior to its war with Mexico, was rooted in a realization of the commercial value of soft gold on the Pacific coast. Along with victory in that war, came an expanded nation – the culmination of a movement begun and greatly furthered by the drive for hides. From exploration to commercial contact with other cultures, the trade in animal skins in California's fledgling commerce solidified its future position as an international economic force.

Notes

1 James Cook, *A Voyage to the Pacific Ocean. Undertaken by the Command of His Majesty, for Making Discoveries in the Northern Hemisphere ... in the Years 1776–80* (3 vols), London: W. and A. Strahan for G. Nicol and T. Cadell, 1784.

2 Ibid., Vol. II, pp. 270 f. and Vol. III, pp. 368 ff.

3 Ibid., Vol. III, pp. 401 ff.

4 Hector Chevigny, *Lord of Alaska. The Story of Baranov and the Russian Adventure*, Portland: Binfords and Mort, 1951, p. 17.

5 Ibid., p. 18.

6 Ibid.

7 Paul Phillips, *The Fur Trade* (2 vols), Norman, OK: University of Oklahoma Press, 1961, Vol. II, p. 42.

8 Adele Ogden, *The California Sea Otter Trade, 1784–1848,* Berkeley, CA: University of California Press, 1941, p. 6.

9 Ibid., p. v.

10 Ibid., p. 2.

11 Ibid.

12 Elliot C. Cowdin, "The Northwest Fur Trade," *The Merchants' Magazine*, XIV (June 1846), 534, quoted in Ogden, *The California Sea Otter Trade*, pp. 4–5.

13 Ogden, *The California Sea Otter Trade*, p. 15. James Gibson, *Otter Skins, Boston Ships, and China Goods*, Seattle: University of Washington Press, 1992, p. 20.

14 Gibson, *Otter Skins*, p. 20.

15 Ibid.

16 Ogden, *The California Sea Otter Trade*, p. 32.

17 Ibid., p. 35.

18 Ibid., pp. 45–65.

19 Ibid., p. 66

20 Ibid.

21 Ibid., p. 95–103.

22 Ibid., p. 96.

23 "Letter From Mr. Wallace," *Haye's Scrap Book*, XLVII, pp. 53–4, quoted in Ogden, *The California Sea Otter Trade*, p. 108. Timothy Flint (ed.), *The Personal Narrative of James O. Pattie* ..., Cincinnati, 1833, p. 387.

24 Iris Higbie Wilson, *William Wolfskill, 1798–1866*, Glendale, CA: Arthur H. Clark, 1965, p. 82.

25 Charles L. Camp (ed.), *George Yount and His Chronicles of the West*, Denver: Old West Publishing Co., 1966, pp. 100–14; Kenneth L. Holmes, *Ewing Young, Master Trapper*, Portland: Binfords and Mort, 1967, pp. 78–81; Job Francis Dye *Recollections of a Pioneer, 1830–1852*, Los Angeles: Glen Dawson, 1951, pp. 28–30; William H. Ellison, ed. *The Life and Adventures of George Nidever*, Berkeley: University of California Press, 1937, pp. 34–46.

26 Ogden, *The California Sea Otter Trade*, p. 140; Robert G. Cleland, *A History of California: The American Period,* New York: MacMillan Co., 1926, p. 9.

27 Robert G. Cleland, *From Wilderness To Empire: A History of California*, New York: Alfred A. Knopf, 1959, p. 68.

28 Cleland, *A History of California*, p. 44. See also, Richard H. Dana, *Two Years Before the Mast*, New York: Random House, 1936, pp. 78–79.

29 George R. Brooks, *The Southwest Expedition of Jedediah Smith, His Personal Account of the Journey, 1826–1827,* Glendale, CA: Arthur H. Clark Co., 1977, pp. 217 and 234.

30 Adele Ogden, "Hides and Tallow," *California Historical Society Quarterly*, Vol. VI, No. 3 (September 1927), p. 255.

31 Cleland, *A History of California*, p. 42.

32 Dana, *Two Years Before the Mast*, p. 274.

33 Cleland, *A History of California*, p. 44.

[34] Ibid., p. 43. For Phelps' quotes, see Adele Ogden, "Boston Hide Droghers along California Shores," *California Historical Society Quarterly*, Vol. VIII, No. 4 (December 1929), p. 305.

[35] Ogden, "Hides and Tallow," p. 261.

[36] Dana, *Two Years Before the Mast*, p. 274–75.

[37] Ogden, "Hides and Tallow," p. 258.

[38] Ibid., p. 296.

[39] Gibson, *Otter Skins*, p. 260.

[40] Dale Morgan, *Jedediah Smith and the Opening of the West,* New York: Bobbs-Merrill Co., 1953, p. 201.

[41] Joseph Grinnell, Joseph S. Dixon, and Jean M. Linsdale, *Fur-Bearing Mammals of California*, Berkeley, CA: University of California Press, 1937, pp. 635–37.

[42] Charles L. Camp (ed.), *George C. Yount and His Chronicles of the West*, Denver: Old West Publishing Co., 1966, p. xii.

[43] Iris H. Wilson, *William Wolfskill, 1798–1866, Frontier Trapper to California Ranchero*, Glendale, CA: Arthur H. Clark, 1965, pp. 144–77.

3

San Francisco's Pacific Exports, 1850–1898

David J. St Clair

The discovery of gold in California in 1848 quickly turned the small port of San Francisco, population 812, into a bustling commercial center. Population soared as miners poured in from all over the world. San Francisco quickly became the world's fastest growing city, reaching a population of 25,000 by 1850. California's non-Indian population of 8,000 in 1848 burgeoned to more than 100,000 in 1850, the result of the "greatest world migration in history to any one single spot for any one single purpose" (Gay, 1967, p. 225). By 1860, California's population had tripled again, reaching 380,000. The 1870 census recorded a population of 560,000, while the 1880 census found 865,000 people residing in the state (Rolle, 1987, pp. 2, 146, 166, 241).

More than 700 ships loaded with fortune seekers docked in San Francisco during the last nine months of 1849 (Bailey, 1996, p. 2). Crews often jumped ship to join the miners in the rush to the gold fields, leaving cargoes to rot in the holds. Ships were abandoned or salvaged for timber or converted to lodgings. California farms and businesses were abandoned in the rush to get rich quick. However, the dreams of quick fortune soon gave way to the reality of hard work in the gold fields and the rigors of coping with California's isolation. San Francisco during the Gold Rush was a remote outpost on the fringe of North America situated more than 2,500 miles west of the nearest manufacturing town of any importance and 15,000 miles removed from world markets (Bailey, 1996, p. 8).

California's rudimentary economy was unprepared for such a population explosion. Most food and commercial supplies had to be imported. Herds of sheep and cattle were driven into the state and ships brought manufactured products, food, building supplies, and machinery. San Francisco's first stone building was built with stones imported from China. Vine cuttings were imported from Europe and bottles were collected in Hawaii and South America for shipment to San Francisco. One of the California's earliest iron foundries was shipped from Chicago to Sacramento as ballast, arriving in 1850 (Bailey, 1996, pp. 8–9). Plentiful gold and scarce products created California's notoriously high Gold Rush prices. However, while high prices attracted ships from around the world, their haphazard arrival in San Francisco often glutted the market, sending prices tumbling.

San Francisco imports are a familiar part of the Gold Rush story. Less appreciated are its exports. Merchandise exports, excluding gold exports, exceeded imports at least by 1859 (San Francisco Chamber of Commerce, 1907, p. 149). In a remarkably short time, San Francisco became a major exporting center. By 1855, San Francisco had already become the nation's eighth largest exporting port (Evans, 1884, p. 11). In 1863, San Francisco ranked third in exports, behind only New York and Boston/ Charleston. In the 1860s, California exports, almost entirely through San Francisco, ranked third among the states. From 1871–80, California exports ranked fourth (Evans, 1884, pp. 233–36).

The traditional view of San Francisco exports has focused almost exclusively on two products – gold and wheat. The California Gold Rush, the world's first major gold discovery of the nineteenth century, pumped unprecedented amounts of gold into the world economy. Very little gold actually stayed in California. For example, from 1854 through 1859, California produced more than $318 million of gold, while exporting more than $292 million of treasure (Boalich, 1914, p. 20; and US Treasury, 1864, p. 188). In other words, gold and silver exports amounted to nearly 92 per cent of California gold production. The Comstock did not begin producing silver until 1859, so Nevada silver was not included in these treasure exports. Mexican and US silver coins were used extensively in nineteenth-century trade with China and were probably counted in these treasure exports. However, California trade with China was still in its infancy before 1859 so the amount of silver coins included in these figures was probably not substantial. Most of California's treasure export was gold and the gold drain explains the contemporary complaints of California merchants about chronic money shortages. It also explains why silver coins, mostly foreign denominations, were the de facto medium of exchange in California during the early years of the Gold Rush (Adams, 1913, pp. vii–xxvii).

Beyond mining, California agriculture quickly developed in response to the population explosion. From tentative beginnings in 1852, California producers were already sending shipments of wheat to New York, Australia, South America, Russian Alaska, and Great Britain by 1854 and 1855 (Paul, 1973, p. 32). By 1859, California wheat production had expanded to the point where export markets became a necessity (Paul, 1959, p. 394). In 1860, half of California wheat was being exported to Liverpool, with additional exports to Australia, New York, and China (Paul, 1959:, p. 395). After a brief lull, significant wheat exports resumed in the mid-1860s. In 1867, 80 per cent of California wheat exports went to Liverpool. California wheat exports in 1868 amounted to more than one-third of the total wheat exports from the United States (Paul, 1959, pp. 396–97).

Thomas Cox has argued that the California Gold Rush rekindled trade with China, trade that had dried up following the demise of the fur trade earlier in the century (Cox, 1969, p. 86). According to Cox, the ships that carried miners to the California gold fields could not be economically returned to Eastern ports in ballast. Consequently, ships were dispatched to Asia carrying any local products that might fetch a price in Asian markets. Cox points to lumber and flour as principal California exports to China. From 1860 through 1865, large quantities of lumber were exported from California, with China being "by far the most important foreign buyer during this period" (Cox, 1969, p. 89). Lesser quantities of quicksilver, hops, leather, butter, barley, beans, oats, wool, potatoes, and hay were also exported from California to Asia (Cox, 1969, pp. 90, 97).

Do gold, wheat, and lumber account for the bulk of California exports in the nineteenth century? What about trade in other products? Was China California's biggest export market? What about trade with other Pacific ports? These questions are the focus of this paper.

The search for answers to these questions immediately encounters a formidable problem – data availability. Data problems are endemic to historical research, but the problem is especially troublesome here because of the way in which trade data were compiled. Trade data aggregation has often made it difficult to find answers to the questions raised above. We have statistics on the volume of exports from individual American ports, statistics on the destination of American exports, and figures showing the export of individual products from American ports. However, we do not have good data showing which products were exported from individual ports to specific destinations (Mears, 1929, pp. 53–55; and Mears, 1935, p. 159).

This paper seeks to address this problem by exploiting two untapped data sources. First, a United States Treasury Department Report in 1864 provides a detailed account of products exported from San Francisco in 1861, 1862, and 1864 (US Treasury, 1864). In addition, the destination of San Francisco exports can be determined from this source. Unfortunately, these data are limited to only these three years.

Second, annual reports issued by the San Francisco Chamber of Commerce can be used to track San Francisco exports during the last two decades of the nineteenth century. The Chamber of Commerce compiled trade data from monthly customs reports, before the data were assembled into the published aggregates. As a consequence, the destination of exports can be determined. We can also track products shipped from San Francisco. In some cases, specific products can be linked to specific destinations. Annual reports from the Chamber of Commerce are available from 1858, however, earlier reports devote more attention to organizational matters than trade figures. Beneficial trade statistics from these reports begin in earnest in 1882 and are used here to provide a picture of San Francisco exports after 1881.[1]

While these two sources cannot provide a complete picture of California exports during the nineteenth century, they do shed some light on an important and little known aspect of the states' economy and its dealings with trading partners across the Pacific.

Gold and silver exports

Table 3.1 shows the destination of San Francisco treasure exports from 1854 through 1863. We do not have a breakdown of treasure into gold versus silver, but it is likely that gold accounts for the bulk of the exports. Comstock silver production was just getting underway toward the end of this period and probably had little impact on these treasure exports. On the other hand, Mexican and US silver coins are included in these treasure exports, but their magnitude cannot be determined from these data.

TABLE 3.1
Destination of San Francisco treasure exports, 1854–63

Destination	*Value ($)*	*Per cent*
Eastern ports	341,659,147	73.7
England	88,306,054	19.0
China	24,957,524	5.4
Panama	5,267,602	1.1
Other countries	3,516,010	Less than 1.0
TOTAL	463,706,338	100.0

Source: Compiled from (US Treasury, 1864, p. 188).

Almost three-quarters of California treasure during this period went to eastern US destinations.Their subsequent disposition (e.g. export to Europe) cannot be determined from these data. England received 19 per cent of California treasure exports while China took 5.4 per cent of the total.

Tables 3.2, 3.3, and 3.4 show San Francisco treasure exports for the period 1882–98. In this later period, Comstock silver was being produced in volume. In addition, railroads were now handling virtually all treasure shipments to eastern US destinations.[2] Note that these shipments were California "exports," but not US exports.

Table 3.2 shows that 39.6 per cent of treasure was shipped east, compared to 73.7 per cent in the earlier period shown in Table 3.1. Table 3.3 shows the four largest recipients of San Francisco treasure exports by sea in the 1882–98 period. These four – China, Japan, India, and Hawaii – account for 97.4 per cent of treasure exports by sea. In essence, these three Pacific destinations, along with India, account

TABLE 3.2
Treasure exports from San Francisco, 1882–98

Year	*By sea ($)*	*Overland ($)*	*Total ($)*
1882	6,149,169	4,234,135	10,383,304
1883	10,729,348	1,569,743	12,299,091
1884	15,837,920	1,849,979	17,687,899
1885	18,804,749	32,378,585	51,062,557
1886	18,209,881	12,435,575	30,645,456
1887	15,413,807	10,315,214	25,729,021
1888	16,547,230	6,002,105	22,549,335
1889	20,265,857	5,717,210	25,983,067
1890	8,667,380	3,516,920	12,184,300
1891	9,074,306	3,698,148	12,772,454
1892	NA	NA	NA
1893	13,052,942	16,534,052	29,586,994
1894	13,978,869	8,671,580	22,650,449
1895	18,799,671	17,153,423	35,953,094
1896	15,510,829	15,233,997	30,744,826
1897	18,756,336	5,176,409	23,932,745
1898	8,694,695	5,379,284	14,073,979
TOTAL	228,492,989	149,866,359	378,359,348
Per cent of treasure exports	60.4	39.6	

Source: San Francisco Chamber of Commerce, *Annual Reports*, various years.

for virtually all sea exports during this period. China alone took 72.2 per cent of these exports. Table 3.4 shows the composition of silver exports from San Francisco as a per cent of treasure exports by sea. The large number of Mexican silver coins in these exports is noteworthy. More than half of the silver exported from San Francisco during this period was re-exported Mexican silver dollars. Nevada mines provided the United States with a supply of silver, but Comstock silver did not automatically displace Mexican silver dollars in America's trade with China. Efforts to increase the circulation of American silver coins in Chinese commerce led to the creation of the American Trade Dollar in 1873.[3] However, these efforts were

TABLE 3.3
Destination of treasure exports by sea from San Francisco, 1882–98 (thousands of dollars)

Year	*China*	*India*	*Japan*	*Hawaii*
1882	4,634	534	831	54
1883	9,595	–	709	357
1884	13,074	274	1,279	1,176
1885	12,490	3,497	2,001	620
1886	11,102	4,098	2,051	923
1887	9,236	2,810	2,680	530
1888	10,359	3,592	2,034	300
1889	13,434	391	4,110	1,284
1890	6,852	48	584	828
1891	6,129	327	1,491	1,027
1892	NA	NA	NA	NA
1893	9,572	224	1,833	976
1894	8,234	–	4,614	607
1895	16,878	–	1,159	401
1896	11,001	35	1,472	1,112
1897	15,037	1,472	904	1,044
1898	7,266	417	–	861
TOTAL	164,894	17,717	27,750	12,102
Per cent of sea exports	72.2	7.8	12.1	5.3
Per cent of total treasure exports	43.6	4.7	7.3	3.2

Source: See Table 3.2

soon abandoned with the passage of the Allison–Brand Act and the Sherman Purchase Act that promoted domestic silver coinage. The large number of Mexican silver coins in San Francisco exports during this period is a testament to their importance in American trade with China.

TABLE 3.4
Composition of San Francisco silver exports, 1882–98

Type	*Per cent of treasure exports by sea*	*Per cent of total treasure exports*
Silver bullion and US silver coin	47.2	28.5
Mexican silver dollars	52.4	31.7
Silver bullion, US silver coin, and Mexican silver dollars	99.6	60.1

Source: See Table 3.2.

Table 3.4, in conjunction with Table 3.3, confirms the composition of the treasure flows shown in Table 3.2. Table 3.4 shows that silver accounted for 99.6 per cent of treasure exports by sea, while Table 3.3 reveals that 97.4 per cent of treasure exports by sea were destined for China, Japan, India, and Hawaii. Consequently, treasure exports by sea were virtually synonymous with silver exports to these three Pacific destinations, plus India. China was clearly the principle recipient of San Francisco silver exports. A meaningful way to view these silver exports to China in the second half of the nineteenth century is to see them in the context of the long-standing flow of silver across the Pacific to China. In this sense, these flows are more of an extension and continuation of earlier trade patterns.[4]

San Francisco Exports, 1861–1863

Table 3.5 shows San Francisco exports by sector for the period 1861–63. Mineral products clearly dominate. Agricultural exports are a distant second, followed by manufactures. Forest product exports were about one-sixth the size of manufacturing exports.

Table 3.6 shows total merchandise exports and merchandise exports to Pacific regions. Merchandise exports exclude gold and silver. The importance of Pacific exports is noteworthy. Thomas Cox observed that, while trans-Pacific trade was too small to have had a real impact on the national economy, it was significant for the Far West (Cox, 1969, p. 86). The predominance of Pacific exports in these figures tends to support and quantify this view.

Table 3.7 shows the destination of San Francisco merchandise exports by country. Great Britain was the largest export market, accounting for virtually all

TABLE 3.5
San Francisco exports by type, 1861–63 ($)

	1861	*1862*	*1863*
Mineral products	42,103,193	44,105,662	47,982,398
Agricultural products	4,314,688	3,698,268	4,277,586
Forest products	69,931	149,560	134,086
Maritime products	21,828	21,868	11,285
Manufactures	962,876	798,191	873,854
TOTAL	47,472,217	48,773,549	53,280,209

Source: Compiled from US Treasury, 1864, p. 188.

TABLE 3.6
San Francisco merchandise exports, 1861–63

Year	*Total exports ($)*	*Exports to Pacific regions ($)*	*Pacific exports as per cent of total exports*
1861	8,184,693	5,346,689	65.3
1862	7,127,172	5,771,955	81.0
1863	8,635,274	6,937,452	80.3
TOTAL	23,947,139	18,056,096	75.4

Source: Compiled from US Treasury, 1864, pp. 186–89.

that flour exports to China are generally attributed to the influence of Chinese immigrants. Contemporary observers credited immigrant Chinese in the US, mostly residing in San Francisco, with overcoming ancient prejudices against a barbarian diet (US Treasury, 1864, p. 190). Finally, Table 3.15 shows lumber exports by sea from San Francisco, the per cent of sea exports sent to China, and China's rank as a recipient of lumber exports. Thomas Cox's claims that lumber exports were an

TABLE 3.7
Destination of San Francisco merchandise exports, 1861–63

Country	*Value($)*	*Per cent of total exports*	*Per cent of Pacific exports*
Great Britain	5,891,043	24.6	–
China	2,680,324	11.2	14.8
Australia and New Zealand	1,876,421	7.8	10.4
Mexico	3,929,221	16.4	21.8
Peru	650,721	2.7	3.6
Japan	81,076	Less than 1.0	Less than 1.0
British Columbia	5,119,856	21.4	28.4
Hawaii	939,616	3.9	5.2

Source: Compiled from US Treasury, 1864, p. 187.

non-Pacific exports. British Columbia and Mexico were the largest Pacific markets, followed by China and Australia and New Zealand.

China did not dominate San Francisco merchandise exports, or even Pacific exports during this period. However, these data suggest that exports to China were clearly more important to San Francisco than to the US economy as a whole. Peter Schran puts US exports to China in the 1861–65 period at 2.5 per cent of US exports (Schran, 1986, p. 239). It is not clear if treasure exports are included in his figures. However, even if we take these figures to be net of treasure exports, China's share of San Francisco merchandise exports is still four times greater than the national share. If treasure is indeed in Schran's figure, then the relative importance to San Francisco of merchandise trade with China was even more pronounced.

Table 3.8 shows leading San Francisco merchandise exports for this period. Wheat was already the largest export, followed by quicksilver. Significant quantities of wool, hides, flour, and copper ore were exported as well. By comparison, lumber exports were relatively insignificant.

Merchandise Exports, 1870–81

Table 3.9 shows San Francisco merchandise exports for the period 1870–81. These are the only figures on exports for this period that can be gleaned from the San

TABLE 3.8
Leading San Francisco merchandise exports, 1861–63 ($)

Product	*1861*	*1862*	*1863*	*Total*
Barley	361,452	131,282	65,044	557,778
Copper ore	135,240	370,200	719,300	1,224,740
Flour	858,425	688,234	767,270	2,313,929
Hides	444,995	947,253	924,567	2,316,815
Lumber	69,931	49,560	123,084	342,575
Oats	156,879	72,045	130,602	359,526
Quicksilver	1,079,850	1,138,961	1,073,078	3,651,415
Silver ores	211,345	34,740	118,109	364,194
Wheat	2,702,434	1,372,572	1,754,116	5,829,122
Wool	519,577	1,009,194	1,119,098	2,647,869

Source: Compiled from US Treasury, 1864, p. 187.

TABLE 3.9
Largest merchandise exports from San Francisco, 1870–81 ($)

Product	*Value*	*Per cent of California merchandise exports*
Wheat	176,734,611	64.4
Flour	29,259,285	10.7
Wool	19,379,327	7.1
Quicksilver	13,093,614	4.8
Wine	6,208,692	2.3
Barley	3,916,355	1.4
Lumber	3,307,378	1.2

Source: Compiled from San Francisco Chamber of Commerce, 1882, pp. 36–37.

Francisco Chamber of Commerce *Annual Reports*. Wheat exports were clearly dominant, followed by flour, wool, and quicksilver. Wine exports were already significant and lumber was again relatively insignificant.

Merchandise Exports, 1882–1898

Table 3.10 shows San Francisco merchandise exports and Pacific merchandise exports for the period 1882–1898. The share of Pacific exports is dramatically lower than the share for 1861–63 previously reported in Table 3.6. Still, Pacific exports remained significant, and show a definite increase over the period at hand. Tables 3.11 and 3.12 suggest that large exports to Great Britain (mostly wheat) were responsible for the lower share of Pacific exports. On the other hand, rapidly rising exports to Japan as the century drew to a close were responsible for the rising share of Pacific exports over the period.

Table 3.12 highlights the magnitude of California exports to England. It also shows the distribution of Pacific trade. Central America and Hawaii were the largest Pacific markets, each accounting for 23 per cent of Pacific exports. China was third with 21.7 per cent. Exports to British Columbia declined dramatically from their level in the 1861–1863 period, while exports to Japan increased dramatically.

Tables 3.11 and 3.12 suggest that California exports were spread throughout the Pacific, not simply destined for China. Indeed, exports to Central America and to Hawaii were greater than exports to China. Perhaps the best way to characterize California's non-English exports is to suggest that California merchants pursued diverse Pacific markets, not simply Chinese or Asian markets.

Table 3.13 shows the size of California wheat (including flour) exports, as well as California's share of US wheat exports. Table 3.14 shows San Francisco wheat and flour exports to England and China. As noted earlier, Rodman Paul supported his argument about the importance of the English wheat market by noting that Liverpool took 80 per cent of the California wheat crop in 1867 (Paul, 1959, pp. 396–97). He also pointed out that California wheat exports amounted to more than a third of US wheat exports in 1868 (Paul, 1959, pp. 396–97).

The figures presented in Tables 3.13 and 3.14 support Paul's view. They also provide a more complete picture of the size of California wheat exports. Wheat and flour exports account for 56.2 per cent of California's merchandise exports after 1881. Table 3.13 also reveals that California continued to enjoy a large share of American wheat exports after 1881. In 1882 and in 1886, California's shares of US wheat exports were only slightly less than the one-third level cited by Paul for 1868. California wheat exports remained strong until the very end of the century.

The importance of the English wheat market for California exports is apparent in Table 3.14. Indeed, much of California's exports during this period might be

TABLE 3.10
San Francisco merchandise exports, 1828–1898

Year	Total exports ($)	Pacific exports ($)	Pacific export's % of total
1882	50,194,014	15,420,151	31
1883	42,010,893	14,301,702	34
1884	34,304,389	12,361,074	36
1885	32,986,021	12,172,745	37
1886	37,147,326	12,480,930	34
1887	29,276,127	12,093,398	41
1888	34,440,500	12,464,500	36
1889	35,240,774	14,099,878	40
1890	35,897,692	14,416,051	40
1891	48,515,234	16,517,521	34
1892	NA	NA	
1893	33,853,345	11,714,551	35
1894	26,410,672	12,427,189	47
1895	33,264,861	14,494,321	44
1896	43,513,996	21,708,274	50
1897	44,280,000	19,785,079	45
1898	35,852,544	21,734,751	61
TOTAL	597,188,388	238,192,115	40

Source: See Table 3.2.

aptly summarized as "one product being shipped to one country." However, care should be taken not to allow the dominance of wheat exports to Britain to obscure other California exports. Without wheat exports to Britain, California exports were still robust and diverse. The success of wheat exports should not be read as the failure of other exports. Wheat and flour exports to China are also shown in Table 3.14. Wheat exports to China were virtually nil, however, flour exports were significant. Although flour exports to China were generally below flour exports to England until the late 1880s, China was a major buyer of California flour. Cox's description of China as a good customer for California wheat is essentially correct, although a Chinese market share that seldom exceeded 50 per cent still left plenty of room for significant wheat exports to other markets. It is also interesting to note

TABLE 3.11
Destination of San Francisco exports, 1882–98
(thousands of dollars)

Year	China	Hawaii	Central America	Australia/ New Zealand	Pacific Islands (ex. Hawaii)	Japan	British Columbia	Asiatic Russia	England	France	Belgium
1882	4,688	2,606	3,726	1,661	560	476	1,583	120	29,762	1,602	2,342
1883	4,254	3,032	3,016	1,204	696	373	1,595	132	25,949	608	920
1884	2,897	2,572	2,899	1,346	683	492	1,319	153	19,516	832	1,409
1885	3,602	2,428	2,359	1,441	395	628	1,190	129	20,194	262	18
1886	3,614	3,057	2,047	1,460	572	592	968	168	20,471	2,708	613
1887	3.090	2,864	2,846	1,186	354	766	804	184	16,544	153	0
1888	2,433	2,837	2,926	2,027	619	684	800	140	18,494	2,783	250
1889	2,657	3,353	3,324	2,399	709	636	908	113	19,286	570	250
1890	3,128	4,179	3,475	1,312	571	747	861	142	16,998	2,182	1,089
1891	3,184	4,100	4,087	1,691	533	738	870	195	17,140	12,447	1,845
1892	NA	NA	NA	NA	NA	NA	NA	NA	NA	NA	NA
1893	2,559	2,985	3,435	813	510	1554	715	143	16,259	424	100
1894	2,409	3,014	3,761	875	431	1,322	454	161	9,657	100	4
1895	2,328	3,455	4,547	1,357	385	1,805	369	247	14,539	14	0
1896	3,279	3,687	5,019	5,142	1,104	2,477	432	568	15,973	93	604
1897	3,948	4,804	3,906	2,569	529	3,038	612	377	17,445	484	817
1898	3,528	6,008	3,306	2,345	727	4,510	1,004	307	9,210	11	9
TOTAL	51,599	54,982	54,680	28,829	9,379	19,839	14,484	3,278	287,436	25,275	10,227

Source: See Table 3.2.

TABLE 3.12
Distribution of San Francisco merchandise exports, 1882–98

	Per cent of total exports	Per cent Pacific exports
China	8.6	21.7
Hawaii	9.2	23.0
Pacific islands (ex. Hawaii)	1.6	3.9
Central America	9.2	23.0
Australia and New Zealand	4.8	12.1
Japan	3.3	8.3
British Columbia	2.4	6.1
Asiatic Russia	< 1.0	1.4
TOTAL PACIFIC	39.9	
England	48.1	
France	4.2	
Belgium	1.7	

Source: See Table 3.2.

important part of California's Pacific trade, and that China was the principal export market for lumber, is not supported by the data in Table 3.15. Lumber was not a significant California export and China was not a major export market for California lumber.[5]

Quicksilver exports

California quicksilver deserves special note. As shown in Tables 3.8 and 3.9, quicksilver was a significant merchandise export. Only wheat exports were larger in the early 1860s. During the 1870s, quicksilver exports ranked fourth – behind wheat, flour, and wool – in merchandise exports. Quicksilver remained a significant export throughout the nineteenth century (St Clair, 1994/95; and St Clair, 1998a).

Quicksilver exports were overwhelmingly a Pacific phenomenon. From 1850 through 1890, more than 95 per cent of California quicksilver was shipped to Pacific

TABLE 3.13
San Francisco wheat and flour exports, 1882–1898
(thousands of dollars)

Year	Export value	California exports as a per cent of US exports
1882	36,164	24
1883	29,199	17
1884	22,618	18
1885	21,755	18
1886	25,816	29
1887	18,124	13
1888	21,711	20
1889	21,396	24
1890	22,113	22
1891	33,105	31
1892	NA	NA
1893	15,911	9
1894	9,020	7
1895	13,181	14
1896	18,670	21
1897	17,784	16
1898	9,078	4
TOTAL	335,645	17

Sources: San Francisco Chamber of Commerce, *Annual Reports*, various years listed in References; and US Department of Commerce 1960, pp. 546–47.

destinations.[6] More than 43 per cent was shipped to China, while Mexico received more than 37 per cent. During this period, California produced more than half of the world output of quicksilver. During its peak production years, California quicksilver mines supplied two-thirds of the world's quicksilver. Since mercury (quicksilver) was virtually indispensable to gold and silver recovery before 1890, California quicksilver had a significant effect on precious metals production in the United States and abroad (St Clair, 1994/95; and St Clair, 1998a). On the other hand, Chinese quicksilver demand was primarily a demand for mercury for use in the manufacture of vermilion, a prized red pigment.

TABLE 3.14
Destination of San Francisco wheat and flour exports, various years (as per cent of California wheat and flour exports)

Year	England		China	
	Flour	Wheat	Flour	Wheat
1879	24.7	87.3	46.1	–
1880	29.6	93.9	45.5	–
1881				
1882				
1883	60.9	92.4	24.4	Neg
1884				
1885	49.9	98.6	33.8	Neg
1886	41.7	80.3	37.5	–
1887				
1888	33.5	81.3	32.6	–
1889				
1890	34.9	78.8	35.1	–
1891				
1892				
1893				
1894				
1895	5.1	97.6	50.7	–
1896				
1897				
1898	9.2	75.8	44.3	Neg

Source: See Table 3.2.

Omitted exports

While the *Annual Reports* of the San Francisco Chamber of Commerce data are an invaluable addition to the historical record, they clearly omit some exports. Not all exports were surveyed and enumerated in these reports. The most glaring omission is manufacturers. The Treasury Department data used in the discussion of exports in the 1861–63 period showed significant manufacturing exports. However, no manufacturer exports were reported in the *Annual Reports*. Did earlier exports of manufactures disappear after 1882?

TABLE 3.15
San Francisco lumber exports, 1876–1898

Year	Value of exports by sea ($)	China per cent of sea exports	China rank
1876	199,894	2.6	#10
1877	267,333	3.9	#8
1878	289,374	–	–
1879	NA	NA	NA
1880	284,776	*	#14
1881	387,587		*
#13			
1882	512,173	*	#20
1883	381,386	*	#12
1884	513,899	*	#18
1885	431,784	*	#12
1886	296,548	*	#22
1887	339,924	*	#16
1888	593,918	*	#12
1889	457,208	*	#21
1890	447,468	–	–
1891	470,264	–	–
1892	NA	NA	NA
1893	NA	NA	NA
1894	333,921	–	–
1895	287,691	–	–
1896	649,359	–	–
1897	471,519	–	–
1898	411,521	2.7	#10

An * indicates less than 1 per cent.

Source: See Table 3.2.

This was not the case. Other sources mention substantial exports of California machinery and industrial product, especially mining equipment and related mining peripherals and supplies, throughout the nineteenth century (Bailey, 1996, pp. viii, 20, 22, 29, 36, 39). California foundries and machine shops developed innovative machinery for California and Nevada gold and silver mines and quickly became major suppliers of mining equipment the world over (Bailey, 1996; St Clair, 1998/99). California mining equipment suppliers dominated export markets, especially through the 1870s, even exporting entire quartz mills (Bailey, 1996: 36). John Hittell also chronicled significant California exports of industrial leather hose and belts, mining machinery, and other industrial products (Hittell, 1882, pp. 520, 27, 643, 646, 612, 614).

In addition, it is clear from a footnote in the 1901 *Annual Report* that manufacture exports were deliberately omitted from Chamber of Commerce reports. The 1901 report enumerated fourteen commodities exported from San Francisco to the Hawaiian Islands in 1898 and 1899. However, a footnote states that "The principle part of the export value is for machinery and other plantation supplies, dry goods, hardware, building supplies, live stock, general groceries and provisions" (San Francisco Chamber of Commerce, 1901, p. 127). While some of the building supplies and general provisions may have been enumerated in the table, it is clear that the machinery, hardware, etc were not included. By my calculation, the fourteen enumerated products only accounted for about two-thirds of California's exports to Hawaii during these years, suggesting that the omitted manufacture exports were quite significant.

Summary

The picture of California exports presented here is not complete, but hopefully it is an improvement over the dearth of data that has been the usual fare in this area. Major features of California's trade include significant trade with Great Britain in wheat, large exports of silver and flour to China, and large exports of quicksilver to China and Mexico. Silver, but not gold, flowed to Pacific markets. In addition, California's trade with Hawaii, Latin America, and British Columbia was often greater than its trade with China. Contrary to Cox's claims, lumber exports in general, and lumber exports to China in particular, were not significant. While lumber exports may have been significant in Oregon or Washington, the figures presented here do not support such a view of California trade. Finally, trade with China and the Pacific was far more important to San Francisco trade than it was to trade with the United States as a whole.

How should one view California's export trade during the second half of the nineteenth century? Having acquired a window on the Pacific in 1846, what did Americans do with it? Was it a springboard to Asia? To China? Was the revival of Pacific trade a by-product of what Cox called the passage to India?

Certainly one of the primary motives for acquiring a window on the Pacific was the prospect of US trade with China. But California exports show a different course of events. China was indeed a significant export market for silver, flour, and quicksilver. However, outside of these products, trade with China does not seem to warrant the importance that Cox and others have claimed. California's exports were not exclusively or primarily focused on China. Indeed, aside from the huge wheat trade with England, San Francisco exports are best characterized as the export of a diverse set of products all around the Pacific. Characterizing this trade as having been exclusively or even primarily "Asian" or "Chinese" seems inappropriate. A passage to India may serve as a good description of the expectations of California merchants, but a "passage to the Pacific" may be a more apt description of the reality of California exports in the second half of the nineteenth century.

This last point bears upon a related issue. Some scholars have argued that the China market, while offering so much promise, never lived up to expectations (see, Schran, 1986; Collins, 1972, pp. 64–103; Varg, 1968). The China trade, always enthusiastically hyped as a savior for American producers seeking exports markets, seldom lived up to its billing. Eager American shoemakers, counting Chinese feet, seldom realized sales commensurate with their dreams. This disappointment was a common theme at the turn of the century, and has been argued by modern scholars as well (Schran, 1986). The data presented here suggest that aside from flour, quicksilver, and silver, China did not dominate California's exports. This does not mean that the Chinese market was insignificant, but the reality of less-than-resounding trade with China was probably disappointing to many California merchants. The data presented here do not speak directly to this issue, but they may be worth consideration in this regard.

Notes

1 San Francisco Chamber of Commerce *Annual Reports* for the years 1893, 1900, and 1901 do exist, but have not come into the author's possession. Consequently, data for 1892, 1899, and 1900 are not available as of this writing.

2 Postal shipments of treasure are not counted in any of the figures cited in this article. There are no reliable estimates of their magnitude or importance.

3 For a discussion of the American trade dollar, see St Clair, 1998b. The remainder of this discussion is from this source.

4 For a discussion of silver flows to Asia in earlier periods, see Flynn and Giráldez, 1994; Flynn and Giráldez, 1995; Flynn and Giráldez, 1996a; Flynn and Giráldez, 1996b; Von Glahn, 1996a; and Von Glahn, 1996b.

5 In Cox's defense, California lumber may have been exported through Oregon, or perhaps Washington. This author cannot find any indication that this occurred, but it seems appropriate to venture the possibility. While San Francisco was the primary port for California exports throughout this period, the possibility of lumber exports through Oregon cannot be dismissed.

6 All of the following figures are from St Clair, 1994/95 and St Clair, 1998a

Referemces

Adams, E., *Private Gold Coinage of California, 1849–55: Its history and its issues*, Brooklyn, NY: Edgar H. Adams, 1913.

Bailey, L., *Supplying the Mining World: The mining equipment manufacturers of San Francisco, 1850–1900*, Tucson, AR: Westernlore Press, 1996.

Boalich, E., *Mineral Production for 1913*, Sacramento, CA: State Printing Office, 1914.

Collins, G., *Gateway to the Orient: San Francisco and the China trade at the turn of the century*, Masters Thesis, San Diego State College, 1972.

Cox, T., "The Passage to India Revisited: Asian Trade and the Development of the Far West, 1850–1900," in John A. Carroll (ed.), *Reflections of Western Historians*, Tucson: University of Arizona Press, 1968, pp. 85–103.

Evans, C. *Exports, Domestic from the United States to All Countries from 1789 to 1883, Inclusive*, Washington, DC: Government Printing Office, 1884.

Flynn, D. and Giráldez, A., "China and the Manila Galleons," in A. Latham and H. Kawakatsu (eds), *Japanese Industrialization and the Asian Economy*, London: Routledge, 1994.

——, "Born with a 'Silver Spoon': The origins of world trade in 1571," *Journal of World History*, Vol. 6, No. 2 (1995), pp. 201–21.

——, "Monetary Substances in Global Perspective: An introductory essay," in D. Flynn, and A. Giráldez (eds), *Metals and Monies in an Emerging Global Economy*, Aldershot: Variorum, 1996a.

——, "China and the Spanish Empire," *Revista de Historia Economica*, Vol. 14, No. 2 (1996b), pp. 309–38.

Gay, T., *James W. Marshall: The discoverer of California gold*, Georgetown, CA: Talisman Press, 1967.

Hittell, J., *The Commerce and Industries of the Pacific Coast of North America*, San Francisco: A.L. Bancroft, 1882.

Mears, E., *San Francisco's Trans-Pacific Shipping*, Kyoto: American Council, Institute of Pacific Relations, 1929.

——, *Maritime Trade of the Western United States*, Stanford, CA: Stanford University Press, 1935.

Paul, R., "The Wheat Trade between California and the United Kingdom," *The Mississippi Valley Historical Review*, XLV (1959), pp. 391–412.

——, "The Beginnings of Agriculture: Innovation vs. Continuity," in George H. Knoles (ed.), *Essays and Assays: California History Revisited*, Los Angeles: The Ward Ritchie Press, 1973, pp. 27–37.

Rolle, A., *California: A history*, Arlington Heights, IL: Harlan Davidson, 1987.

San Francisco Chamber of Commerce, *Thirty-Second Annual Report*, San Francisco: Murdock & Co., 1882.

——, *Thirty-Fourth Annual Report*, San Francisco: Murdock & Co., 1884.

——, *Thirty-Sixth Annual Report*, San Francisco: Murdock & Co., 1886.

——, (1887) *Thirty-Seventh Annual Report*, San Francisco: Murdock & Co., 1886.

——, *Thirty-Ninth Annual Report*, San Francisco: Commercial Publishing, 1889.

——, *Forty-First Annual Report*, San Francisco: Commercial Publishing, 1891.

——, *Forty-Second Annual Report*, San Francisco: Commercial Publishing, 1892.

——, *Forty-Sixth Annual Report*, San Francisco: Commercial Publishing, 1896.
——, *Forty-Seventh Annual Report*, San Francisco: Commercial Publishing, 1897.
——, *Forty-Ninth Annual Report*, San Francisco: Commercial Publishing, 1899.
——, *Fifty-First Annual Report*, San Francisco: Commercial Publishing, 1901.
——, *Fifty-Sixth and Fifty-Seventh Annual Reports*, San Francisco: Neal Publishing, 1907.
Schneider, J., *Quicksilver: The complete history of Santa Clara County's new Almaden Mine*, San Jose, CA: Zella Schneider, 1992.
Schran, P., "The Minor Significance of Commercial Relations between the United States and China, 1850–1931," in E. May, and J. Fairbank (eds), *America's China Trade in Historical Perspective: The Chinese and American Performance*, Cambridge, MA: Harvard University Press, 1986, pp. 237–58.
St Clair, D. ,"New Almaden and California Quicksilver in the Pacific Rim Economy," *California History*, LXXIII, Vol. 4 (1994/95), pp. 278–95.
——, "California Quicksilver in the Pacific Rim Economy, 1850-1890," in S. Miller, A. Latham, and D. Flynn (eds), *Studies in the Economic History of the Pacific Rim*, London: Routledge, 1998a, pp. 210–33.
——, "American Trade Dollars in Nineteenth Century China," in D. Flynn and A. Latham (eds) *Pacific Centuries*, London: Routledge, 1998b.
——, "The Gold Rush and the Beginnings of California Industry,"*California History*, Vol. LXXVII, No. 4 (1998/99), pp. 185–208.
US Department of Commerce, *Historical Statistics of the United States: Colonial times to 1957*, Washington, DC: Government Printing Office, 1960.
US Treasury Department, *Statistics of the Foreign and Domestic Commerce of the United States*, Washington, DC: Government Printing Office, 1864. Citations are to the Johnson Reprint: New York (1972).
Varg, P., "The Myth of the China Market, 1890–1894," *American Historical Review*, LXXXIII (1968), pp. 742–58.
Von Glahn, R., "Myth and Reality of China's Seventeenth-Century Monetary Crisis," *The Journal of Economic History*, Vol. 56, No. 2 (1996a).
Von Glahn, R., *Fountain of Fortune: Money and Monetary Policy in China, 1000–1700*, Berkeley: University of California, 1996b.

4

Powerhouse Economies of the Pacific A Comparative Study of Gold and Wheat in Nineteenth-Century Victoria and California

Warwick Frost

The comparative method is a useful tool for understanding the development of the countries and regions of the Pacific. It has especially been used for comparing and contrasting the regions of recent European settlement, which include the USA, Canada, Australia, and New Zealand. However, the comparative method has rarely been used for the (eastern) Pacific coast of Australia and the (western) Pacific coast of the USA.

In particular the two powerhouse economies of the nineteenth-century Pacific, Victoria and California, have only occasionally been the subjects of comparative studies. The cause of this is mainly teleological. Looking backwards from the dawn of the twenty-first century, California appears too advanced, too rich, and too "Californian" to be compared with anywhere else in the Pacific, or on Earth. Victoria may also be Western, advanced and wealthy, but nowhere on the scale or style of California and indeed in the twentieth century it has lost its Australian pre-eminence to New South Wales. Such a loss of domination is unthinkable for California. Australian scholars may think of comparisons for Victoria, but it is very hard for those on the other side of the Pacific to consider California as anything but unique and therefore beyond comparison. An example of this view is Rothstein who argued that due to gold, for a short time, "in the 1850s the Pacific slope resembled Australia's more than it did the other sections of the United States," but from the 1860s onwards the comparison was no longer valid as the American Pacific Slope progressed far more rapidly than the Australian Pacific Slope (Rothstein, 1975, pp. 273–74).

The few comparative studies of California with Victoria tend to concentrate on specific themes in which the two states share a common history. Two recent examples illustrate this. The first is David Goodman's *Gold Seeking: Victoria and California in the 1850s* (1994). California (1848 onwards) and Victoria (1851 onwards) were the two great gold rushes of world history and thrust these two isolated underdeveloped pastoral economies into the world spotlight. Goodman's interest is in how the participants in these rushes thought about the social impact of these revolutionary events. Significantly, Goodman is inclined to dwell on the differences between the two gold rushes rather than the similarities, especially the different types of society and the different customs which developed.

The second is Lionel Frost's *The New Urban Frontier: Urbanisation and city building in Australasia and the American West* (1991). Frost argues that nineteenth-century Victoria and California saw the development of "Pacific Cities," low density spacious cities which contrasted to the crowded European style cities which had previously developed in regions of recent European settlement. Melbourne and Los Angeles were the best examples of these new style cities (others included Denver, Oakland, Auckland, Vancouver, and Adelaide). Due to high incomes generated through providing services to their rich hinterlands, the inhabitants of these cities were able to afford suburban housing and lifestyles, parks, and wide streets and to avoid overcrowding and slums.

The purpose of this paper is to argue that the potential of the comparative tool extends well beyond these two topics. To further illustrate the value of comparison, this paper presents two case studies. The first is the effect of gold on the economic and population growth of California and Victoria. The second is the wheat industry, particularly the decline of wheat-growing in California and the central part of Victoria.

The effect of gold

Before gold, California and Victoria were isolated minor pastoral European settlements on the Pacific Rim. However, Victoria was far more developed than California; just prior to the discovery of gold, its capital Melbourne had a population of 23,000, whereas San Francisco's population was less than 500. Victoria's success was entirely due to the export of wool; not only was much of the state highly suited to its production, but it was initially pioneered in New South Wales and Tasmania and was simply landed in Victoria as a fully viable and established industry. The returns from wool meant that Victoria was rapidly (though lightly) settled and by the early 1840s indigenous society had collapsed and the indigenous population was severely reduced. In contrast, California had not really established a staple before gold. Whereas Victoria was sandwiched between the established colonies of New South Wales and Tasmania, California was very isolated from the older American states. Up to 1848, settlement was sparse and mainly coastal and the greatest shock to the indigenous peoples would come after the discovery of gold.

Gold greatly accelerated population growth, as shown in Table 4.1. What is perhaps surprising is how much higher the population of Victoria was than that of California in the 1850s through to the 1870s. In 1850 (the year California achieved statehood and Victoria became a separate colony to New South Wales), California had about 30 per cent more population than Victoria. However this gap was due to the earlier discovery of gold. By 1853 (two years after gold was discovered), Victoria's population was 195,000, double that of California's two years after gold. By 1860, Victoria's population was 150,000, or about 40 per cent, greater than

TABLE 4.1
Population of California and Victoria
(thousands)

	1850	1860	1870	1880	1890	1900
California	93	380	560	865	1,208	1,485
Victoria	71	530	710	850	1,119	1,192

Source: *United States Census of Population*, 1850–1900; Victoria, 1973, pp. 1069–70.

California's. In 1870 the gap was still 150,000 in Victoria's favor. Then, in 1880 California pushed narrowly ahead, a lead that was maintained in 1890. However, by 1900 California's population was nearly 300,000, or 25 per cent, greater than Victoria's.

How can Victoria's greater population up to the 1870s be explained? There are three possibilities. First, gold-mining in Victoria remained important throughout most of the nineteenth century, with new discoveries and the development of deep-lead mining. Second, in 1861 the Victorian government began to make land available for small family farmers under the Selection Act. In contrast, in California until the 1880s much of the best land would remain tied up by speculators and court action over disputed Mexican land grants. Third, for immigrants, Victoria was the most attractive of the Australian colonies, whereas California was perhaps not as attractive as the mid-western states which were closer to eastern markets.

One significant difference of the 1860s and 1870s was in British migration. At the 1860 Census, 61 per cent of California's population had been born in the USA, 12 per cent in Britain (England, Scotland, Ireland and Wales), 11 per cent in Europe and 9 per cent in China. In contrast, the 1861 Census of the much larger Victorian population showed that 29 per cent had been born in Australia, 60 per cent in Britain, 3 per cent in Europe and 5 per cent in China. Put another way, in 1860 California had 45,000 British and Victoria in 1861 had 320,000. In 1870 63 per cent of California's population was American born and 14 per cent British, whereas in 1871 49 per cent of Victoria's population was Australian born and 45 per cent British. In making a decision to travel half-way around the world to seek gold or other opportunities, the British overwhelmingly chose their colony in Victoria in preference to California. It is tempting to speculate that if gold had not been discovered in Victoria, where these British would have migrated to, indeed would they have left Britain?

Population growth in the key cities of San Francisco and Melbourne, as shown in Table 4.2, paralleled the general pattern of California and Victoria. Even though San Francisco was 200 miles and Melbourne was 100 miles from the main goldfields, they both functioned as major ports and service centers for the miners. Melbourne was significantly larger than San Francisco throughout most of the nineteenth century. In 1860 it held over twice the population of its Californian counterpart. San Francisco grew rapidly in the 1860s, but by 1870 Melbourne was still some 25 per cent larger. In 1880 they drew roughly level, then "Marvellous Melbourne" went through its great boom. Between 1880 and 1890 Melbourne's population soared by over 70 per cent and of Victoria's population increase of 269,000 over that period, 202,000, or 75 per cent, went to Melbourne. In comparison, San Francisco grew by 32 per cent and in 1890 was only three-quarters of the size of Melbourne. During the depression of the 1890s Melbourne's population fell (to 444,000 in 1894), but it saw in the new century still larger than San Francisco.

TABLE 4.2
Population of San Francisco and Melbourne
(thousands)

	1850*	**1860***	**1870**	**1880**	**1890**	**1900**
San Francisco**	35	59	162	274	364	439
Melbourne	23	140	203	281	483	494

* Population of Melbourned in 1851 and 1861.
** San Francisco also includes the cities of Oakland, Alameda, and Berkeley.

Source: *United States Census of Population,* 1850–1900; Victoria, 1973, pp. 1069–70.

The chief difference between the influence of gold on California and Victoria, was in the development of gold towns, as shown in Table 4.3. Initially miners in both regions congregated in mining camps, tent cities of up to 30,000, which could quickly disappear with the news of better strikes. In time, some of these were transformed into towns with permanent buildings and a range of functions. Those that made the transformation did so because their gold was more extensive or deep underground and required the commitment of capital and time to find. Some towns developed because they combined gold with other activities, such as servicing agriculture or transport routes.

TABLE 4.3
Population of gold towns in California and Victoria
(thousands)

	1860/1	1870/1	1880/1	1890/1	1900/1
VICTORIA					
Ballarat	22.1	47.2	41.1	43.4	46.8
Bendigo	13.6	28.6	35.6	34.1	39.2
Castlemaine	13.0	9.3	8.6	6.0	6.9
Stawell	0.2	5.2	7.3	5.2	5.3
Clunes	1.7	6.1	5.8	3.5	2.4
Maryborough	2.5	2.9	3.3	5.0	5.6
Creswick	4.7	4.0	3.7	3.1	3.1
Daysleford	1.9	4.7	3.9	3.8	3.4
CALIFORNIA					
Grass Valley	3.8	7.1	6.7	6.8	4.7
Nevada City	3.7	4.0	4.0	2.5	3.3

Sources: *United States Census of Population,* 1860–1900; Census of Victoria, 1861–1901.

In Victoria two gold towns, Ballarat and Bendigo, rose to major prominence. Both discovered in 1851, they remained as major gold producers throughout the nineteenth century. By 1871 Ballarat had a population of 47,000, nearly a quarter the population of Melbourne, and Bendigo had 29,000. Indeed in 1871, Victoria's eight largest gold towns had a combined population equal to half the population of Melbourne. For the rest of the century Ballarat's population was over 40,000 and that of Bendigo around 35,000. As well, there were a number of smaller gold towns. Some, such as Castlemaine, were the slowly declining remnants of vast 1850s mining camps. However, others, such as Stawell, Clunes, Maryborough, and Daylesford, experienced significant growth in the 1860s, 1870s, and 1880s as they became centers of underground mining.

Nothing like Ballarat or Bendigo developed in California. The two largest of the Californian gold towns, Grass Valley and Nevada City, were at their peak, 15 per cent and 8 per cent the size of Ballarat respectively. Grass Valley was also significantly smaller than Castlemaine, the third largest Victorian gold town and Nevada City was smaller than all eight of the Victorian towns listed.

TABLE 4.4
Population of non-gold towns in California and Victoria
(thousands)

	1860/61	1870/71	1880/81	18909/1	1900/01
CALIFORNIA					
Sacramento	13.8	16.3	21.4	26.4	29.3
Los Angeles	4.4	5.7	11.2	64.2	125.4
Stockton	3.7	10.4	10.2	14.4	17.5
Marysville	4.7	4.7	4.3	4.0	3.5
San Jose	4.6	9.1	12.6	18.1	21.5
San Diego	0.7	2.3	2.6	16.2	17.7
Fresno	–	–	–	10.8	12.5
VICTORIA					
Geelong	23.0	21.4	20.7	22.6	23.4
Warrnambool	2.2	3.8	4.8	6.6	6.4
Echuca	0.2	1.6	4.8	4.4	4.1

Sources: *United States Census of Population,* 1860–1900; Census of Victoria, 1861–1901.

Whereas regional urban growth in Victoria occurred in gold towns, in California urban development was in non-gold towns (see Table 4.4). In 1860, no Californian town other than San Francisco was as large as Melbourne, Ballarat or Geelong. In 1880, Sacramento, the capital and second-largest town, was half the size of Ballarat and about 60 per cent the size of Bendigo. Even as late as 1900 only San Francisco and Los Angeles were bigger than Ballarat.

Why did Ballarat and Bendigo develop as large regional cities, whereas no Californian gold town followed a similar path? There are two probable explanations. The first is that the rich deposits of these two towns lasted longer than those in California. Throughout the nineteenth century gold remained a major industry for Ballarat and Bendigo, providing employment and retaining population. The second (and perhaps more important) is that Ballarat and Bendigo were surrounded by an extensive agricultural hinterland and that over time they (and to a lesser extent the other gold towns) became service and transport centres. In particular the combination of gold, agriculture, and railways made Ballarat a foundry city (Bate, 1978, pp. 123–28).

In contrast all of California's gold towns were in the foothills of the Sierra Nevada with limited agricultural potential. California's agricultural heartland was the Central Valley, to the west of the gold towns, and its produce was carried further west to the coast. It was towns such as Sacramento and Stockton, which had initially developed as river ports for the goldfields, which made the transformation to agricultural service centers. Even though they had no gold, they were the closest Californian towns in their functions to Ballarat and Bendigo. Without other industries to service, the gold towns tended to decline. Grass Valley and Nevada City only retained their population after the 1850s as they were on the main transport route to the mines in Nevada (Mann, 1982, p. 78)

The Victorian gold towns were not only significantly larger than their Californian counterparts, they were also grander and more imposing, still the most visible difference today (Frost, 1998). In 1897 Mark Twain was impressed that, "Ballarat is a town of only forty thousand population; and yet, since it is in Australia, it has every essential of an advanced and enlightened big city" (Twain, 1996, p. 197). While Ballarat was the grandest, most of the other Victorian towns were also spaciously laid out with their main streets dominated by substantial buildings of brick and stone.

The wealth and civic pride of the Victorian gold towns was most obviously manifested in their public architecture. Government surveyors laid out Ballarat, Castlemaine, and Beechworth on grid patterns with wide streets surrounding the Gold Commissioners' Camps. Most towns had large botanic gardens and extensive sporting grounds (in the summer of 1861/2 Ballarat, Castlemaine and Beechworth hosted matches against the visiting English cricket team, one of the world's first international sporting contests). Public buildings, particularly town halls, post offices, and railway stations, dominated the skyline with the seemingly mandatory clocktowers. The pattern of strong governmental presence was set early; by 1854 the Government Camp at Ballarat held 230 inhabitants and cost about 90 per cent of the revenue collected from licences (Bate, 1978, p. 47).

At Maryborough, the government railway station built in 1890 (when the town's population was only 5,000) was as large as that in Ballarat and far larger than that in Bendigo. The visiting Mark Twain was forewarned,

> Don't you overlook that Maryborough station, if you take an interest in governmental curiosities. Why, you can put the whole population of Maryborough into it, and give them a sofa apiece, and have room for more. You haven't fifteen stations in America that are as big, and you probably haven't five that are as half as fine. Why it's perfectly elegant. And the clock! Everybody will show you the clock. There isn't a station in Europe that's got such a clock (Twain, 1996, p. 253).

Victoria's gold towns are still dominated by their public buildings. The Victorian

State Government Heritage Register records and protects buildings and structures of state significance. In 1995 it listed 249 nineteenth-century sites in gold towns (about 40 per cent of all non-metropolitan sites). Of these, 133 were government buildings or structures, nearly all made of brick or stone. They included 26 railway structures and stations, 21 courthouses, 21 schools, 11 police buildings, three prisons, 11 hospitals, eight town halls, eight post offices, four libraries, two art galleries, and three schools of mines. Ballarat had 17 registered government sites, and Beechworth, whose population has remained at about 3,000 since the gold rushes, had 13 (Victoria, 1995). For all their tourist appeal today, Nevada City, Placerville, Columbia and the other Californian gold towns never had that same level of public infrastructure.

Agriculture and declining wheatfields

Initially the gold rushes led to an expansion of agriculture in California, but a contraction in Victoria (Gerber, 1999, pp. 139–45). Then from the 1860s onwards, agriculture grew rapidly and soon was regarded as more important than gold-mining in both regions. In California, wheat was the major crop throughout the nineteenth century, reaching a peak of 3.6 million acres in 1884. By 1900 California grew 2.7 million acres of wheat, over two million acres of hay, one million acres of barley, nearly half a million acres of orchards, 1.7 million cattle, and 1.5 million sheep. Victoria was more pastoralist and less intensively farmed. It had five million sheep before the gold rushes and ten million by 1870. By 1900 Victoria (about 60 per cent of the area of California) had nearly 11 million sheep, 1.6 million cattle, 2.1 million acres of wheat (which would double by 1930), a half a million acres of hay, and nearly 50,000 acres of orchards (Victoria, 1973, pp. 1084–90; Frost, 1994, pp. 30, 61).

In both California and Victoria, wheat-growing was the cornerstone of the agricultural economy after the initial gold finds. However, both regions also experienced rapid declines in wheat-growing. In California, where wheat was mainly grown in the Central Valley, wheat acreage fell from 3.1 million acres in 1896 to 1.6 million acres in 1904 and to less that half a million acres in 1909. In 13 years California's wheatfields shrank by 85 per cent. In Victoria, wheat initially dominated what may be termed Central Victoria (which included Melbourne, Geelong, and the goldfields). In 1871 Central Victoria recorded a peak of 235,000 acres, by 1876 it had fallen to 109,000 acres and by 1894 29,000 acres. In 23 years Central Victoria's wheatfields had shrunk by 88 per cent (Frost, 1994, pp. 29–31).

Two regions on opposite sides of the Pacific experienced major rapid declines in their commercial wheatfields. In both the cause of the decline have been matters of great debate. By comparing the two, a better understanding is possible.

The decline of wheat in Central Victoria has generally been viewed as due to falling prices. The last third of the nineteenth century saw a great worldwide increase in wheat production and a consequent fall in prices. It has been argued that as price fell below 60 pence a bushel, established wheat farmers could not compete with newcomers on the ever expanding wheat frontier to the north, who had the advantage of cheap land, larger holdings, and virgin soil (Wadham et al., 1957, p. 17; Dunsdorfs, 1956, pp. 128–37).

Table 4.5 compares average wheat acreage and average wheat prices for Central Victoria. It shows that the rate of decline in acreage was far greater than the decline in prices. Most significantly between the early and late 1870s prices hardly changed, while harvest costs fell (Frost, 1994, p. 160), yet this was the period of greatest acreage decrease.

TABLE 4.5
Central Victoria, indices of average wheat acreage and average wheat prices, 1867/70–1896/1900
(1867/70 = 100)

Year	Index of wheat acreage	Index of wheat prices
1867/1870	100	100
1871/1875	90	87
1876/1880	59	84
1881/1885	43	73
1886/1890	29	67
1891/1895	24	54
1896/1900	41	58

Source: Calculated from Frost, 1994, pp. 29–32, 123.

Table 4.6 compares indices of acreage and price for California. In the 1870s and early 1880s wheat acreage grew significantly despite a major fall in the price of wheat In the late 1880s and 1890s wheat acreage fell and then rose in line with price changes. However, in the first decade of the twentieth century wheat acreage dropped significantly, even though the price of wheat rose. If anything, the relationship between price and acreage in California was the reverse of what may reasonably be expected.

Taking the tables for California and Central Victoria together, there is little support for the view that price was a significant factor in the decline of wheat.

TABLE 4.6
California, indices of average wheat acreage and average wheat prices, 1867/70–1906/10
(1881–85 = 100).

Year	Index of wheat acreage	Index of wheat prices
1867/1870	29	136
1871/1875	71	142
1876/1880	64	120
1881/1885	100	100
1886/1890	91	93
1891/1895	65	78
1896/1900	79	87
1901/1905	56	95
1906/1910	31	101

Source: Calculated from W. Frost, 1994, pp. 29–32, 123.

What are the other possible explanations? Probably the most popular for California is that of soil exhaustion. Californian wheat-growing was called "bonanza farming." Farms were on a huge scale, with large capital expenditure at harvest time but little attention to fertilizing. The growers aimed for a bonanza, low costs and low yields per acre, but a massive total profit due to its sheer scale.

Bonanza farming was criticized from the outset as not "real" farming. As early as 1872 one commentator complained of soil problems due to the lack of rotation and fallowing (Player-Froud, 1872, pp 138–39). In 1880 E.W. Hilgard warned,

> This kind of farming … is doomed to speedy termination and that [though] for the while being it enriches individuals it is of very doubtful permanent benefit to the country. The exhausted wheat fields must wait for the coming generation of more careful farmers – true husbandmen, not skimmers of the soil – to be rehabilitated (Hilgard, 1880, p. 77).

Later writers have been just as critical. Bean and Rawls decried bonanza farming as, "a kind of soil mining, ruthlessly carried on year after year without fertiliser or rotation" (Bean and Rawls, 1988, p. 187; see also Paul, 1958, p. 411, and Pisani, 1984, p. 6).

However, there is little statistical evidence to support this view. Between 1880 and 1889, the years of great expansion, the average wheat yield was 12.5 bushels per acre. From 1891 to 1895, the peak, it was 12.7 bushels. From 1896 to 1900, the beginning of the fall, the average was 11.6 and from 1901 to 1905 it was 11.0. From 1906 to 1910 it was 15.7 (calculated from United States Yearbook, 1891–1910). The changes are just too small to be seen as significant, since it was not likely that farmers would abandon wheat on the basis of a fall of about one bushel per acre or about 10 per cent of their previous yield.

The situation was similar for Central Victoria. Recent writers have argued that wheat was abandoned due to lack of manuring and rotation (Dingle, 1984, p. 103; Lines, 1992, p. 102). However, again the statistical evidence points in another direction. Between 1866 and 1870, as acreage expanded, the average was 16.7 bushels per acre. From 1871 to 1875, the peak, it was 15.5 bushels. From 1876 to 1880, the decline, it was 15.2 bushels. Between 1881 and 1885 it was 17.8 bushels and between 1886 and 1890 15.5 bushels (calculated from Victoria, 1867–73 and Victoria, 1874–91). Again there was no significant fall that would force the farmer to give up wheat. Rather, the problem may have been later historians overestimating the decline in yields through an over reliance on anecdotal evidence.

A third explanation is that farmers voluntarily abandoned wheat in favor of other agricultural products which were becoming increasingly profitable. These high-value products were those demanded by the increasingly wealthy urban domestic and export markets and included meat, butter, milk (and the fodder for the livestock), fruit and fresh vegetables. Such an explanation has been popular for California, where wheat has come to be seen as a transitional phase before the shift to irrigation and more intensive farming (Roske, 1968, pp. 395–407; Bean and Rawls, 1988, p. 187; Pisani, 1984, pp. 94–95, 120–23, 191).

The evidence for this explanation is an overwhelming mass of anecdotal evidence that Californian wheat farmers voluntarily shifted to more intensive activities. An example of this evidence was provided by Victorian politician Alfred Deakin who visited California in 1885. Deakin reported that, "The land and water which will produce 25 to 35 bushels of wheat at 2s 6d [30 pence] per bushel, will produce under fruit trees, a crop worth twenty or thirty times as much" (Deakin, 1885, p. 48).

For Central Victoria, there is very little in the way of anecdotal evidence of why farmers abandoned wheat. However, for Victoria it is possible to construct extensive price indices of a wide range of agricultural products (to an extent that is not possible for California). These indices are shown in Table 4.7. Of the ten available price indices, between 1867/1870 and 1881/1885 wheat experienced the greatest decline, that of 26 per cent. In contrast butter rose by 35 per cent, fowls and eggs by 15 per cent, beef by 16 per cent and mutton by 8 per cent. These price increases for other products would have been a major factor in encouraging wheat

TABLE 4.7
Agricultural Price Indices, Victoria, 1867/70–1881/85
(1867/70=100)

	1867/70	1871/75	1876/80	1881/85
Wheat	100	87	84	74
Oats	100	98	82	75
Hay	100	96	89	88
Beef	100	122	92	116
Mutton	100	121	98	108
Pork	100	101	93	95
Milk	100	93	82	85
Butter	100	112	111	135
Fowls	100	114	111	115
Eggs	100	120	113	115

Source: Frost, 1994, p. 172.

farmers to *voluntarily* withdraw from wheat-growing. In voluntarily rather than involuntarily changing the wheat farmers of Central Victoria behaved similarly to their counterparts in California.

Further areas for comparison

Gold and wheat are two examples of how comparisons between California and Victoria can lead to a greater understanding of developments within these two regions. Beyond these, there are other topics which would benefit from the comparative approach. The effect of European settlement on the indigenous population and the natural environment are popular fields of study in both regions and our understanding could be enhanced by comparison. The experiences and impact of non-Anglo groups (and in the nineteenth century both California and Victoria had significant numbers of Chinese, Germans, and other Europeans) are areas that lend themselves to comparative studies. Andrew Markus's, *Fear and Hatred: Purifying Australia and California 1850–1901* (1979), is a pioneering comparative study of racism, which unfortunately has not been further built on in the 20 years since it was published. Sucheng Chan's, *The Bittersweet Soil: The Chinese in California agriculture, 1860–1910* (1986), is an excellent highly-detailed study, but not only is there no comparable work for Victoria, Chan's research is virtually unknown in Australia. Agricultural history provides further opportunities, especially in land tenure systems, machinery, dairying, orchards, and wine-making. Apart from the recognition that Victoria's irrigation schemes were modelled on California (Frost, 1992; Frost and Harvey, 1997), little has been achieved on comparing irrigation in the two regions. A recent work, Ian Tyrrell, *True Gardens of the Gods: Californian–Australian environmental reform, 1860–1930* (1999), highlights the advantages of comparative environmental history. Many more possibilities wait to be explored.

References

Bate, Weston, *Lucky City: The first generation at Ballarat 1851–1901*, Melbourne: Melbourne University Press, 1978.

Bean, Walton and Rawls, James, *California: An interpretative history*, 5th edn, 1st pub. 1968, San Francisco: McGraw-Hill, 1988.

Chan, Sucheng, *The Bittersweet Soil: The Chinese in California agriculture, 1860–1910*, Berkeley: University of California Press, 1986.

Deakin, Alfred, "Royal Commission on Water Supply. First Progress Report: Irrigation in western America, so far as it has relation to the circumstances of Victoria," *Victorian Parliamentary Papers 1885 (2)* (1885).

Dingle, Tony, *The Victorians: Settling*, Sydney: Fairfax, Syme & Weldon, 1984.

Dunsdorfs, Edgars, *The Australian Wheat-growing Industry 1788–1948* , Melbourne: Melbourne University Press, 1956.

Frost, Lione, *The New Urban Frontier: Urbanisation and city building in Australasia and the American West*, Sydney: New South Wales University Press, 1991.

Frost, Lionel, "Government and Economic Development: The case of irrigation in Victoria," *Australian Economic History Review*, Vol. 32, No. 1 (1992).

Frost, Warwick (1994), "The Decline of Wheat-growing, 1850–1910: A comparative study of East Anglia, California and Central Victoria," PhD Thesis, La Trobe University.

Frost, Warwick and Harvey, Sarah, "Forest Industries or Dairy Pastures? Ferdinand von Mueller and the 1885–1893 Royal Commission on Vegetable Products," *Historical Records of Australian Science*, Vol. 11, No. 3 (1997).

Frost, Warwick, *Gold Tourism and the 150th Anniversary of the Discovery of Gold in California*, Melbourne, report to the Celebration of the 150th Anniversary of the Victorian Gold Rushes Committee (1998).

Gerber, James, "Gold Rushes and the Trans-Pacific Wheat Trade: California and Australia, 1848–1857," in Dennis O. Flynn, Lionel Frost, and A.J.H. Latham (eds), *Pacific Centuries: Pacific and Pacific Rim history since the sixteenth century*, London: Routledge, 1999.

Goodman, David, *Gold Seeking: Victoria and California in the 1850s*, Sydney: Allen and Unwin, 1994.

Hilgard, E.W., "Report on the Physical and Agricultural Features of the State of California," *United States Census of Agriculture 1880*, Vol. 23 (1880).

Lines, William, *Taming the Great South Land: A history of the conquest of Nature in Australia*, Sydney: Allen and Unwin, 1992.

Lloyd, Christopher, "Australian and American Settler Capitalism: The importance of a comparison and its curious neglect," *Australian Economic History Review*, Vol. 38, No. 3 (1998), pp. 280–305.

Mann, Ralph, *After the Gold Rush: Society in Grass Valley and Nevada City, California 1849–1870*, Stanford: Stanford University Press, 1982.

Markus, Andrew, *Fear and Hatred: Purifying Australia and California 1850–1901*, Sydney: Allen and Unwin, 1979.

Paul, Rodman, "The Wheat Trade between California and the United Kingdom," *The Mississippi Valley Historical Review*, Vol. 45, No. 3 (1958).

Pisani, Donald, *From the Family Garm to Agribusiness: The irrigation crusade in California and the West, 1850–1931*, Berkeley: University of California Press, 1984.

Player-Froud, J.G., *Six Months in California*, London: Longmans Green, 1872.

Roske, Ralph, *Everyman's Eden: A history of California*, New York: Macmillan, 1968.

Rothstein, Morton, "West Coast Farmers and the Tyranny of Distance: Agriculture on the fringes of the world market," *Agricultural History*, Vol. 49, No. 1 (1975).

Twain, Mark, *Following the Equator: A journey around the world, Volume 1*, 1st pub. 1897, Hopewell, NJ: Ecco Press, 1996.

Tyrrell, Ian, *True Gardens of the Gods: Californian–Australian environmental reform, 1860–1930*, Berkeley: University of California Press, 1999.

United States of America *Yearbook of the United States Department of Agriculture* (1891–1910).

United States of America, *United States Census of Population* (1850–1900).

Victoria, Census of Victoria, *Victorian Parliamentary Papers* (1861–1901).

Victoria, Statistics of the Colony of Victoria – Production, *Victorian Parliamentary Papers* (1867–73).

Victoria, Statistical register – production, *Victorian Parliamentary Papers* (1874–91).

Victoria *Victorian Year Book 1973: Centenary edition* (1973).

Victoria, *Victorian Heritage Register* (1995).

Wadham Samuel, Wilson, Kent, and Wood, Joyce, *Land Utilization in Australia*, 3rd edn, 1st pub. 1939, Melbourne: Melbourne University Press, 1957.

5

New Zealand and the Gold Rushes of the Mid-nineteenth Century

Kenneth E. Jackson

Gold discoveries have variously been described as the product of random chance or the product of more systematic forces endogenous to the economic system. Amongst Antipodean historians Geoffrey Blainey is in the forefront of those who have proposed that there is a clear link between economic conditions and the pattern and timing of mineral discoveries, rather than their resulting from force of happy circumstance. He prefaced one of his articles with the statement that:

> A mystique seems to bathe the discovery of mineral fields. In hundreds of books and articles on economic theory and economic history, discovery is interpreted as essentially an accident, an event almost as mysterious as the fall of a meteorite. Nevertheless there is evidence that the discovery of mining fields, even in the era of romantic bonanzas, was sensitive to economic conditions and open to rational explanation (Blainey, 1970, p. 298).

Whilst it is tempting to believe in a rational set of economic forces operating in this field as in other parts of everyday economic activity, empirical investigation has so far suggested any such claims are somewhat extravagant; it can be argued that serendipity is equally valid as an explanatory process. Blainey's approach represented an extension of Kondratieff's original suggestion of a relative price or opportunity cost effect, with the position in the business cycle as a key determinant: that gold remains stable as other prices fall in the downswing, raising its relative value and thus increasing the incentive to seek it out at such times. This logic was felt to hold the promise of much explanatory power.

Historical investigation, however, has suggested it provides little, if any, greater accuracy of explanation than other approaches, such as that of writers who suggest that the simple process of increased overall population levels, and with it increased density of population in areas where minerals lay hidden, leads to an increased likelihood that the discovery will occur. This particular alternative is difficult to argue against because of its generality, but for the same reason it is of limited use in terms of developing much in the way of a predictive economic model of anything more than a very general kind. It is left here as the residual, if Blainey's approach is found wanting.

When prediction on the periodicity of gold discoveries is linked to so called long swings, or Kondratieff waves, with an approximate 50 year periodicity, it is generally acknowledged that there are insufficient reliable observations of economic data for the approach to be tested fully, which is sad since the underlying idea appeals to economic logic. Such an approach is only intended to indicate periods when finds are more likely and in Blainey's terms relates to initial discoveries, not to the timing of their economic exploitation. Why one would engage in search without the intention of simultaneously discovering and exploiting such a find, however, does seem to weaken the logical force of the argument more than somewhat.

In terms of the general economics of the approach, Blainey and his followers are in essence concentrating on the supply-side, with available capital and labor being sucked into the industry in times of relatively high returns, the opportunity costs of searching for gold are reduced in depressed economic times. There is, simultaneously, the appearance of some increase in the demand for gold due to its increased purchasing power, but the principal thrust is through the supply side and the reduction in the opportunity costs of search.

By contrast, the economic explanations of the *outcomes* of gold discoveries in Australia and elsewhere have been approached with a far greater degree of rigor, through the investigations of institutional developments and applications of property rights approaches (for Australia specifically see La Croix, 1992 and for New Zealand Jacobsen, 1998) and the application of supply-side shocks models to the historical evidence in the seminal work of Maddock and McLean (1984). The outcome for the Australian economy as viewed by these latter two writers was clear and unequivocal. Within the Australian economy the impact of gold was felt in two ways, through a resource movement effect, which operated in a universally adverse fashion on other sectors and through an income effect that was mainly positive to the non-tradeable sector and scarcely relevant to the world price-taking tradeable sector.

The main aim of this paper is to undertake an initial exploration of the implications of such an approach to the New Zealand experience in the middle of the nineteenth century. It starts from the intuition, generated from the history books, that compared to the Australian experience revealed by Maddock and McLean, the New Zealand impact was initially far less in scope and in the longer run far less lasting. This would be a finding which is in stark contrast to the impression to be gained from reading some of the non-New Zealand standard historical accounts of gold discoveries and their impact elsewhere, including Blainey himself:

> Meanwhile national historians sought explanations of mineral discovery in the Americas, Australia, New Zealand, South Africa and *all those lands where the finding of rich minerals marked the beginning of the eras of spectacular development* (Blainey, 1970, p. 298).

The general New Zealand historical accounts of the period are far more restrained in the tenor of their findings. Keith Sinclair described the impact as not a negligible contribution, *but far less than in Victoria or Australia in general,* placing more emphasis on local effects than on national ones (Sinclair, 1980, p. 107). Others were more concerned with detailing the fears of the social impact held by the founding fathers of settlements such as Presbyterian Otago or Church of England Christchurch that gold discoveries would bring in disreputable and unruly elements, rather than being concerned with the economic impacts of a mineral boom (for example see Reed, 1947, p. 228). How do these thoughts on the impact of gold discoveries upon New Zealand stand up to close examination?

There are four component parts to this paper after the introduction. The first part is an attempt at a brief examination of endogenous economic explanations for initial gold discoveries in the New Zealand case. This is followed by a short consideration of the impact of Australian discoveries on the New Zealand economy. The third section, the longest by far, represents an initial attempt at assessing the impact of the New Zealand rushes, to the extent that the available evidence permits. Whilst more work remains to be done some of the gaps in the historical account from a New Zealand perspective are narrowed. The fourth section draws together some general conclusions and points the way to work remaining to be done.

Causes and timing of discoveries in New Zealand

To say that the rushes in Australia prompted a search for gold in New Zealand is to state the obvious. Along with other colonies in Australasia after the initial payable finds of 1851, inducements were offered to those who could find such a substantial deposit of gold in New Zealand. Typically sums of the order of £500 were offered by most of the provincial Governments to encourage finds in their area. Some finds were made as early as 1852 and 1853 (Reed, 1947, p. 229) with payable finds dating from 1857 around Nelson in the South Island (Parsons, 1904, p. 73). All of these finds predate Gabriel Read's 1861 major discovery which was followed in short order by more general discoveries and the major rush.

Blainey's use of Kondratieff's work as a starting point in attempting to produce an endogenous, economically based explanation seems to have little support from the dates of initial discoveries here. His claim was based on two effects observable during troughs and initial upswings in the business cycle. At such times those underemployed or unemployed in other occupations were not only more likely to trade "leisure time" off against searching for precious minerals, but had the increased returns resulting from a constant gold to currency relationship as against generally declining commodity prices. Cheaper capital costs for new ventures at such times could also have stimulated the search.

Unfortunately, despite the apparent logical appeal of the approach, the historical investigations made so far fail to bear it out. Several writers have examined specific historical cases of mineral discovery and found Blainey's approach wanting, including authors such as Morrissey and Burt (1973), who find fault with the approach both in a general sense and with specific reference to Queensland gold mines, and Davies (1985) who gives an South Australian based copper mining response which is also negative in its conclusions. With copper rather than gold it is the reduction of opportunity costs of search that is important, the purchasing power maintenance argument fails since copper along with other minerals is more rarely linked directly to the currency value in the way that gold was in the nineteenth and early twentieth century.

What is observable in the New Zealand case in the search for gold is that throughout the 1850s the newly opened British market for wool exports from New Zealand had led to a strong growth in flock numbers and increasing wool export receipts, along with those coming from agricultural produce exports to Australia. By the early 1860s the share of receipts coming from minerals was the dominant component as may judged from Figure 5.1. Minerals rise to over 70 per cent by value, squeezing the relative share of pastoral (wool) exports although the latter are still growing in absolute terms. At the top of the graph the relative share of agricultural exports peaks at 1855, when it accounted for over 50 per cent of total exports. (See tables at end of paper for more complete details of exports and other series.) Such effects were not the stuff of downturns in the business cycle or even initial upswings. Basically economic conditions at this time it would appear were generally those associated with an expansionary phase with only a very few exceptions.

Price changes and National Income figures are available in very general and questionable estimate terms from the late 1850s (Rankin, 1992, p. 60). These, however, do suggest strong, but massively fluctuating growth from the end of the 1850s and very early 1860s as can be seen from Table 5.1 with the more authoritative Greasley and Oxley estimates for 1865 onwards, given in parentheses as an indicator of the possible unreliability of the Rankin figures.

The more recent and reliable estimates by Greasley and Oxley (1999, p. 27) given above in brackets, are more reliable than Rankin's earlier ones, but unfortunately for current purposes they do not start until 1865, by which time the initial impact of the gold shock was past.

Given the wide fluctuations exhibited by the data, nothing other than general trends should be relied upon in inferring outcomes from this data set. If resort is made to other indicators of activity levels such as the available evidence of the growth of bank assets and liabilities, which run from 1857 and on which the above figures are based, the indications are for a period of strong growth from the late 1850s to a plateau around 1865 to 1867 (Bloomfield, 1984, p. 386). Financial

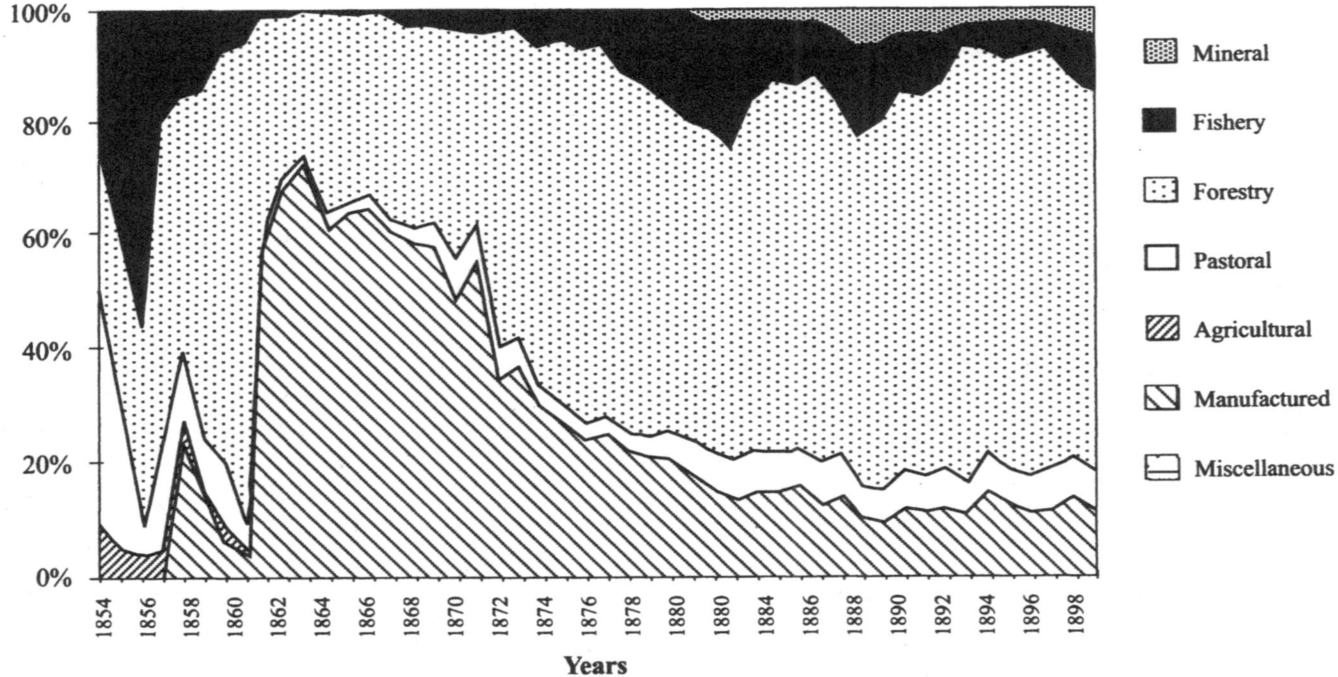

FIGURE 5.1
Percentage share of exports by category

Source: After Bloomfield, 1984, p. 263.

SUMMARY TABLE 5.1
GNP Estimates

Year	GNP nominal Rankin (£000,000)	GNP nominal Greasley and Oxley (£000,000)	GNP per capita real Rankin (%)	GNP per capita real % calculated from Greasley and Oxley
1859	4.4		4.7	
1860	5.8		5.5	
1861	6.6		22.5	
1862	10.6		−10.5	
1863	12.2		1.3	
1864	14.6		−1.1	
1865	15.8	(14.1)	6.0	(−5.14)
1866	18.4	(14.1)	−12.1	(−9.39)
1867	16.5	(14.1)	5.7	(2.48)
1868	18.5	(14.8)	−4.4	(11.05)
1869	16.9	(16.0)	−4.6	(−8.38)
1870	16.3	(14.8)		

expansion may not have been exactly correlated with real economic expansion, but expansion there was, although the 1861 and 1862 values given overstate the amount of real expansion and contraction. Rapid expansion was there at the time of the gold discoveries, which is not in conformity with the Blainey thesis.

Looking specifically at Blainey's explanation here, there is only anecdotal evidence to support his approach. There is a well-reported claim of widespread unemployment in the deep south of the country in the early 1860s, including a petition of 1,010 signatures to the Provincial Council in Otago in October of 1861 asking for relief from distress (Sutch, 1969, p. 63). This, however, is after the initial gold discovery, even after the large one of that year by Read, so does not really conform to, or give much support to Blainey's approach. In addition much of the unemployment was regional and centered on the North rather than the South where the gold discoveries occurred. The 1850s were generally an expansionary phase, although the development of wool production was land rather than labor intensive. Little if any Blainey type incentives to search for minerals seem likely. Any of those thinking in this way were far more likely to head for Victoria and the greater certainty of known finds at this time.

Matthews' (1990) serendipity version of accidental discovery, or something like La Croix's description of discoveries in California, Australia, and Nevada as "unexpected" (1992, p. 204) seems more apt in this case, rather than trying to estimate the operation of the trade cycle and to accord to it the explanatory power that Blainey would have us do.

The impact of Australian discoveries on New Zealand

Some of the very prosperity indicated by rising export receipts, bank assets, and liabilities as detailed in the tables and graphs at the end of the paper, can be attributed to the initial gold discoveries in Australia. The increased income and wealth effects of such discoveries led to higher demand levels for agricultural produce, with some of this being supplied from New Zealand (Condliffe *et al.*, 1938, p. 95). The resource movement effect from the Australian agricultural sector into gold mining and prospecting also impacted negatively on Australian producers' cost structures to the advantage of their New Zealand counterparts. Exports of agricultural produce expanded through the 1850s, although the overall impact was somewhat restricted, with less than 50,000 acres being under cultivation in the agriculturally export-based areas of the South Island by 1857 (Parsons, 1904, p. 73). A similar impact has been recently documented by Gerber (1999), for California with the maturing of a large grain production industry, although in this case the gold rush came first, in contrast to the New Zealand case where the Australian discoveries induced an exporting grain industry in advance of New Zealand gold finds. That apart the similarity of Australia's impacts on grain production in both California and New Zealand is significant, yet little noted in the literature.

Besides the positive boost of an income and wealth effect upon New Zealand, there was also a negative resource movement effect in the sense of a loss of population to Australia as some of the inter-colonial migrants wanting to try their luck on the gold fields were from New Zealand alongside those from other Australian colonies. Exact numbers are somewhat difficult to estimate, but are likely to have had a small but significant effect upon the economy.

New Zealand and the impact of its own gold rushes

Maddock and McLeans' consideration of the Australian gold rush of the 1850s and its impact on the economy had major implications both for the economic history of the topic and for the more general economics literature on the topic. In part Corden's 1984 article on the subject of supply-side shocks was a response to points raised by their work, especially on the topic of immigration.

Maddock and McLeans' version of the model is capable of being applied directly to the historical real world with a minimum of problems resulting from any unreality in its basic assumptions. The core model has such assumptions, but they are far less restrictive in their impact and appear easier to relax in order to bring the model closer to historical reality than is the case with most economic models.

The economic experience of the mid-nineteenth-century gold rushes in New Zealand can be viewed against this framework of analysis of a small open economy confronted with a primary commodity boom. Maddock and McLean's model uses a fixed exchange rate variant for the nineteenth-century Australian case (1984, 1049) which seems appropriate in the New Zealand case too, since the local currency was effectively linked directly to sterling, as was Australia's, thus most of the trade was being conducted within a sterling currency area.

The economy is modeled as being composed of three sectors: two tradeable goods and one non-traded. Tradeables have their prices fixed on world markets, which are effectively given for the local economy. The non-traded sector, by contrast, has prices, which are flexible within the system. A boom in one of the tradeables has effects on the other two sectors which are explored through Corden and Neary's resource movement and spending effects (1982).

Gold is taken as representative of a booming tradeable sector, wool as the lagging tradeable sector and services as the non-tradeable sector. These will suffice as broadly representative, accepting that there are problems for the modern application of these models, such as those of defining the service sector as non-tradeable. What Maddock and McLean found for Australia was that the inter-sectoral factor mobility usually associated with the appearance of a boom did occur in this example, but that it was accompanied by an extensive international mobility of labor, which had been given little prominence in the theoretical literature to that date. It was this aspect of their work that prompted Corden's later response and refinement of his own work. The twin aims of their paper: "using theory, to illuminate our history, but also making use of history to examine theory" (Maddock and McLean, 1984, p. 1050), were effectively accomplished.

The finding that international labor mobility played an important part in the consequential economic impact and adjustment process resulting from the discovery of gold prompted comment that this was merely what many had already said on the historical front. The direct explicit use of the model, however, did more than just confirm this generalized statement. Something of the results of the complex interaction of the adjustment process were set out for further examination. Overall relative price movements for products, labor market prices and import and export prices (given the small open-economy assumption) all behaved much as the model would lead one to expect (Maddock and McLean, 1984, p. 1054).

Some of the previous historical accounts of shortages and gluts resulting from the gold boom therefore need to be re-examined more closely, as did the question of the slower growth in wool production in the 1850s. Again the model suggested possible answers through the impact of the rush on the cost of inputs into the wool industry such as transport from farm gate to port.

The general findings were that in the short run, two years or so in this case, the internal resource movement effects into the booming gold sector put a cost squeeze on the other sectors, which was particularly felt in the case of the other tradeable, wool. The non-tradeable sector, represented by services, was able to recoup some of the cost increases by virtue of its greater price flexibility. In the longer term, labor immigration compensated somewhat for shortages created internally and the effects of increased spending tended to dominate the resource movement effects, particularly for the service sector (Maddock and McLean, 1984, p. 1064). Wool apparently suffered some relative problems, but wool producers gained by being able to switch to meat production at enhanced prices.

At its conclusion the study throws up the interesting thought that living standards rose little as a result of gold. Population increased rather than per capita income. The supposition that it was the discovery of gold which led to a per capita income amongst if not the highest in the world at the time of the gold rushes, both for Australia in the 1850s and New Zealand in the 1860s (Pomfret, 1981, p. 133; Dowie, 1966, p. 119), thus needs to be reconsidered.

From the immediate point of view, the importance of population flows was brought starkly into view. A similar conclusion is possible for the subsequent gold rush across the Tasman, in New Zealand, where the economic impact of gold has been viewed as equally if not more dramatic but relatively fleeting and localized. The inflow of migrants it attracted, however, was said to be an important factor in the development process of the country. A full investigation of the model is somewhat hampered by a lack of detailed statistical data and must await further research, but some general thoughts can be ventured.

There was a large population inflow, as can be judged from Table 5.2, which summarizes information in Tables 4 and 5 at the end of the paper. The inflow served the same, if not an enhanced, equilibrating role as had been accomplished in the Australian case. The inflow to New Zealand from Australia in particular was sufficiently quick in its response to mean that only very briefly was a labor resource movement effect noticeable on lagging and non-tradeable sectors. Wool exports rose by more than double in quantity terms between 1861 and 1864 along with an extension of the acreage under crops, from 226,000 acres to 383,000 (Bloomfield, 1984, pp. 283, 170).

SUMMARY TABLE 5.2
Population migration

Year	Net inflow
1861	16,222
1862	20,991
1863	35,120
1864	8,527
1865	12,309
1866	7,599
1867	4,859
1868	860
1869	3,641

The latter expansion could be taken to represent, in part at least, the spending effect upon the demand for foodstuffs amongst the influx of migrants plus the existing population. The European population in New Zealand nearly doubled between the census years of 1861 and 1864, rising from approximately 99,000 to about 172,000 (Bloomfield, 1984, p. 42).

The speed with which the population increase was achieved suggests that the immediate resource movement effect was muted if not neutralized in the New Zealand case. It is also probable that the population growth enhanced the spending effect and that this had some important consequences for the long run subsequent growth of secondary industry in New Zealand. When Gabriel Read set things alight in 1861 there was only one joint stock company operating. The subsequently rapid growth in popularity of this form of enterprise can be partly attributed to the 1860 Joint Stock Companies Act which made it easier to form such a company and partly to the long term spending effects from the supply-side shock. This would be consistent with growth in the non-traded goods and services sector. In the short run a considerable amount of the spending went into imports rather than local products. Relatively cheap back freight rates from Britain from commodity export carrying ships also tended to reduce any natural protection to domestic producers afforded by distance.

As can be seen from Table 5.6 there was still a more than doubling of numbers employed in the classifications of Trade, Commerce and Manufacturing and of Artificers and Skilled Workers at the height of the gold rush, 1861–64 (Bloomfield, 1984, p. 130). The anticipated, and in Australia, observable downturn in the rate of growth of wool output does not seem to occur in this case, except in relative terms. The non-traded goods sector appears to flourish in a way which is to be expected and the Maddock and McLean message of the need to take account of the equilibrating potential of an inflow of migrants into the labor supply is backed up by an apparently swifter response. Here an application of theory leads to some interesting hypotheses and questions for further investigation.

The inflow of migrants and the accompanying release of wealth and income into the system were not without their drawbacks. As can be seen from the trade balance figures in Table 3, there was a legacy of a large and increasing deficit being accumulated, with imports rising much faster than export receipts. After the initial enthusiasm and dissipation of a great store of wealth, the bills remained to be paid and there was evidence of a deleterious impact of an effective appreciation of the real exchange rate, fixed though it might have been in nominal terms. To the extent that local wages and prices rose, imports became relatively cheaper and there was certainly evidence of a high propensity to import. Local basic manufacturing development may not have entirely benefited from the shock and along with the wool sector may have grown far more slowly than would have been the case without the discovery of gold, leaving the population inflow as the major long term benefit.

The price effects can be seen from anecdotal evidence to have impacted largely on the immediate area of the individual gold rushes. From 1857 to 1864 prices for agricultural produce and transport rose, with claims of cartage over a 45-mile journey between Dunedin and the gold fields of Cromwell and Clyde costing £600 at the peak of price rises (Parsons, 1904, p. 74). These were, however, local in their incidence rather than national. More specific data on prices in general and wages in particular has at this stage to await further investigation.

There is enough scattered information to suggest that a story consistent with the supply-side shocks approach is to be found here.

In conclusion

Further investigation might suggest that the initial impact was felt in a New Zealand which was already part of a trans-Tasman economy. That both a resource movement and spending effect were felt in factor and goods markets, as the result of the gold discoveries in New South Wales and Victoria, although the statistical data is somewhat sketchy for this period. As the impact of these shocks died away, towards the end of the 1850s, they were replaced by a new shock originating in New Zealand itself. The swiftness of the "international" labor response to this latter shock, was due to the proximity to New Zealand of a large population. A far larger part of a relatively unified trans-Tasman labour market was to be found in Australia. Seventy thousand immigrants represented a near doubling of New Zealand's 1860 European population. Such a figure represented only some 7 or 8 per cent of Australia's population at the same date. Australia had had to wait far longer for its immigrant response to the gold shock. The more rapid wiping out of any internal resource movement effect in New Zealand was therefore only to be expected.

The findings concerning the importance of international migration in the Australian case are repeated and enhanced in the subsequent New Zealand experience. A totally heretical hypothesis would be to suggest that it is remarkable not that so many were attracted into New Zealand by the discovery of gold, but rather that so few actually came.

It is the richness of institutional detail and problems of imperfections of the system under study that form the basis of the historical interest. The unique character of each case study means they cannot alone serve as a model, but this does not imply that a new model has to be invented for each case. There are similar mechanisms at work in the New Zealand, Californian, and Australian cases, but the speed, strength of the impact, and the eventual outcomes are all different in terms of the detail. By considering the interaction between them it can be seen that there was a Pacific rim economy effect as well as their own internal impacts, and that this effect was not confined to the population shifts between them.

Sinclair may be right in saying that gold was not insignificant, more right than he intended, for if the relative growth of wool exports are looked at then a shock as sudden as that New Zealand received in 1861 took time to digest in the long run structural transformation of the economy. There was also a lasting legacy from the growth of import demand as well as export increase. Wool and secondary manufacturing grew less fast than otherwise would have been the case. An appreciation in the real exchange rate allied with cheap backfreight shipping costs from Britain hindered New Zealand's manufacturing development.

After the decline of gold there were further adjustments to be made both internally and externally. Employment in basic manufacturing expanded, as it had to do if population was to be retained, since wool did not provide massive employment opportunities, but it was only with the advent of refrigeration, effectively in the 1890s, that an alternative strong source of employment was generated, in primary processing rather than general secondary manufacturing.

The Blainey hypothesis regarding the provision of an economic basis to the causes of gold finds is not supported by this investigation. The bank deposit data and the national income estimates derived from them, whilst questionable as to their detailed year to year fluctuations, are useful in terms of broad trends and orders of magnitude and are not consistent with the Blainey view. The looser population density or serendipity approaches cannot be tested and are thus neither refuted nor proven in the New Zealand case.

The impact of the Australian rushes on New Zealand also appears to have been limited, although this may be more the result of the paucity of data for that period than any real effects. The initial analysis of the available data on income growth and export receipts from the late 1850s and the New Zealand gold discoveries, however, are strongly suggestive of a major shock on the New Zealand economy, with the possibility of some de-industrialization and a slowdown in the rate of growth of the major tradeable sector, the wool trade. Questions relating to the conventional wisdom of the impact including the role of the equilibrating flow of immigrant labour, which was rapid and in the end probably of greater significance economically than the rush itself, are raised with more definitive answers awaiting further study.

Note

This is a revised version of a paper presented to the "Pacific Centuries" Conference at the John Muir Center for Regional Studies, University of the Pacific, Stockton, California, April 1998. My thanks to an anonymous referee, to the participants of the 1998 Pacific History Conference and to the participants in the 1999 Conference of the Australian and New Zealand Economic and Maritime History Conference for their comments and improvements to this paper. The responsibility for any remaining faults and blemishes remains my own.

Figures and tables

1 Gold production and exports (Jacobsen, 1998, p. 358), all production classified as exports at this time.

Years	Volume (oz.)	Value (£)
1857	10,437	40,442
1858	13,534	52,464
1859	7,336	28,427
1860	4,538	17585
1861	194,031	751,873
1862	410,862	1,591,389
1863	628,450	2,431,723
1864	480,171	1,856,537
1865	574,574	2,226,474
1866	735,376	2,844,517
1867	686,905	2,698,862
1868	637,474	2,504,326
1869	614,281	2,362,995
1870	544,880	2,157,585
1871	730,029	2,787,520
1872	445270	1731261
1873	505,337	1,987,425
1874	376,388	1,505,331
1875	355,322	1,407,770
1876	322,016	1,284,328
1877	371,685	1,496,080
1878	310,486	1,240,079
1879	287,464	1,148,108
1880	305,248	1,227,252
1881	269,561	1,080,790
1882	254,204	1,002,720
1883	248,374	993,352
1884	229,946	921,797
1885	237,371	948,615
1886	227,079	903,569
1887	203,869	811,100
1888	201,219	801,066
1889	230,211	808,549

Years	Volume (oz.)	Value (£)
1890	193,193	773,438
1891	251,996	1,007,488
1892	238,079	954,744
1893	226,811	913,138
1894	221,615	887,839
1895	293,491	1,162,164
1896	263,694	1,041,428
1897	251,645	980,204
1898	280,175	1,080,691
1899	389,558	1,513,173
1900	373,616	1,439,602

2 Commodity share of exports (Bloomfield, 1984, p. 263).

Years	Mineral	Fishery	Forestry	Pastoral	Agri-cultural	Manu-factured	Misc.	TOTAL
1853	22	109	67	54	303			
1854		11	75	70	106			321
1855		9	14	93	151			366
1856		11	42	146	48			318
1857	93	12	47	177	56			369
1858	52	8	37	254	56			458
1859	28	12	55	340	33			551
1860	18	4	24	444	28			589
1861	753	5	29	524	7			1,370
1862	1,591	9	27	674	12			1,423
1863	2,432	8	45	843	4			3,485
1864	1,858	3	86	1,088	1			3,402
1865	2,226	3	59	1,159	20			3,713
1866	2,845	1	95	1,372	15			4,520
1867	2,700	2	93	1,598	38			4,645
1868	2,505		96	1,533	117			4,429
1869	2,365		178	1,423	102			4,225
1870	2,164		327	1,831	149			4,823
1871	2,813	14	282	1,735	183			5,282
1872	1,741	11	285	2,855	192			5,191
1873	1,997	5	277	3,022	152			5,610

Years	Mineral	Fishery	Forestry	Pastoral	Agri-cultural	Manu-factured	Misc.	TOTAL
1874	1,516	5	165	3,092	324			5,251
1875	1,419	11	192	3,557	250			5,829
1876	1,274	11	177	3,599	366			5,673
1877	1,486	6	189	4,002	325			6,327
1878	1,255	6	184	3,661	610			6,016
1879	1,146	9	191	3,457	701			5,743
1880	1,231	10	310	3,512	958			6,353
1881	1,007	7	352	3,251	1,075			6,061
1882	934	6	399	3,615	1,169	121	9	6,253
1883	905	13	503	3,766	1,537	121	8	6,855
1884	1,000	22	505	4,337	969	104	6	6,942
1885	954	18	469	4,334	688	121	8	6,592
1886	1,002	18	402	4,138	689	110	28	6,387
1887	804	15	509	4,506	588	124	5	6,551
1888	988	19	582	4,506	906	233	21	7,255
1889	885	20	527	5,607	1,424	570	11	9,045
1890	839	17	582	6,135	1,290	548	17	9,429
1891	1,113	17	639	6,295	894	420	21	9,400
1892	1,045	12	618	6,271	1,036	368	17	9,366
1893	1,004	10	626	5,843	717	346	13	8,557
1894	970	10	536	7,012	318	225	15	9,085
1895	1,259	15	575	6,008	326	189	18	8,390
1896	1,126	19	577	6,669	572	198	15	9,177
1897	1,081	19	565	7,232	495	198	7	9,596
1898	1,175	20	761	7,694	411	254	10	10,325
1899	1,644	24	818	8,010	914	378	12	11,800
1900	1,560	22	863	8,787	1,231	549	13	13,055

3 Trade statistics (*Official Statistics of New Zealand*, various years).

Year	Exports (£000)	Imports (£000)	Balance (£000)
1853	303	598	–295
1854	321	891	–570
1855	366	813	–447
1856	318	711	–393
1857	369	993	–624
1858	434	1,141	–707

Year	Exports (£000)	Imports (£000)	Balance (£000)
1859	521	1,551	−1,030
1860	549	1,548	−999
1861	1,339	2,494	−1,15
1862	2,358	4,626	−2,268
1863	3,343	7,025	−3,682
1864	3,051	7,001	−3,950
1865	3,503	5,595	−2,092
1866	4,396	5,895	−1,499
1867	4,479	5,345	−866
1868	4,269	4,986	−717
1869	4,090	4,976	−886

4 Approximate share of population by Province (Bloomfield, 1984, p. 32).

Year	1841	1851	1861	1871	1881	1891	1901
Auckland	30.0	35.0	25.0	25.0	23.0	21.5	22.0
Taranaki	10.0	6.0	2.0	2.0	2.5	4.5	4.5
Hawkes Bay	–	–	2.5	2.5	2.5	4.5	4.5
Wellington	35.0	25.0	12.5	8.0	12.0	15.0	19.0
Marlborough	–	–	–	2.5	2.0	2.0	2.0
Nelson	22.5	16.0	11.0	8.0	5.0	5.0	5.0
Westland	–	–	–	5.0	3.0	2.5	2.0
Canterbury	2.5	12.0	17.0	19.0	22.5	20.0	19.0
Otago	–	6.0	27.0	24.0	21.5	18.5	16.0
Southland	–	–	3.0	4.0	6.0	6.5	6.0
Total	100.0	100.0	100.0	100.0	100.0	100.0	100.0

5 Population and migration (*Official Statistics of New Zealand*, various years).

5.1 Population

Year	Population total	Males	Females
1854	32,554	17,914	14,640
1855	37,192	20,781	16,411
1856	45,540	25,356	20,184
1857	49,802	27,606	22,196
1858	59,413	33,679	25,734

6 Occupational groups (Bloomfield, 1984, p. 130).
Major groups of occupations 1858–71 (a)
Total number employed

Year	**1858**	**1861**	**1864**	**1867**	**1871**
Trade, commerce and manufactures	1,813	3,283	7,625	10,194	11,079
Agricultural and pastoral	4,416	7,469	12,089	18,863	20,587
Mechanics and artificers (b)	4,579	5,783	12,118	13,695	16,026
Mining	(c)	11,138	12,527	20,372	21,226
Clerical professions	145	196	235	292	347
Legal professions	74	94	153	161	229
Medical professionals	123	178	231	280	270
Teachers	206	390	612	928	1,337
Surveyors	110	194	290	305	292
Other educated professions	297	392	204	244	308
Labourers	4,061	5,607	12,639	13,025	14,312
Domestic servants	1,927	2,808	6,202	7,259	7,017
Miscellaneous	2,592	4.245	10,492	6,883	8,881
Mariners	(c)	(c)	3,495	3,537	3,032
No occupation stated (d)	38,985	57,244	93,282	122,630	151,450
TOTAL POPULATION	59,328	99,021	172,158	218,668	256,353

Notes: (a) Excluding Maoris (b) Skilled workers included from 1864
(c) Included in Miscellaneous (d) Mostly dependants

Year	Population total	Males	Females
1859	71,593	41,107	30,486
1860	79,711	45,394	34,317
1861	99,021	61,062	37,959
1862	125,812	79,680	46,132
1863	164,048	105,978	58,070
1864	172,158	106,508	65,578
1865	190,607	117,376	73,231
1866	204,114	125,080	79,034
1867	218,668	131,929	86,739
1868	226,618	134,621	91,997
1869	237,249	140,112	97,137

5.2 Migration

Year	Arrivals	Departures	Net change
1861	22,339	6,117	16,222
1862	34,290	13,299	20,991
1863	45,730	10,610	35,120
1864	20,931	12,404	8,527
1865	18,916	6,607	12,309
1866	14,893	7,294	7,599
1867	11,126	6,267	4,859
1868	8,723	7,863	860
1869	8,903	5,262	3,641

References

Blainey, Geoffrey, "A Theory of Mineral Discovery: Australia in the nineteenth century," *Economic History Review*, 2nd series, Vol. XXIII (1970), pp. 298–313.

Bloomfield, G.T. , *New Zealand: A handbook of historical statistics*, Boston: G.K. Hall & Co., 1984.

Condliffe, J.B. and Airey, Willis T.G., *Short History of New Zealand*, 6th edn, Auckland: Whitcombe and Tombs, 1938.

Corden, W.M. and Neary, J.P., "Booming Sector and De-industrialisation in a Small Open Economy," *Economic Journal*, Vol. 9 (1982), pp. 825–48.

Corden, W.M., "Booming Sector and Dutch Disease Economics: Survey and consolidation," *Oxford Economic Papers*, Vol. 36 (1984), pp. 359–80.

Davies, Mel, "Blainey Revisited: Mineral discovery and the business cycle in South Australia," *Australian Economic History Review*, Vol. XXV (1985), pp.112–28.

Dowie, J.A., "A Century-old Estimate of the National Income of New Zealand," *Business Archives and History*, Vol. 6 (1966), pp. 117–31.

Gerber, James, "Gold Rushes and the Trans-Pacific Wheat Trade: California and Australia, 1848–57," in Dennis O. Flynn, Lionel Frost, and A.J.H. Latham (eds), *Pacific Centuries: Pacific and Pacific Rim history since the sixteenth century*, London: Routledge Press, 1999, pp. 125–51.

Greasley, David and Oxley, Les, "Measuring New Zealand's GDP 1865–1933: a cointegration-based approach," paper to meeting of New Zealand Econometrics Working Group, Auckland (1999).

Jacobsen, V. (1998), "The Development of Gold Mining Law in New Zealand," PhD thesis, University of Waikato.

La Croix, Sumner J., "Property Rights and Institutional Change during Australia's Gold Rush," *Explorations in Economic History*, Vol. 29 (1992), pp. 204–27.

May, Philip Ross, *The West Coast Gold Rushes*, Christchurch: Pegasus Press, 1967.

Maddock, R. and McLean, I., "Supply Side Shocks: The case of Australian gold," *Journal of Economic History*, Vol. XLIV (1984), pp. 1047–67.

Matthews, Derek, "Serendipity or Economics? Tin and the Theory of Mineral Discovery and Development, 1800–1920," *Business History*, Vol. 32 (1990), pp. 15–48.

Morrissey M. J. and Burt R., "A Theory of Mineral Discovery: A note," *The Economic History Review*, 2nd ser., Vol. XXVI (1973), pp. 497–505.

Parsons, Frank, *The Story of New Zealand*, Philadelphia: C.F. Taylor, Equity Series, 1904.

Pomfret, R., "The Staple Theory as an Approach to Canadian and Australian Economic Development," *Australian Economic History Review*, Vol. 21 (1981), pp. 133–46.

Rankin, K., "New Zealand's Gross National Product: 1859–1939," *Review of Income and Wealth*, Vol. 38 (1992), pp. 49–69.

Reed, A.H., *The Story of Otago: Age of adventure*, Wellington: A.H & A.W. Reed, 1947.

Sinclair, Keith, *The Pelican History of New Zealand*, Auckland: Penguin Books, 1980.

Sutch, W.B., *Poverty and Progress in New Zealand: A re-assessment*, Wellington: A.H. & A.W. Reed, 1969.

6

Gold Rush California Bound: New Evidence from French Passenger Lists

Annick Foucrier

On January 24, 1848, James Marshall noticed a shining flake on the ground of a sawmill he was building at Coloma for Johann Sutter. This was not the first discovery of gold in California, and probably not even the first gold found in this region, but the conjunction of a local event and of the almost simultaneous annexation of this Mexican territory by the US started a major worldwide migration. Spreading of the news was the result of convergent efforts. For Samuel Brannan, it was an opportunity to sell his goods for a large profit; for US President James Polk, it was a justification for war with Mexico; for American politicians and land speculators (often the same), it made it possible to attract people to new territories; for journalists, it meant an increase in newspaper sales. After a Presidential speech on December 5, 1848, the information became official, and gold fever spread along the East coast as well as through Europe (Kurutz, 1997).

Some French residents already in California were among the first to arrive in the Sierras, taking advantage of their knowledge of the country, and of previous relations with Indians they already used as laborers. Those first to discover mines made fortunes. To name a few, *Don Pedro's Bar* was named for Pierre Sainsevain, *Sicard's Bar* for an old French sailor, the *Fourcades* (later Mokelumne Hill) for two brothers from Guitres (Gironde) (De Saint-Amant, 1854; Foucrier, 1992, 1999b). Claude Chana discovered Auburn: with three French Canadians and 25 Indians, he was reported to have gathered $25,000 in gold between May 1848 and October 1849. In July 1848, Charles Roussillon, Pierre Sainsevain, Antonio Suñol, a Californian, and 125 Indians gathered eight pounds of gold a day. Others are remembered in place names: the great number of names including *French* in the Mother Lode (*French Gulch*, *French Corral*, *French Ravine*, *French Hill*) testify to their presence (Pence, 1987), although they could have been applied to French from France as well as to French Canadians, as was the case for *French Camp*.

Mainly paupers?

Still, the topic of French influence has been somewhat neglected. Most studies accent the arrival of paupers, the *Lingots*, and discrimination suffered by French miners, especially through the 1850 Foreign Miners' tax against which the French reacted vigorously. But the approximately 3,000 Lingots, among whom were many women and children, did not fully represent the migration of 25,000 to 30,000 French people. The archives of the consulate invite bias too, since the consul emphasized problems he had to solve in order to strengthen his claims for financial support. Nevertheless, even the consul mentioned the successes of French miners and merchants (Nasatir, 1934, 1954; Lemonnier 1944; Shepard 1955; Chalmers 1991). Very recently, the French have also been the subject of inconsistent fantasies, including the incredible assertion that Napoleon III (or Louis-Napoleon) placed Parisian prostitutes on California-bound ships to rid the French capital of them.

My purpose here is to reconsider French participation in this world migration, as part of a larger study of the migrations and presence of French people in California, from 1769 to the present day (Foucrier, 1999a). It is social history "from the bottom up." It is also economic history, since it is still conventionally assumed that immigrants were mainly destitute people seeking survival at the cost of uprooting themselves. Descriptions of Irish paupers and Italian or Polish unskilled laborers come to mind. The French fit poorly into this picture, so explanations for leaving France usually involve religious or political considerations (e.g. Huguenots at the end of the seventeenth century, or aristocrats at the time of the French revolution). The fact that the stream of French migration has been small (compared to other nationalities) but continuous, has been noted but not explained. French immigrants have sometimes been credited with adaptability, but there has been no real attempt to study their mobility.

The sources

Gold Rush migration makes a good case study. A quantitative approach to this migration is possible because of the existence of sources of unusual quality, French passengers lists (Foucrier 1999a). They are reliable, since captains copied them from passports issued by prefects using data furnished at the local level by mayors. The lists provide each traveler's name (although married women were usually added on their husbands' passports without detailed information), age, profession, place of birth (village or city, county), place of residence (village or city, county), city where passport was issued, ship, date the ship left France, and date of arrival in San Francisco. Captains also recorded those who changed their minds and stayed in ports along the way. Because of the unstable situation in California, there are no equivalent American sources for these early years.

Analysis of passports in French county archives reveals that people of all social backgrounds left, but artisans, merchants and gentlemen were over-represented. Farmers were under-represented. Letters of application for passports show that a majority were able to provide a signature, and often to write a letter. They frequently expected to return soon to France with money gathered from mining or from "practicing their profession." Once in California, some decided to stay, and asked relatives to come. Many applications during the years 1851–57 mentioned an intention to join husbands or fathers, or to settle in California. The lack of passport designation of a specific French county of origin does not imply that nobody born in that county left for California; rather, it often reflects the fact that the migrant had first migrated within France, and only later asked for a passport to a foreign county.

The French passengers lists confirm this hypothesis. They offer a unique opportunity to study the social, regional, familial, and professional characteristics of migration. They help to elucidate the historical context of departures, and force reconsideration of the simplistic image of "unemployed and discontented Parisians" as stereotypical immigrants.

The first French to arrive directly from France reached San Francisco on September 14, 1849, after spending 173 days on the ship *Meuse* (previously used as a whaler). My study considers 30 ships that left Havre for San Francisco between March 24, 1849 (the *Meuse*) and August 31, 1851 (the *Fortune*), and reached San Francisco from September 14, 1849 to April 9, 1852. I added one ship from Saint-Malo (the *Montalembert*, July 13, 1850) and one that left for Chagres on September 4, 1850 (the *Revanche*). Thus, I have a sample of 1,722 passengers (after having excluded those who did not board, or who left before San Francisco). They represented the French pioneers of the California Gold Rush. There is a small bias, however, since passenger lists from Bordeaux were burnt. But a preliminary study of 105 passports from Bordeaux between February 1849 and May 1850 reveals exactly the same features.

From all over France

The majority of passengers were men. The average age was 31.70 years, with the great majority between 20 and 41; 3 per cent were over 50, and 1 per cent under 15. Women accounted for 8.6 per cent, a rather high percentage for a pioneer group. Their average age was 29.15 (see the graphs in the appendix). Of women over 20, half were unmarried and the other half were married or widowed.

These lists include 8.5 per cent foreigners, mainly Swiss, Belgians, Piemonteses, Germans, and refugees from Poland. The greatest number of French came from Paris, although a majority was born outside Paris (see Map 1 in the appendix). A newspaper from San Francisco, the *Alta California*, correctly noted in 1853 that French immigrated from all parts of France: Paris, Marseilles, Lyons, Normandy, Brittany, Alsace (*Alta California*, May 13, 1853). Some origins are not surprising, namely the major cities, such as Paris with its suburbs in the departments of Seine and Seine et Oise, Lyons, and the port of Havre. Lorraine, Normandy, and Brittany were well-known regions of emigration. The valley of the river Seine and the northern part of France, from the Parisian region to the border with Belgium, are mentioned less often as regions of origin, but Paris was for these migrants a first destination (the same was true of Lyons for people from Isère). A greater surprise comes from rural departments, for example Jura and Puy-de-Dôme.

A comparison between Map 1 and another map drawn from the residences (see Map 2 in the appendix) shows Paris as the major place of departure. This can be explained by an initial migration within France prior to migration to America. The fact that many migrants had lived first in Paris is important, since they had become familiar with urban life, and with the language spoken in Paris. Though they might have been raised to speak some dialect, and they may have spoken French with the accent of their region of origin, they had experienced a kind of cultural assimilation, which, in a foreign country, would become a factor of national cohesion.

The situation may have been different for migrants lacking the initial Parisian migration experience, such as those who left from Jura, Puy-de-Dôme, Meuse, and Moselle, in Lorraine, the last two departments well-known for dialects that are close to German. Ariège and Hautes Alpes are two departments from the mountains, where seasonal migrations were frequent.

Some historians have emphasized economic crisis in explaining the great number of departures. For others, such as Roger Lotchin (1997), migrants to the Gold Rush were more attracted by the lure of gold (pull factor) than they were repelled by economic and political difficulties back home (push factors). In the French case, previous domestic migrations of many from small villages to cities bear testimony that their situation was already uncertain before 1848. The years 1846–48 were indeed years of economic crisis. Demographic pressure in rural provinces was at its peak and had stimulated them to leave, as had been done traditionally, usually on a seasonal basis. Thus, migrants left their villages to go to Paris in the 1840s, but the economic and political situation had worsened and the capital was unable to provide enough jobs. Some had already left to go to South America, Louisiana, or New York. In the words of the French consul in San Francisco, this migration was "positive for France, since it helped her to get rid of too much population, and it created new markets abroad for French products" (quoted in Foucrier, 1999a, p. 122).

The occupations

Professions are known for 1,273 of the men who left France for California (see graph in the appendix). It is possible to compare them with a smaller sample of 122 emigrants who left the region of Lorraine for California during the same period (March 1849 to March 1852), a group studied by Camille Maire (1980). The largest group of men – landlords, capitalists, professionals and teachers – comprised 33 per cent of the total, twice the proportion found for the Lorraine group. Likewise, "servants" were three times as numerous. "Farmers" were almost the same percentage, but only half as many declared "no profession ." "Artisans, laborers and clerks" amounted to 45.4 per cent as opposed to 55.7 per cent for the Lorraine group. So, migrants in the larger group (France) were better-off than migrants leaving from this rural region (Lorraine). They also had more education and savings. This is a general phenomenon, since the cost of the trip to the West Coast was higher than to the East Coast.

The categories themselves are not totally satisfactory. "Landlord" was a term used for rich proprietors as well as for small farmers. A "merchant" might involve retail or wholesale operations. And we don't know whether "artisans" were working independently or as hired hands. Another occupational classification scheme – such as the one used for the 1870 US census – might be more instructive.

Migrants already engaged in commerce in France (traders, dealers, clerks in stores) comprised 19.6 per cent (21.2 per cent, if grocers are included). They were the first to leave for California, less intent upon digging for gold than to take advantage of new consumer markets. Professionals (10.4 per cent, including clergymen, architects, artists, doctors, lawyers, teachers), personal services (domestic servants, 2.7 per cent) and highly skilled luxury craftsmen (3.5 per cent) together totaled 16.6 per cent of all immigrants. They provided services for wealthy customers; their journey far from Paris is explainable (like a similar case in the 1790s) by economic crisis (1846–50) and revolution (1848) that together ruined the luxury labor market in Paris. Instead of waiting for an improved situation to arrive, these service providers left for destinations where they hoped to find a rich and spendthrift clientele. Thus, study of the service sector illustrates that even relatively modest providers, like coachmen, were able to leave when perceiving new opportunities. Farmers and farm laborers comprised only 7.4 per cent of the migrants. Semi-skilled or unskilled workers (laborers) comprised a mere 8.1 per cent. Probably most were too poor to finance a trip to such a far away land (the cost of third class ship passage was 500 to 600 francs). Artisans (pre-industrial minus grocers and luxury crafts) comprised 22.5 per cent, a relatively high proportion. The amazing variety of trades involved attests to the power of the general economic crisis in France at the time. Another aspect deserves notice. Professions related to food consumption (like bakers, butchers, millers, brewers) were represented (5 per cent), but hotelkeepers and restaurateurs were seldom mentioned. Since these occupations are among those most often associated with the French in California (as well as elsewhere in America), they must have resulted from adaptation to local market conditions.

Women

Women migrants were mostly urban workers in France. A high percentage came from Paris (73 per cent, actually 85.6 per cent if one includes the suburban county of Seine), although only 22 per cent were Paris born. But they had previously lived in a large city. A majority were unmarried, and most traveled alone or in the company of a friend. Half declared an occupation. Of these, a majority worked in traditional female activities, such as in clothing (dressmakers, seamstresses, washerwomen, milliners) or as domestic servants. But one was a teacher of languages, two were shop girls, and several were shopkeepers (a baker, a florist, a cream seller, a shoemaker, a feather seller). It is notable that 11 were investors and 10 were artists or actresses (30 per cent together). Some of these stockholders were probably courtesans. The actresses deserve mention. There were eight (10 per cent of the women who declared an occupation), a far greater percentage than the percentage of male artists (five in number, 0.3 per cent of declared male occupations). Some observers, like Albert Bénard or De Massey, have suggested that actresses went to California to get rich by displaying charm more than talent, but this is not a pertinent issue (Bénard, 1980; De Massey, 1927). Among these female passengers were Madame Marie Adalbert, wife Wagner, Mademoiselle Elisa Racine and Mademoiselle Eléonore Florentin, who arrived in November 1850 on the *Vesta*, and became directors of the first French theater in San Francisco, the *Adelphi* on Commercial street, and of one of the first theatrical companies in California, the *French Vaudeville Company*. Such women were cultural pioneers (Banner, 1983). Generally, these women appear to have been more educated and more independent than the average immigrant woman in the United States (Gabaccia, 1994). They were proponents of cultural change and have often been credited with the introduction of Parisian fashion (and a certain taste for large spending) to the California frontier.

Another point is worth noting: the high percentage of French women who declared an occupation in France conflicts with California censuses that failed to report such activities. Two explanations might be proposed: these women may have achieved sufficient wealth in California to afford to stay at home, as middle-class women would do at the time. This was probably true for some, but was very unlikely for others with husbands who were bakers, or who ran small shops requiring cashiers and labor of entire families. An alternative hypothesis involves bias on the part of census takers (as well as on the part of mainstream society) against declaration of female labor. In any case, the use of censuses should consider such issues so as not to underestimate the extent and variety of occupations served by women.

The Golden Ingots

Contrary to the mythical and popular image of the French in the Gold Rush, adventurers, soldiers of fortune, and prostitutes – although high in profile – actually comprised a very small minority. For those emigrants who already intended to leave France, the discovery of gold provided an additional prospect; for others who had been hesitating, it provided an additional opportunity. Many emigration societies were created to facilitate departure by providing information and passage aboard ships. These organizations may have been ill-informed and poorly managed, but they were indeed instrumental in directing people to California.

One such society is particularly well-known, not because it was representative of this migration – quite the contrary! – but because its archives have survived. Historians depend upon the availability of documents, such as those left by the society of the "Lottery of the Golden Ingot." It was created on August 3, 1851 through governmental decision, with the avowed purpose of gathering sufficient funds to transport 5,000 unemployed workers to California and to help them settle there. Thus, 4,025 people left France between October 1851 and January 1853. Because a certain number preferred to remain in ports on the way, only 3,293 reached California between February 1852 and May 1853. A more detailed and statistical study than offered here is needed, but these immigrants appear to constitute a second migrant wave with specific features. As in the first wave, most were born in villages or small towns, and many had been previously attracted to Paris by the promise of earnings from national workshops. But they were poorer than other migrants, their passages having been paid by the *Lottery*. Most were able to sign their names, however, and to declare occupations such as craftsman or small shopkeeper. There was certainly pronounced opposition to the Regime among them, and the French government no doubt desired to get rid of them. But the high percentage of married women and children should be considered before blindly accepting the image of dangerous revolutionaries applied by some authors, notwithstanding remarks by the American consul in Marseilles who announced in April 1851 the arrival of "some of the great desperadoes," "worse than Italian Banditti." Summoned by the San Francisco Committee of Vigilance in September 1851, the French Consul assured the Committee "that no apprehension need be entertained that the government of France would sanction the shipment to this country of any of its convicted felons, that it had ever been foreign to their policy to do so, and that under the existing Constitution of the Republic, it would not be in the power of the Government to take any such action without the authority of some special Law for the purpose, and that no such law had ever been enacted" (Williams, 1919, pp. 662–64). On February 10, 1852, the *Alta California* published an article retelling the whole story, quoting two letters from authorities in France who assured the Committee that there was no criminal among "the future French

Californians," "all honest people emigrating voluntarily."

Once in California, most of these migrants proceeded first to the mines, but soon many thought better and returned to San Francisco where they tried to practice their professions as bakers, butchers, cooks, tailors, or hatters. Others became laundry workers, a much needed profession at the time. The French consul, at first wary, admitted in 1853 that most of these migrants were better off than when they had arrived, and noticed that some had been pretty successful.

In the mines

In the mines, the French clung together both for protection and for better information, since very few were able to speak English. Some, especially early arrivals, were successful. Anecdotal evidence helped create a reputation for being very lucky, like the story of the three Frenchmen who unearthed a tree stump, only to find gold worth $5,000 in the cavity. Another case involved a Frenchman trying to catch frogs for breakfast on Mokelumne Hill in November 1848. Noticing a sparkle, he dug up a nugget worth $2,150 with a knife. An envious miner later recalled another occurrence at Steep Gulch:

> Steep Gulch became famed as a Frenchman's treasure box. A small colony of them working on Middle and Big Bars of the Mokelumne River were the first to hear and take advantage of the sailor's discovery and many of them returned to La Belle France with the wealth they dug from the banks of the gulch. It was a long remembered event in Mokelumne Hill when the first thirty or forty of them departed for France. A boniface named Leger, gave a big dinner to the Frenchmen about the Hill, and the quantity of wine that was drunk and the number of times the Marseillaise was sung was never equaled before or since. As the stage could not take the number who were going away at one time, the party decided to go to Stockton on horseback, so they selected a captain and bought or borrowed enough horses and mules for each man to have a mount. Amidst great enthusiasm they departed and as quite a number of them had never been astride a horse before, their efforts at mounting and keeping in the saddle were extremely ludicrous. They arrived at Stockton after much mental distress, sore of body and sailed away with about a ton of gold (Peters, n.d., p. 135).

In every mining town where they were numerous enough, there was a "French Town" for sharing a French way of life. Some British travelers declared they were able to recognize French miners from their capacity to bring comfort to the wilderness, from their skill in making culinary miracles with the monotonous daily diet of the miner: flour, ham, and beef. They reported too that French emigrants were eager to get news from France, a need transformed into nostalgia for some.

After a hard week's work, the French liked to gather on Sundays for large reunions, sometimes numbering as many as 50 to 100 persons. Great quantities of beef were cooked, many bottles of wine were uncorked, and the French would have a good time, laughing, singing, and discussing French politics (Paquette, 1996; Borthwick, 1929; Marryat, 1952; Chamberlain, 1879, p. 83).

Conclusion

Pioneer Frenchmen of the Gold Rush were more educated, more likely to have some capital, and also more mature than most immigrants. This helps to explain some of their success. Many among them actually did return to France with some gold, and there should be further scholarly investigation about the impact of this gold on local consumption trends in France during the Second Empire.

The Gold Rush is a turning point in the history of emigration from France. The economic crisis of 1846–50 had two sides. The last traditional crisis coming from grain shortage comprises one important aspect. France's first industrial crisis, accompanied by bankruptcies and unemployment formed another aspect. Similarly, the emigration of French people to California appears to have been a reaction to traditional domestic demographic pressures, while at the same time involving establishment of new migration channels that led to further waves of departure.

References

Banner, Lois W., *American Beauty*, Chicago: University of Chicago Press, 1983.

Bénard de Russailh, Albert, *Last Adventure. San Francisco in 1851*, trans. C. Crane, San Francisco: Westgate Press, 1931.

Bénard de Russailh, Albert, *Journal de voyage en Californie à l'époque de la ruée vers l'or, 1850–1852*, edited by Sylvie Chevalley, Paris: Aubier, 1980.

Borthwick, J.D., *The Gold Hunters*, New York: Book League of America, 1929.

Chalmers, Claudine, "L'aventure française à San Francisco pendant la ruée vers l'or, 1848–1854," unpublished PhD, University of Nice, 1991.

Chamberlain, W.H., *History of Yuba County, California, with Illustrations*, Oakland, Calif: Thompson & West, 1879.

De Massey, Ernest, *A Frenchman in the Gold Rush, the Journal of Ernest de Massey, Argonaut of 1849*, trans. Marguerite Eyer Wilbur, San Francisco: California Historical Society, 1927.

De Saint-Amant, Pierre Charles, *Voyages en Californie et dans l'Orégon*, Paris: L. Maison, 1854.

Foucrier, Annick, "Pierre Vignes, the Other Brother," *The Californians* 10, 4 (1992), pp. 17–26.

—, *Le rêve californien: migrants francais sur la côte Pacifique, XVIIIe–XXe siècles*, Paris: Berlin, 1999a.

—, "Le grand rêve californien," *L'Histoire*, 238 (1999b), pp. 58–64.

Gabaccia, Donna, *From the Other Side. Women, Gender and Immigrant Life in the US, 1820–1990*, Bloomington, Indiana: Indiana University Press, 1994.

Krebs, Albert, "La ruée vers l'or des Français en Californie," *Rapports France-Etats-Unis* (1952), pp. 49–58.

Kurutz, Gary, *The California Gold Rush. A Descriptive Bibliography of Books and Pamphlets covering the years 1848–1853*, San Francisco: The Book Club of California, 1997.

Lemonnier, Léon, *La ruée vers l'or*, Paris: Gallimard, 1944.

Lotchin, Roger W., *San Francisco 1846–1856. From Hamlet to City*, New York, Urbana: University of Illinois Press, 1997.

Maire, Camille, *L'émigration des Lorrains en Amérique, 1815–1870*, Metz: Centre de recherches en relations internationales de l'université de Metz, 1980.

Marryat, Frank, *Mountains and Molehills*, Stanford, CA: Stanford University Press, 1952.

Moerenhout, J.A., *The Inside Story of the Gold Rush*, San Francisco: California Historical Society, 1935).

Nasatir, A.P., *The French in the California Gold Rush*, New York: American Society of the French Legion of Honor, Franco-American Pamphlet Series 3, 1934.

—, "Alexandre Dumas fils and the Lottery of the Golden Ingots," *California Historical Society Quarterly*, 33, 2 (1954), pp. 125–42.

Paquette, Mary G., *Then Came the French. History of the French in Mokelumne County, California*, Sonora, CA: The Tuolumne County Historical Society, 1996.

Pence, Ellsworth, "French Place Names in California," *Pacific Historian*, Vol. 31, No. 1 (1987), pp. 59–79.

Peters, C., *The Autobiography of Charles Peters*, Sacramento, California: The Lagrave Co, n.d.

Shepard, William F., "Parisian Paupers in the California Gold Rush," *Proceedings of the First Annual Meeting of the Conference of California Historical Societies*, Stockton, CA: College of the Pacific, 1955, pp. 31–45.

Williams, Mary Floyd (ed.), *The Papers of the San Francisco Committee of Vigilance of 1851*, Berkeley: University of California Press, Publications of the Academy of Pacific Coast History 4, 1919.

Appendix

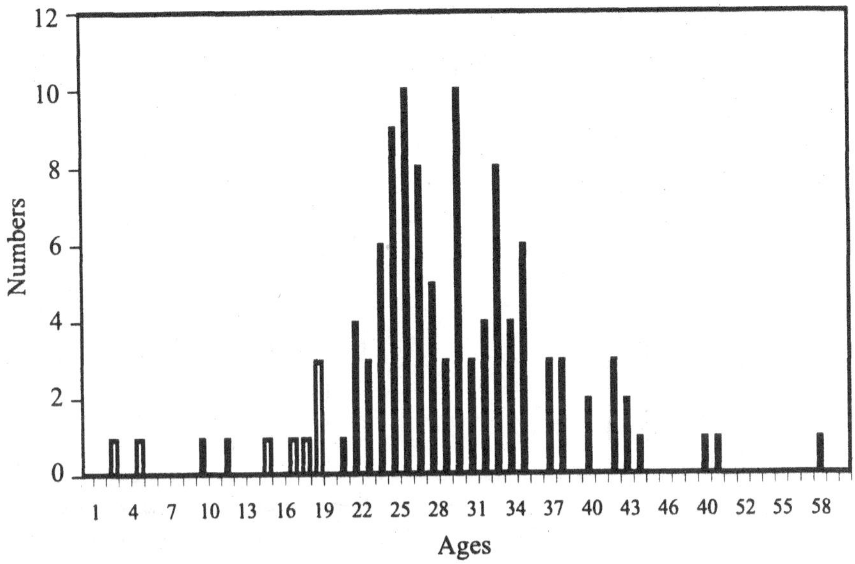

Passengers (women)

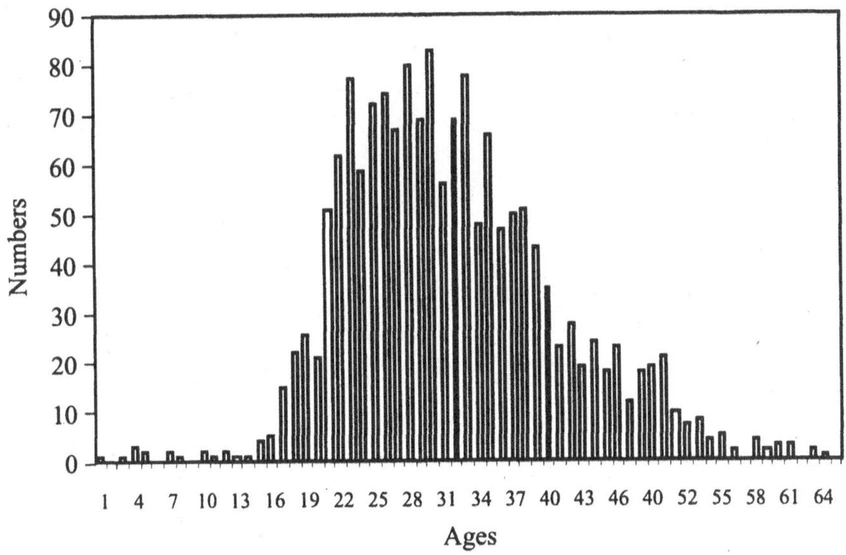

Passengers (men)

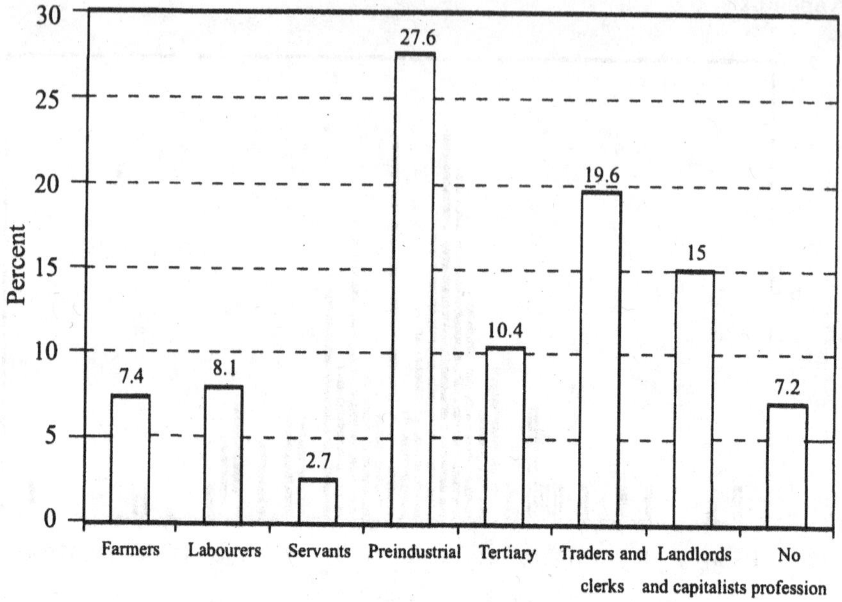

Occupations of French male passengers (1849–51)

Source: Passengers lists, Havre.

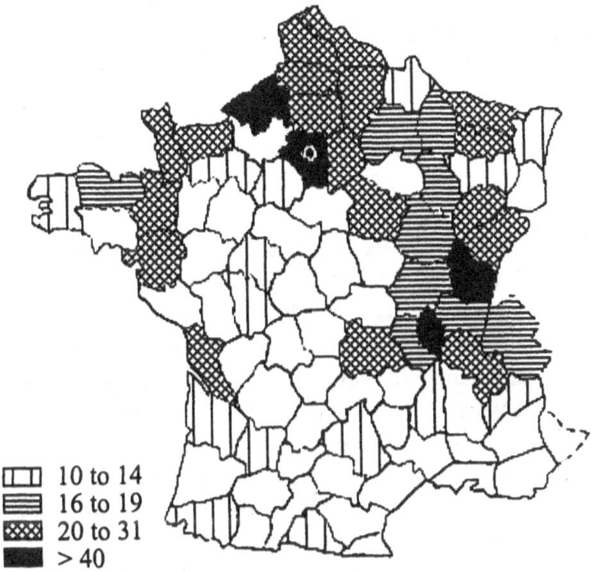

MAP 1
Places of birth of passengers (N = 1406)

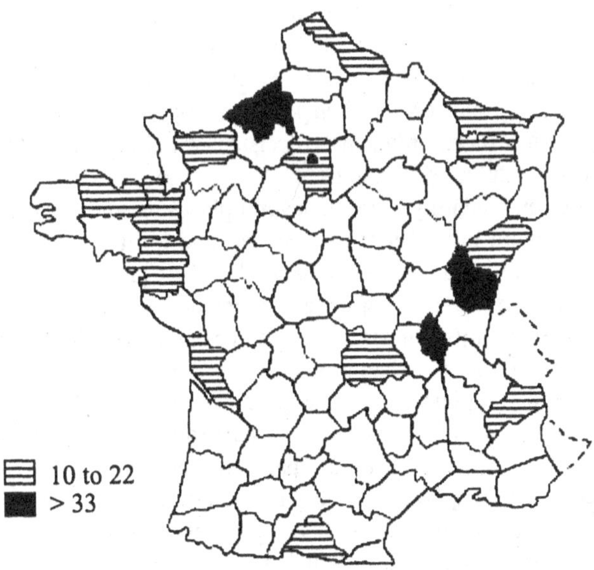

MAP 2
Residences of passengers (N = 1477)

7

The Rim of Fire: Pacific Rim Cities and the Problem of Fires

Lionel Frost

One of the attractions of studying Pacific history is the opportunity to explore some important themes of human history in an arena where there have been significant and long-lasting contrasts and connections between individual cases. Comparisons can be made on an international basis, over long periods of time, of the ways in which different societies have responded to common problems. One major issue which all societies have had to deal with during periods of economic growth is the growth of cities. Cities possess the ability to transform economies because they can provide clusters of labor with diverse skills and are the location of effective transport facilities which provide access to large markets. As a result, they are good places to do business and a fertile setting for technological change. For people in their hinterlands, cities can provide job opportunities which mop up surplus or displaced land workers, while urban demand for food and raw materials may encourage primary producers to become more efficient. Yet cities can prosper only if these economic advantages are not offset by the congestion costs which result from the need to house and service dense clusters of people. No city can remain an effective place to work and do business if the advantages of doing so are outweighed by these congestion costs. When people attempt to solve urban problems by reducing congestion costs they often make decisions which are difficult to reverse and create problems for future generations.

During the nineteenth century cities in several places around the Pacific Rim grew rapidly. They were typically very crowded and built quickly of cheap, flammable materials. Water supplies were generally inadequate. No city had any really effective means of fire-fighting once a major blaze had taken hold. As a result, most cities were highly combustible lumps of capital. But while the problem of large-scale, multi-building fires had in some cases been brought under control by the end of the century, it persisted in other places. Around the Rim one can see examples of cities coping with the same problem, but producing markedly different outcomes. A comparative perspective reveals that there were multiple ways in which city-dwellers used the capital, land, and building materials which were available to them to find ways to minimize the damaging effects of fire. Where peoples' choices were constrained by decisions which had been made in the past, even rational behavior could lead to an outcome which failed to maximize economic well-being.

This chapter will outline the nature of the nineteenth-century urban fire problem around the Pacific Rim, consider why it diminished in significance in some places but not others, and examine the economic costs of recurrent fire risk and damage. The conclusion will consider the implications of these findings for the general issue of how well societies can cope with city growth.

City growth and the problems of fires

Before the nineteenth century, most of the Pacific Rim's major cities were Asian ones (Jones, Frost, and White, 1993, pp. 136–39). The nineteenth century saw an urbanized and industrialized Europe exert an increasing global impact through a relentless search for new resources, land, and markets. Cities, some of them completely new, grew rapidly in the Americas and Australasia, while many Asian cities experienced a new burst of growth as well. European traders and settlers were looking for opportunities to establish capitalist production by gaining access to untapped markets, and cheap labor and land. In a few cases, the interaction with indigenous populations that resulted was beneficial to the latter, but for many societies the arrival of Europeans was a disaster. Wherever a surplus was produced for market, towns grew; the larger the surplus and the more productive the activity which created it, the greater the expansion of urban jobs.

Gold rushes in California in 1848, Australia in 1851, and British Columbia in 1858 lured prospectors from all over the world. During the 1850s the total population of the Pacific Rim states of California, Oregon, and Washington increased from 106,000 to 444,000 (Jones, Frost, and White, 1993, p. 89), and that of the colony of Victoria rose from 76,000 to 540,000. In 1858 the Victorian goldfields population reached a peak of 150,000; 40,000 of these were Chinese (McCarty, 1998, p. 89). Melbourne, which had been established by pastoralists from Tasmania during the 1830s, boomed during the gold rushes and by 1861 had 129,000 inhabitants, twice as many as San Francisco. European trade and colonization created several such "instant cities" (Barth, 1975), but strong urban growth impulses were also felt in Asia. Treaty port status brought a new burst of population growth to several cities. For instance, Hankow, an important port city on the Yangtze River, was largely destroyed during the Taiping Rebellion (1850–65), but recovered strongly and its population reached around the one million mark by 1890 (Rowe, 1984, pp. 38–42). Shanghai, the largest treaty port, grew spectacularly from 149,000 inhabitants to over three million by 1930 (Jones, Frost, and White, 1993, p. 137). Urbanization was also rapid in Japan after the Meiji Restoration, when the country was opened up to Western influences and trade in manufactured goods was developed successfully. In parts of several cities one could see evidence of the transnational nature of this process: a district in San Francisco was called Sydney Valley; Ballarat had a place named Canadian Gully and a Chinatown called Hong Kong; Bendigo had a California Gully; in Shanghai there was a replica of the Liverpool waterfront.

Before the gold rushes, Australian cities were in a dire physical condition. When the Sydney Municipal Corporation was established in 1842, 50 years of virtually unplanned growth had left the city with severe problems. "Most roads were no more than tracks. No water or sewerage had been laid on. ... Building regulations were minimal and often honored in the breach" (Fitzgerald, 1992, p. 39). In Melbourne, attempts to dam the Yarra River to increase supplies of drinking water led to serious flooding in 1839, 1841, 1842, 1843, 1844 (twice), 1848, and 1849. Like Sydney, the town was unsewered. The streets were unlit and in poor condition: two children drowned in gullies in Elizabeth Street in 1842 (Cannon, 1991, p. 95, 102, 113, 126). On the eve of the gold rush, San Francisco was much smaller than Melbourne, being little more than a village of one thousand inhabitants. "It boasted few improvements of any kind; its architecture was an undistinguished collection of adobes and rude frame buildings" (Lotchin, 1974, p. xviii). Flat land near the bay was at a premium.

The gold rushes were not the time to remedy these defects. Many people stayed in San Francisco or Melbourne for only a short time on their way to the diggings. Wages were high but excess demand for housing and food drove up rents and prices. San Francisco was a "helter-skelter assembly of canvas tents, wooden shacks, and warehouses" (Issel and Cherney, 1986, p. 13), built compactly on the flat ground close to the bay. Under the pressure of population growth resulting from the gold rush, the city's retail, wholesale, manufacturing, and residential areas were packed close together (Lotchin, 1974, p. 16). In Melbourne, the existing stock of shelter was simply inadequate to meet the needs of thousands of immigrants. "Where are we to put them?" asked the *Argus* in 1852. "We are crammed already. Our houses are already too full for either health or decency .... We cannot build fast enough with bricks or stone, and houses must be had, and that within these few months." One-third of Victoria's population was still living in rough, impermanent shelter by 1861 (Butlin, 1964, pp. 215–17). South of Melbourne's Yarra River, a large area of tents and shanties, known as Canvas Town, appeared quickly in response to shortages of housing (Daley, 1940, pp. 26–27). In 1852, a *Sydney Morning Herald* reporter contended "that a worse regulated, worse governed, worse drained, worse lighted, worse watered town of note is not on the face of the globe ... in a word, nowhere in the southern hemisphere does chaos reign so triumphant as in Melbourne" (*Sydney Morning Herald*, November 4, 1852).

The gold towns themselves were rough, raw places, where not many people planned to stay for very long. Most were prepared to live cheaply in primitive conditions. Most of the gold-seekers in the Ballarat area were within walking distance of the town's Main Street, which "was probably the most boisterous mile and a half of road that has ever existed in Australia" (Bate, 1978, p. 96). It was "as noisy, smelly, bustling, as congested as an Asian market, as wild as an American frontier town, as wealthy as London's Lombard Street, and as seamy as the back alleys of Naples" (Bate, 1978, p. 96). Caked with mud half the time, and a cloud of dust the rest, Main Street was flanked by hundreds of businesses, built close together and lined with canvas and calico. "Flames from unstable candles and oil lamps waited greedily for the chance to spread, stoves and fireplaces lacked proper hearths and chimneys, and large stocks of gunpowder, paint and turpentine were bound to encourage fire" (Bate, 1978, p. 111). Sacramento was "built originally of muslin, calico, canvas, sails, logs, boards, tin, and boxes" (Larsen, 1978, p. 78). In the towns of America's Pacific Northwest, abundant local forests provided investment opportunities in cutting and sawmilling, and most building was done in flammable local softwoods such as red cedar and Douglas fir. During this early "wild west" stage, crowding and primitive building made these towns as flammable as a box of matches.

In contemporary Asian cities, population growth also placed a strain on the urban physical fabric. Fitzgerald's (1987: 226) observation that in Sydney during the second half of the nineteenth century there was a "steady deterioration of the physical environment as rapid population growth proceeded without adequate provision of the amenities likely to preserve the quality of living and the health of the citizens" could be applied equally to, say, Hong Kong. City growth typically resulted in housing shortages and low standards of water supply and sanitation. In most cases, cheap housing built of flammable materials was run up to meet the need for shelter.

On the backstreets of Edo, people lived in two-roomed huts measuring only 9 feet by 12 feet. These huts "had roofs of the flimsiest and most combustible sort. They burned merrily when there was a fire" (Siedensticker, 1983, p. 14). Hankow was built on sandy foundations close to forests which provided abundant timber. Even its rich merchants built their houses of wood, without any fire-proofing of walls, roofs or gates. "And if the less wealthy could not be counted upon to build natural firebreaks, even less could the laboring classes, with their wooden or thatch houses. Most hazardous of all were the rush-mat lean-tos of the indigent, which with great predictability filled in any open space" (Rowe, 1989, p. 159). Cooking and heating was done on small charcoal-burning braziers and these could easily topple over during earthquakes. Town water supplies were not reliable. A maze of narrow streets and alleys made escaping and fighting fires difficult. Shopkeepers and craftsmen allowed their work areas to encroach on the street and this reduced the effectiveness of streets as firebreaks and a means of safe, easy access to and from fires. Wooden bridges and hundreds of river craft provided combustible material which helped fires to jump rivers and canals. According to Rowe, the usual places where fires started in Hankow were commercial warehouses, where combustibles such as kerosene, vegetable oils, medicinal chemicals, alcoholic beverages, wicker and rattan goods, timber, textiles, and fireworks were stored. Rowe adds that the problem of arson was chronic (Rowe, 1989, p. 158).

Not surprisingly, these cities did burn, extensively and with great frequency. Indeed, there is a long history of conflagration in Chinese cities in particular (Frost, 1997). During the Song and Mongol dynasties, soldiers were stationed in towns to watch for and fight fires. Marco Polo reported that in Hangzhou, capital of the Mongol dynasty, each of the city's 12,000 bridges was guarded by ten soldiers, who watched for fires, enforced a curfew after which all fires and lights were extinguished, and helped citizens to evacuate in times of conflagration (Polo, 1958, pp. 219–21). Nevertheless, damaging fires still broke out, and in Hangzhou major fires in 1201 and 1208 each destroyed over 50,000 houses (Balazs, 1964, p. 73). During the Qing dynasty 220 major fires were recorded in Chinese cities, including 17 which each destroyed thousands of houses (Chao Erh-sun, 1937, pp. 206–207). Fire was also a major problem in Japanese cities. Over 800 major fires have been recorded in Edo (Tokyo) since 1602, 13 of them caused by earthquakes. Some of these were vast conflagrations, such as the fire of 1657, which started accidently and was spread by strong winds. The fire destroyed three-quarters of the city and killed 100,000 people (Nouet, 1990, pp. 105–106).

The scourge of fires continued in Asian cities though the nineteenth century. On clear, dry nights, fires burning in Edo – the "Flowers of Edo" – were one of the great sights of the city (Inouye, 1910, p. 29). In 1806, when a Dutch merchant learnt that a fire had broken out nearby: "We paid scarcely any attention to the news for fires are so frequent in Edo. Every beautiful night has its fire" (quoted by Nouet, 1990, p. 161). During the last decade of Tokugawa rule, "there were two great fires in 1858 and numbers of lesser but still major fires" (Siedensticker, 1983, p. 22). During the Meiji era, there were five great fires in the Kanda district (two within a few weeks of each other in 1881), four in Yoshiwara and three in Nihombashi (Siedensticker, 1983, p. 62–64). So combustible was the city and so frequent its fires "that no house … could expect to last more than two decades" (Siedensticker, 1983, p. 14). Hankow "was notorious throughout China as a tinderbox. Indeed, to many its very name was synonymous with 'fire'" (Rowe, 1989, p. 158). There were great fires there in 1810, 1846, 1849, 1864, 1887, and 1892, and "smaller neighborhood blazes were an almost daily event" (Rowe, 1989, p. 92). Some idea of the regularity of fire damage is conveyed by the fact that in one year – 1880 – there were over 200 important fires (Rowe, 1989, p. 158). Flooding was another serious problem which occurred almost every year. People who lived in Hankow accepted the fact that disasters would occur and anticipated that their houses would need to be rebuilt at unpredictable intervals.

As urbanization spread around the Rim, so did the fire problem. In 1886 a fire started in Vancouver which burned the town to the ground. According to Rudyard Kipling (1900, p. 54) the process took only 16 minutes. San Francisco's first major fire, in December 1849, was followed by four more in the next 12 months. There were two major fires in 1851 and further fires in 1852 and 1854 (Larsen, 1978, p. 78). Sacramento suffered fires in 1851, 1852, 1854, and one in 1859 which razed seven-eighths of the town (Larsen, 1978, p. 78). Miraculously, Melbourne's Canvas Town did not burn down completely, but in both Melbourne and Ballarat there was a string of small fires in the early 1850s, all of which were thankfully extinguished before developing into conflagrations.

After the fire in San Francisco in 1851, which destroyed 70 per cent of the total stock of buildings, it was reported that "frame buildings burned like tinder ... brick buildings with iron shutters and doors, gave way, and crumbled into ruins. ... such was the fierceness of the flames that they leapt across streets 100 feet wide, and ignited the buildings as if they were made of touchwood" (*The Times*, July 3, 1851). In 1906, San Francisco was again devastated, by an earthquake and series of fires, many of which resulted from arson because insurance policies did not allow claims for earthquake damage. Virtually all of the city east of Van Ness Avenue was destroyed and around 3,000 people were killed (*San Francisco Chronicle*, April 14, 1996). Again fire departments were overwhelmed and ineffective. The 1851 fire was a typical event in the history of gold rush San Francisco – and in the history of large Pacific Rim cities during this era – but in the San Francisco of the early twentieth century the fire problem had been brought so firmly under control that the 1906 disaster was an aberration.

By contrast, the fires in Tokyo and Yokohama started by the dreadful Great Kanto Earthquake of 1923, which killed 140,000 people, were not an aberration. They were started by cooking braziers toppling over and were fed by wooden houses until the flames grew big enough and hot enough to create a firestorm (Hadfield, 1991, pp. 1–14). This was a disaster in which the level of destruction was exceptional, but was essentially a replay of earlier disasters in Asian history. Even today, Japanese cities are characterized by timber houses (which bend and sway, rather than collapse, in earthquakes) and have few open spaces which are capable of providing firebreaks.

Responses to the problem

Cities are an example of what may be called "complex adaptive systems," which are made up of individual agents who can only survive and prosper by developing procedures to cope with and react to what other agents in the system are doing (Waldrop, 1992, pp. 144–97). To live and work in an urban environment, individuals had to adapt to the hazards which were created by the clustering of buildings and other people. In adapting to the problem of fire, the first priority was to get back into business as soon as possible. After a fire burnt out most of central Seattle in

1889, merchants were back at work the next day, doing business under canvas (Turbeville, 1985: 109). Factories and shops which were destroyed by fire needed to be rebuilt quickly, with new equipment and stock, if owners were to keep their business connections open. It was a commonly held belief among merchants that after a fire "if a shop had not resumed business within three days ... it had no future" (Siedensticker, 1990, p. 8).

No fire or other natural disaster destroyed any of these cities completely. Major ports such as Hankow and San Francisco were too economically valuable to be abandoned but this does not mean that when disasters occurred they were of minor economic significance and therefore ephemeral. An observer noted after a fire in Hankow in 1810 that, "because this is such a center for the collection of merchandise, it was not difficult to rebuild – within a month most major buildings had risen again" (quoted by Rowe, 1989, p. 159). Such fast rebuilding was a strategy that people developed to prevent complete devastation when fire occurred.

In pre-industrial times, towns had been built and organized in a way which enabled residents to minimize the cost of housing, infrastructure, and transport. Economic activity was usually concentrated around one or more key points, such as a marketplace or bazaar or dockside area. From these, a tangle of narrow, crooked streets and alleys linked houses and workshops in other parts of the city. Hankow retained this townscape pattern because, as a visitor commented in 1851, "an inch of land is worth an inch of gold" (Rowe, 1989, p. 65). The three main thoroughfares followed the shoreline of the Yangtze and Han Rivers and were crossed by dozens of lanes and alleys, giving a large number of workers access to the city's main commercial sites and places of work (Rowe, 1984, p. 24). Because walking was the basic means of transport the proximity between residence and workplace and between production and point of sale made it easier for people to go about their business. Low-income groups could only afford to live in such a city if they reduced their housing costs by crowding into small houses in densely built-up areas.

In Asian towns, where timber was the basic building material, people responded to a high level of fire risk by building houses cheaply and furnishing them sparely, so that when disasters occurred the loss of capital was kept to a minimum. These houses were the architectural equivalent of a ballpoint pen: they were functional, but disposable, with their loss causing no great economic harm to their owners. As one observer noted, "the actual loss of property is not so great as might at first sight be supposed; for it is a notorious fact that houses in Tokyo are not so carefully constructed as in Kyoto and other cities, and the greater risk from fire incurred in the capital discourages the building of costly houses unless they are to stand on extensive grounds" (Inouye, 1910, p. 30). These houses were considered to be not worth giving a coat of paint, and when they were destroyed they were rebuilt in the same fashion, in cheap, flammable materials.

Furthermore, people kept the savings they would need to pay for rebuilding safe in fireproof containers: in Edo the wealthy used small fireproof warehouses, while "the lower classes kept emergency baskets ready in conspicuous places, and dug pits under their floors with ingenious arrangements that caused flooding when heated, and so, it was hoped, preserved such valuables as had been put away in time" (Siedensticker, 1983, p. 64). At the time of the Great Kanto Earthquake of 1923, Tokyo merchants had made preparation for fires by keeping reserves of waterlogged timber close to a river and by keeping inventories in fireproof warehouses.

By behaving in this way, individual city-dwellers were able to turn a risky and dangerous situation to their advantage. Because houses were built to basic standards, they could be replaced cheaply and this made it possible for people to be able to bear the costs of living in economically prosperous, but fire-prone cities. By minimizing the effects of recurrent fire damage, people were able to cope with the risks which were created when population growth increased the number of naked flames and the supply of combustible materials. Quick rebuilding after fires helped people to stay in town and stay in business.

Rowe writes that in Hankow, "the daily threat of fire spawned a mentality of stoic acceptance that astonished visitors, Chinese as well as foreign" (Rowe 1989, p. 159). What these observers misunderstood was how people in fire-prone cities had learnt to cope with the problem. City-dwellers adapted to the hazards which were created by the clustering of people and buildings, using rules of thumb which held that the best way to minimize likely future fire damage was to build cheaply and make plans to rebuild quickly. This strategy would have been handed down by teaching and confirmed when fires did occur. That there was "stoic acceptance" of the fact that fires would happen in the future did not mean that people merely awaited their fate without developing any strategy to ensure that their personal loss would be kept to a minimum. These cities and their inhabitants were able to ride out disasters, which was an accomplishment.

There was a price to pay for this strategy, however. When buildings which had been destroyed by fire were rebuilt in cheap flammable materials they would provide ample fuel for the next fire. As long as rebuilding was done in this way, cities would be locked in to a path of recurrent fire damage. Because the risk of fire created uncertainty about whether durable capital goods could be protected, it was rational for people to invest unproductively.

To bring the fire problem under control would have required a degree of trust and cooperation between members of society which is difficult to achieve in an urban setting. This is the essence of the problem which game theorists have dubbed the "Prisoner's Dilemma" (Waldrop, 1992, pp. 262–63). If two prisoners are kept in separate cells and questioned by police about a crime they committed jointly, they have a choice of either remaining silent ("cooperating" with each other, in which case they will both be set free because of lack of evidence) or informing on the other ("defecting," and so be set free while the partner is punished). Thus if only one prisoner defects, the silence of the "cooperating" prisoner is taken as an admission of guilt. If both defect, both will be punished. Because there is no way for the prisoners to be sure that the other will not defect, both betray each other. Each prisoner is worse off because they defected rather than cooperated with each other, but if one prisoner had cooperated, he or she would have been *much* worse off if the other prisoner had not done the same. In a situation where mutual trust does not exist, what is rational behavior for individuals leads to the least desirable outcome for everyone.

This is a hypothetical situation, in which people have imperfect information. In reality, many decisions about cooperation and trust have to be made on a day-to-day basis. People who interact on a regular basis develop a reputation and it is likely that people whose past behavior suggests that they can be relied upon not to defect will cooperate with each other for mutual benefit. Game theorists have taken this into account by considering what would happen if choices had to be made repeatedly and if people had perfect information about each other's past conduct. In the so-called *iterated* Prisoner's Dilemma, the rational strategy is for people to cooperate at first, continue to do with others who do the same, and refuse to cooperate with those who defect (Waldrop, 1992, pp. 262–65). In the long run, people will cooperate voluntarily with those whom they can trust.

While there were well-intentioned individuals and groups which did attempt to "cooperate" to contain the problem of fire, most people continued to "defect" to reduce their living costs. In Hankow, a wealthy merchant distributed fire-retardant matting to poor households for several years "but his efforts were never followed up by others and had no significant impact" (Rowe, 1989, p. 160). Some citizens donated land, or funds to allow the government to purchase land, to establish "fire lanes" – open spaces to provide firebreaks and make evacuation and fire-fighting easier, but in thickly settled Hankow it was virtually impossible to keep the lanes clear of squatters. Fire-fighting was done by private companies, which were funded by guilds and benevolent halls, but it was difficult to coordinate their efforts and get their engines through city streets which were narrow in any case, and often blocked by stall pedlars and wheelbarrows (Rowe, 1989, pp. 163–8).

If urban residents fail to develop voluntary institutions which encourage people not to behave in ways which create high social costs, the next best solution is to have a third party which has the power to establish regulations against "defecting" behavior and to punish transgressors. The principal objection to this solution has been outlined by Douglass North: third-party enforcement is not costless and these costs may be sufficient to outweigh any benefit which society derives (North, 1990, p. 54–60). A government may attempt to treat the problems of environmental damage created by Prisoner's Dilemma situations by putting in place regulations and minimum standards, but these are likely to be unenforceable if they impose extra costs on the bulk of the population. No city administration could insist that buildings be constructed in nonflammable materials if timber, bamboo, and thatch were freely available and cheaper than bricks and tiles. Thus in 1872, when Tokyo's governor ordered that the Ginza district, which had been destroyed by fire, be rebuilt in brick, many of the buildings stood vacant because they cost ten times as much to build as did wooden ones. After that, Tokyo remained a wooden city and government efforts to combat the problem of fires were confined to the widening of streets and the purchase of land to build firebreaks (Siedensticker, 1983, pp. 58–61).

In the "wild west," echoes of the Asian response to high fire risk can be detected. In San Francisco, one businessman built three buildings in different parts of town to reduce the risk of them all being lost in one blaze (Lotchin, 1974, p. 18). The string of fires in Sacramento in the 1850s suggest that rebuilding there was being done in flammable materials. But frontier towns soon managed to escape the damaging cycle of recurrent fire damage. Their rough edges were smoothed as a housing stock of vastly improved quality and adequate systems of water supply were built to meet continued population growth. By the early twentieth century little of the combustible cities of the gold rush era remained. The jumble of roughly built housing and workplaces had given way to specialized downtown business districts, built of steel and masonry, surrounded by suburbs with houses which were usually built on large lots and reasonably fire-safe, despite in many cases being built of wood. Gas or electricity had largely replaced naked flames for lighting, heating, and cooking.

In his *New towns in the new world*, David Hamer argues that people saw new towns as agents of civilization, with urban progress representing a crucial moral triumph over the "primitive" aspects of "new societies." Fires "were more often than not welcomed because they destroyed the past and provided the opportunity for a fresh start" (Hamer, 1990, p. 171). In the ashes boosters saw only the opportunity for a phoenix-like emergence of a new city, not simply rebuilt but built to a better standard than before.

City governments attempted to bring this about by tightening up fire regulations for new construction and improving infrastructure. The rebuilding which was required after major fires presented cities with an opportunity to improve their urban physical fabric. After a fire in 1856, the Ballarat municipal council banned buildings with canvas roofs and walls and attempted to control the use of wooden chimneys. As fires cleared away primitive, flammable structures, rebuilding tended to be done in brick (Bate, 1978, p. 111). Thus when the United States Hotel was burnt to the ground, the owners quickly "set up a bar among the ashes to take advantage of the thirst of sightseers. Within three weeks, with the help of fellow Americans, they had rebuilt more solidly and larger than ever" (Bate, 1978, p. 104). After major fires, San Francisco, Seattle, and Vancouver introduced zoning laws and regulations forbidding the construction of flammable buildings in the burnt-out areas (Roy, 1980). The Seattle fire in 1889 enabled the city to rebuild the downtown area with a new layout of regraded streets, a sewerage system, and a municipalized water supply (Turbeville, 1985). The 1886 fire encouraged Vancouver, which also had to deal with a typhoid epidemic that year, to construct reliable water supply and sewerage infrastructure. The *per capita* cost was high, as the city's population was then only 8,000, but voters regarded the new infrastructure as a good investment which would attract settlers and capital (Andrews, 1984). In 1857 Melbourne opened what was probably the largest reservoir in the world, outside the city at Yan Yean. San Francisco obtained a reliable water supply in 1858, and by 1880 large storage reservoirs had also been built in Oakland and Los Angeles (Lotchin, 1974, p. 183; Frost, 1991, p. 149).

Fire regulations were effective in these towns because business and housing did not have to stay close to the old downtown. In most places there was room to move. Hemmed in by its hills and bay, San Francisco was able to open up more land by means of plank roads (and later streetcars) and landfills. Some of the steepest hills were leveled. New residential areas were added to the grid of streets so that people could avoid high-rent areas. Artisans and small manufacturers began to relocate to peripheral areas. More middle-class houses were built on the high ground. Ferries to Oakland began operating in 1851. In Melbourne, there was a grid of 99-foot wide streets, separated by narrow lanes, which acted as firebreaks: only one fire, in 1897, has ever come close to burning out a whole block, and none has ever crossed a city street (Wilde, 1991, p. 211). Outside the central grid, and abundance of parkland was laid out. In towns such as Adelaide and Christchurch, wide streets and squares within the city centre, and a belt of permanent parkland surrounding it, would have acted as firebreaks if a major fire had ever broken out.

Beyond the downtown area, homeowners could not be compelled to build in brick, because in most cases timber was still the cheaper building material. As Turbeville observes of Seattle after its great fire, "it is presumptuous to think that a city surrounded by the great forests of the continent, populated by people with two centuries of woodworking experience, and whose major industry was the cutting, processing and shipment of timber, would turn overnight to unfamiliar, expensive, and often unavailable building materials, no matter how great a tragedy might have suggested such a change" (Turbeville, 1985, p. 109). Nonetheless, in most new suburbs there was enough open space to reduce the supply of combustible materials per unit of land. In Oakland, as a journalist noted in 1887, "nearly all the houses are built on lots sufficiently large to give room for a garden" (quoted by Scott, 1985, p. 80). The Melbourne suburbs of Fitzroy, Collingwood, and Richmond, which had been subdivided in the late 1830s and during the 1840s, filled up quickly during the gold rush with houses on small lots connected by narrow lanes and alleys. Concern about the public health implications of this unplanned, dense development prompted the colonial government to reorganize its Survey Department in 1852. New suburbs such as Carlton, St. Kilda, and Emerald Hill (South Melbourne) were laid out with wide streets, public squares, and sites reserved for parkland, schools, and churches (Grant and Serle, 1957, p. 76). In Los Angeles and other western cities, there was a general reaction against multi-family houses (10,000 of which burnt in Boston in a 1908 fire) "without proper provision for light, air, yards, lawns, trees, shrubs, flowers, and individual home units" (quoted by Bottles, 1987, p. 80). Cities and their boosters energetically promoted suburban real estate, served by mass transit, to open up areas which were more private and spacious.

The development of such suburbs greatly reduced the spread of fire by helping to confine blazes to single buildings. This fire safety reduced the risk of constructing wooden houses, which were being made progressively cheaper by new building methods and lower cost materials (Doucet and Weaver, 1985). Working-class housing was quite durable and fire-safe, even though built of inexpensive and impermanent materials (Frost and Jones, 1989). Capital did not have to be used unproductively to provide reserves of liquid assets and building materials in case of fire, and was instead injected into the city-building process. By the First World War, the standard and spaciousness of housing was demonstrably higher than it had been half a century earlier.

Strong government played a major part in this, by setting out fire regulations, building water supply schemes, and providing public transport and other suburban infrastructure (either directly, as was generally the case in Australia, or indirectly by providing subsidies to private companies). But such a positive role was possible because average incomes were high and few people had to cut urban living costs to the bone. As an observer of San Francisco in 1889 put it: "Aside from drink and vice, and the calamities of vice, there is no deep poverty here" (quoted by Issel and Cherny, 1986: 101). These were prosperous commercial cities and chronically short of labor, but because the costs of migrating to them was so high, poor and unskilled immigrants were few in number, while the spending of migrants who could afford the fares added to the level of aggregate demand. The cities were a product of, and tangible evidence of, the affluence of the average worker. Even though suburban sprawl inflated the cost of infrastructure provision, voters were willing and able to approve expensive projects such as Melbourne's sewerage system, and the building of an aquaduct from the Owens Valley to Los Angeles (Reisner, 1993, pp. 58–89). People preferred to buy or rent new suburban houses, spending up to 30 per cent of an average laborer's wage to do so, even though there was plenty of cheaper, but older housing available close to city centres (Frost, 1991, pp. 116–18). The suburbs were so accessible and affordable that few people had to live in substandard housing. There was no large body of refugees, like that which poured into Hong Kong after the Chinese communist revolution, and no large squatter camps, like that which burnt to the ground in Hong Kong in 1953, leaving 50,000 people homeless.

Conclusions

Throughout history, people in several parts of the world have found themselves in cities where there was a major risk of fire disasters. In some cities people coped by building as cheaply as possible to minimize their losses and hoarding liquid assets to pay for post-fire rebuilding, which was done in cheap flammable materials. They had no choice, for they had inherited a housing stock and townscape from their predecessors, who had reacted in the same way to the fire problem. What was rational behavior by individuals in the circumstances reduced the productivity of investment, impacted on the lives and investments of others, and perpetuated the fire problem.

Similar issues are being played out in Third World cities today. Wherever people overuse common resources – such as rivers and canals to dump wastes, or areas of vacant ground to build shanties – they are making decisions which may seem rational, but which create an outcome which is far from desirable for the rest of society. A "Tragedy of the Commons" situations may occur in which there is no incentive for individuals to conserve resources, because no-one else can be prevented from overusing them. Negative externalities – such as when a fire starting in one house spread to others – may go unchecked. If history can tell us how such problems have been solved in the past, we will have useful information about what needs to be done in the present and future.

The Pacific Rim is a useful arena for studying such problems, because during the nineteenth century several cities grew rapidly and shared the same vulnerability to fire disasters. In some regions, the problem was soon brought under control and after fires cities were rebuilt to higher standards of safety and amenity. Here fires were symptomatic of growing pains, rather than a chronic condition. Rising incomes, and the contribution of governments, which provided effective infrastructure and enforcement of regulations and property rights to control externalities, made the improvement possible. Knowing this aspect of the urban past can point the way towards the creation of a better urban future.

References

Andrews, M.W., "The Best Advertisement a City can Have: Public health services in Vancouver, 1886–1888," *Urban History Review*, 12 (1984), pp. 19–27.

Balazs, E., *Chinese Civilization and Bureaucracy: Variations on a theme*, New Haven: Yale University Press, 1964.

Barth, G., *Instant Cities: Urbanization and the rise of San Francisco and Denver*, New York: Oxford University Press, 1975.

Bate, W., *Lucky City: The first generation at Ballarat, 1851–1901*, Carlton: Melbourne University Press, 1978.

Bottles, S.L., *Los Angeles and the Automobile: The making of the modern city*, Berkeley and Los Angeles: University of California Press, 1987.

Butlin, N.G., *Investment in Australian Economic Development 1861–1900*, Canberra: Australian National University Press, 1964.

Cannon, M., *Old Melbourne Town: Before the Gold Rush*, Main Ridge: Loch Haven Books, 1991.

Chao Erh-sun, *Ch'ing-shih kao* [Draft History of the Ch'ing Dynasty], Mukden, 1937.

Daley, C., *The History of South Melbourne*, Melbourne: Robertson & Mullens, 1940.

Doucet, M.W. and Weaver, J.C., "Material culture and the North American house: the era of the common man, 1870–1920," *Journal of American History*, 72 (1985), pp. 560–87.

Fitzgerald, S., *Rising Damp: Sydney 1870–90*, Melbourne: Oxford University Press, 1987.

Fitzgerald, S., *Sydney 1842–1992*, Sydney: Hale & Iremonger, 1992.

Frost, L., *The New Urban Frontier: Urbanisation and city-building in Australasia and the American West*, Sydney: New South Wales University Press, 1991.

—, "Coping in Their Own Way: Asian cities and the problem of fires," *Urban History*, Vol. 24, No. 1 (1997), pp. 5–16.

Frost, L.E. and Jones, E.L., "The Fire Gap and the Greater Durability of Nineteenth Century Cities," *Planning Perspectives*, 4 (1989), pp. 333–47.

Grant, J. and Serle, G. (eds), *The Melbourne Scene 1803–1956*, Sydney: Hale & Iremonger, 1957.

Hadfield, P., *Sixty Seconds that will Change the World*, London: Pan Books, 1991.

Hamer, D., *New Towns in the New World: Images and perceptions of the nineteenth-century urban frontier*, New York: Columbia University Press, 1990.

Inouye, J., *Home Life in Tokyo*, London, 1910.

Issel, W. and Cherny R.W., *San Francisco, 1865–1932: Politics, power, and urban development*, Berkeley: University of California Press, 1986.

Jones, E., Frost, L., and White, C., *Coming Full Circle: An economic history of the Pacific Rim*, Boulder: Westview Press, 1993.

Kipling, R., *From Sea to Sea and other Sketches: Letters of travel*, London: Macmillan, 1900.

Larsen, L.H. (1978), *The urban west at the end of the frontier*, Lawrence: The Regents Press of Kansas.

Lotchin, R.W., *San Francisco 1846–1856: From hamlet to city*, New York: Oxford University Press, 1974.

McCarty, J.W., "Gold Rushes," in G. Davison, J. Hirst, and S. Macintyre (eds), *The Oxford Companion to Australian History*, Melbourne: Oxford University Press, 1998.

North, D.C., *Institutions, Institutional Change and Economic Performance*, Cambridge, 1990.

Nouet, N., *The Shogun's City: A history of Tokyo*, Folkestone: Norbury, 1990.

Polo, M., *The Travels of Marco Polo*, trans. R. Latham, Harmondsworth: Penguin, 1958.

Reisner, M., *Cadillac Desert: The American West and its disappearing water*, New York: Penguin Books, 1993.

Rowe, W., *Hankow: Commerce and society in a Chinese city, 1796–1889*, Stanford: Stanford University Press, 1984.

—, *Hankow: Conflict and Community in a Chinese City, 1796–1895*, Stanford: Standford University Press, 1989.

Roy, P.E., *Vancouver: An illustrated history*, Toronto: James Lorimer, 1980.

Scott, M., *The San Francisco Bay Area: A metropolis in perspective*, Berkeley and Los Angeles: University of California Press, 1985.

Siedensticker, E., *Low City, High City: Tokyo from Edo to the earthquake*, London: Allen Lane, 1983.

—, *Tokyo Rising: The city since the great earthquake*, New York: Knopf, 1990.

San Francisco Chronicle, April 14, 1996.

Sydney Morning Herald, November 4, 1852.

The Times, July 3, 1851.

Turbeville, D.E. III, "Cities of Kindling: Geographical implications of the urban fire hazard on the Pacific northwest coast frontier, 1851–1920," unpublished PhD thesis, Simon Fraser University (1985).

Waldrop, M.W., *Complexity: The emerging science at the edge of order and chaos*, New York, 1992.

Wilde, S., *Life under the Bells: A history of the Metropolitan Fire Brigade, Melbourne 1891–1991*, Melbourne: Longman Cheshire, 1991.

8

World War I, the American Interior, and Pacific Markets: A Look at Distant Impacts

Nancy J. Taniguchi

This paper argues for a view of Pacific trade based on an analysis of regional market networks. This perspective supplements traditional emphases on coastal areas or on national economic policies, and potentially yields different results. It uses eastern Utah coal – a "hand-maiden industry" for copper, sugar, and railroads – as a test case.

The notion of trade networks and their unifying power is nothing new. Historian Fernand Braudel postulated this kind of unity for the Mediterranean world of Philip II's Spain, describing interactions built on centuries of commerce. More recently, journalist and historian Frank Gibney, echoing Braudel's approach, wrote *The Pacific century*, partly to awaken a somnolent America to the importance of events on her western shore. Against a historic backdrop of trade routes to China, Pacific whaling, Chinese labor in America, and US imperialism, he postulated America's growing awareness of the importance of Pacific interaction as a post-World War II phenomenon. In his scenario, our involvement in a series of Pacific wars – World War II, Korea, Vietnam – created the first significant American awareness of her Pacific neighbors. But, he claims, "It took a massive shift in the economic balance of power to make Americans take notice" of the area ... an "economic takeoff that began with Japan in the early sixties."[1] His contemporary article in *The Wilson Quarterly* gave a few trade statistics: "By 1979 American trade with Pacific Rim countries had grown greater than with Europe. By 1989 our $297 billion commerce with East Asian countries was more than one-third heavier than our total trade with Europe – and growing."[2]

The power of these statistics is obvious and impressive from the national perspective. But if one looks at a region – in my case, an inland region with an economy based largely on extractive industry – the timing and dynamics of Pacific economic importance emerges differently. In the late nineteenth and early twentieth centuries, the American intermountain region – specifically Utah's coal district – turned to Pacific markets. Its entrepreneurs sought to achieve vertical integration in the wake of realigned transportation connections mandated by the federal government during World War I. The wartime experience only coincidentally opened up the Pacific Basin to intermountain trade, but a persistent West Coast orientation followed and is maintained to the present. The purpose of this paper, therefore, is to describe the events of that pivotal period in a landlocked area that nonetheless opened its door – long before those major wars pinpointed by Gibney – to the notion of the importance of Pacific trade. While the fates of three major industries – coal, copper, and sugar – are intertwined in this study, the litmus test is coal. A mineral of little intrinsic worth, coal has nonetheless determined the success of other industries that historically relied on its availability. The resilience of Utah's coal industry and its growing Pacific focus add a new dimension to the study of international market networks.

Perhaps the shift described by Gibney has been neither so recent nor so sudden as might appear from a national, rather than a regional, perspective. The exploration of a regional reorientation, furthermore, begs the question of how one defines and analyzes a national economic trend. The study of several regions and their turn toward Pacific trade should revise or refine the chronology for national awareness postulated by Gibney. These studies, however, and a synthesis of their findings, remain in the future.

First, some background on the historical connections of the Utah coal industry. Coal has always been regarded as a "handmaiden" industry – important as a contributor to the growth of other, more lucrative, enterprises. At its commercial inception in the 1880s, Utah's coal industry fueled railroads then expanding across largely treeless mesas, salt flats, and mountains. Steam engines which could rely on wood in other parts of the United States needed coal to penetrate the last reaches of the western frontier. The first railroad to invade Utah's coal district, the Denver and Rio Grande Western, was a sister line to Colorado's Denver and Rio Grande. This corporation, led by William Jackson Palmer, had originated to tap the mines of Colorado and transport their riches to another Palmer-sponsored enterprise, the silver-lead smelter at Durango, Colorado.[3] This smelter ran on coal as coke (a specially processed coal derivative which, when burned, generates a very high heat). Consequently, from its beginnings, Utah's coal industry was tied into a larger market network, but was oriented eastward.

Central Utah coal development burgeoned apace with railroad and smelting needs. The D&RGW, or Western (as it was locally known), located, patented, and developed Utah's major commercial coal belt, a huge arc of deposits stretching west along the Book Cliffs from the Colorado border into east-central Utah, where it hooks south under the Wasatch Plateau.[4] Although the Union Pacific Railroad (UP) had traversed Utah well north of this region with the driving of the famous "Golden Spike" in 1869, its goal – to span the nation – took it near the settlements of northern Utah, thus skirting Utah's "last frontier." Only a decade later, as population pressures and ecclesiastical priorities drove settlers southeast of the Wasatch Front mountain range, would geological scouting parties, sponsored by the D&RGW, find Utah's major coal deposits.[5] All the Western trains ran on coal, so their very lives depended on a sufficient supply. An increased supply stimulated further mine development, as noted by a Rio Grande spokesman in 1883: "...

when his [Palmer's] road entered Utah, coke was selling for around $20 a ton, a figure that shortly dropped to $10. This permitted a large number of low grade mines to reopen … . His road also claimed to have reduced the rates for shipping lead eastward [to the Durango smelter] as much as 66 per cent … ."[6] Thus, the commercial development of Utah coal grew hand-in-hand with the growth of UP's competitor railway line (the Western), which, in a classic application of vertical integration, also acquired or developed virtually all the commercial coal mines and obtained a true monopoly on coking coal within Utah Territory.[7]

Coking coal had particular value because it supplied the smelting trade, which needed to achieve very high temperatures in order to smelt ore. In the late nineteenth century, hard rock mining, and its attendant need for coke, expanded dramatically throughout the Intermountain West. Utah was no exception. Initially, miners rushed in to develop veins of gold, silver and lead (just as processed in the Durango smelter, as already noted). Then, the lenient Windom Tariff, which admitted Mexican ores virtually tax-free, was replaced by the McKinley Tariff of 1890. This new law not only ended the free movement of silver north into the United States – its intended purpose – but also caused American capital to flow into the construction of American-financed mining operations south of the border, further destabilizing the silver-lead industry, of which copper was a byproduct.[8] This impact, coupled with the collapse of the French copper syndicate in 1889 and the national Panic of 1893, caused many western mining magnates to turn to copper as their leading money-maker.[9]

A prime example of this impulse – and a market for Utah coal – was the development of copper mining at Butte, Montana. The developers, headed by Marcus Daly, had entered copper mining by way of experience with gold and silver mines in California, Nevada, and Utah in the 1840s through the 1870s. By late 1882 Daly's men had struck a vein of chalcolite, the richest deposit of copper sulfide ever discovered.[10] This discovery dovetailed nicely with the new uses of electricity. At the American Centennial Exposition in Philadelphia in 1876, Alexander Graham Bell had demonstrated the transmittal of speech through copper wire, and in 1882 New York had begun running street lights on electricity, by connecting Thomas Edison's newly-patented light bulbs to its municipal generator by copper threads.[11] In 1884, Anaconda's smelter was completed, its production of up to 5,000 tons a month all produced by burning coke.[12] Production burgeoned so that in 1904 Anaconda signed with the largest eastern Utah coal producer to provide 150–200 tons of coke per day, seven days a week.[1]

In Utah, the Highland Boy property in Bingham Canyon, just west of Salt Lake City, matched this regional trend. In 1897, it was undergoing further gold exploration (to take advantage of the newly-developed cyanide process) when miners broke through into a magnificent ore channel of copper sulfides. The resultant assay yielded three times more copper than anticipated, shifting the purpose of the mine away from gold and leading to the first commercial copper shipments by the middle of the year. In 1899, Bingham's developers erected the first Utah smelter designed primarily for copper ores.[14] Soon competitive interests had built nearby a lead smelter and two other copper smelters. All of them forged agreements with the Rio Grande Western Railway Company for motive power, and with its mines for coal and coke.[15]

As ore smelting increased, it dumped rich, sulfurous fumes over orchards and livestock when the wind came from the south, harming plants and beasts. Aggrieved farmers filed suit in Utah's federal district court, which in 1906 perpetually enjoined the defendant companies from smelting sulfide ores of certain properties and from discharging the resultant gasses into the air. This suit effectively caused the closure of most smelters by 1908 and led to the exploitation of porphyry coppers instead of copper sulfides.[16]

These porphyry ores were extracted through open-pit mining, originated at Bingham in 1906 with the introduction of a gigantic steam shovel. Three others were purchased by mid-1907 at a total cost of $72,981, a terrific capital investment in a still-struggling industry.[17] These behemoths, as well as the railroads that had long been hauling ores from mines to smelter and to markets, and the smelters themselves, all ran on coal. As the United States electrified in the late nineteenth and early twentieth centuries, the demand for copper soared, as did the demand for coal.

This coal had other uses, too. It heated homes in Salt Lake City, at an estimated rate of 2,000 tons per day for domestic use alone in January 1908.[18] It powered factories, such as the beet-sugar industry of the Utah-Idaho Sugar Company, first incorporated as the Utah Sugar Company in 1889. This industry built on the foundations of earlier experiments in sorghum cane sugar (which won the $5,000 prize offered by the Utah territorial legislature) and the initiation of beet sugar manufacture in Alvarado, California.[19] With the backing of officials of the Church of Jesus Christ of Latter-day Saints (LDS, or Mormons), a sugar factory was built at Lehi, Utah – the fourth in the nation. Its internal machinery, designed by Edward F. and Harold P. Dyer, formerly of Alvarado, California, pioneered American sugar-manufacturing design. Upon its completion in 1891, sugar beets were sliced and boiled in huge vats heated by coal. Then, in the centrifugal room, the molasses was spun off and the sugar poured into sacks, which were then taken directly to market by coal-powered locomotives.[20] This production was stimulated by a federal bounty of two cents a pound on all domestically-produced sugar, which remained in effect from 1890 to 1894.[21] World-wide, the demand for sugar was increasing dramatically, peaking in America in 1909 at 52.1 pounds per year per household.[22] By that time, the Utah sugar interests had erected another plant in Utah and three more in Idaho, which merged as the Utah-Idaho Sugar Company in 1907.[23] All of these ran on coal.

From the beginning, therefore, Utah coal was part of a regional trade network, originally spanning the miles from eastern Utah to the Rio Grande-affiliated smelter at Durango, Colorado and to the Anaconda smelter at Butte, Montana; to Salt Lake City in competition with the UP-dominated coal trade, and to Utah and Idaho sugar manufactories. These economic connections were strained and extended as the nation reeled under the Panic of 1907.

The economic tremors occasioned by this Panic illustrate the contemporary extent of the intermountain network run on Utah coal. Concern for its effects were first voiced in the coal district newspaper in August. The majority of local coal was being converted to coke for smelting uses, and the biggest local mine was already six months behind on orders. By September, Salt Lake smelters were so desperate for fuel that they were trying to get West Virginia coke at about $12 a ton, as opposed to less than $8 they paid for the local product, when it could be had. But without the coke, their furnaces might freeze up due to inactivity.[24] Meanwhile, the Wyoming coal operators, to keep their mines humming, had increased wages and shortened hours, leading to a influx of "American miners into all the coal camps," which were fully manned for the first time in 25 years. So-called coolie labor was being eliminated.[25] Utah miners who left for Wyoming would count themselves lucky when, by the beginning of October, all the coke ovens at one major mine were shut down because of the idling of smelters at Butte and Anaconda.[26] Men who left took their pay one-third in cash, two-thirds in checks, or half-and-half, due to the inability of banks to provide sufficient specie. Even Salt Lake City banks were issuing certificates instead of cash, and limiting their depositors to a $200 withdrawal weekly.[27]

Ramifications mounted. Trying to capture new markets, by December 1907 400 tons of coal had left eastern Utah for San Francisco. This strategy seemed so promising that for the first time ever, the price of coal was reduced at the mines (as opposed to reductions by retailers) early in 1908, allegedly to attract the Nevada and California trade.[28] In a letter to the statistician of the US Geologic Survey, the Utah State Coal Mine Inspector neatly summed up the Panic's domino effect:

> The recent monetary disturbance has affected the coal mining industry in Utah very materially. After the closing of the mine and smelters in Montana, it was necessary to close the 204 coke ovens at Castle Gate. This was followed by the closing of several metal mines and smelters in Utah, which partially closed down three of our coal mines, and caused a reduction of working forces all along the line.[29]

Those laid off included employees of the D&RG Railroad, whose general manager explained that freight and passenger business had declined due to the closing of smelters and mines; furthermore, no more construction than necessary was being planned.[30] Throughout January and February, mines continued closing, while others ran with reduced forces. This idling during a usually peak demand time was occasioned only partly by the Panic; another contributing factor was the mild winter weather, reducing the need for home heating fuel.[31] Western coal production had dwindled so severely that in May 1908, when President Theodore Roosevelt decided to send his "Great White Fleet" cruising throughout the Pacific, Australia offered to provide the necessary coal and Japan was believed to be waiting in line as well. The coal district newspaper grumbled that it would be better to provide the US Navy with an American product, and the taxpayers should not begrudge the price tag of almost two million dollars for mining and transporting the necessary 266,000 tons.[32]

The Pacific flow of Utah coal – real and potential – helped revive the industry. By August 1908, the newspaper touted local recovery from the depression and, in a move probably calculated to spur mine production, the State Coal Mine Inspector publicly warned of a coming "fuel famine." During his summer inspection tour, he found only 8,000 tons of coal in storage, one-tenth of the previous year's stockpile. He warned of the demands of the upcoming beet harvest, and noted hundreds of disabled railroad cars along the route between Salt Lake City and the Bingham smelters.[33]

Assisting in coal distribution, a settlement between railroad magnates E.H. Harriman and George Gould eased transshipment between the Oregon Short Line and D&RGW, respectively, facilitating the flow of Utah coal into Wyoming which had been stymied since 1905. One reason for this rapprochement lay in the strike of Wyoming topmen (outside mine workers) who led the underground miners out as well. The only way intermountain smelters (controlled by many of the same men as the railroads, or by their friends and business associates) could meet all their production demands with the Wyoming miners out on strike was to admit Utah coal to the Wyoming market.[34] While this strike was short-lived, the effect of the shutout was not. The D&RG, which had sought its own Pacific connection when faced with the intransigence of the Oregon Short Line, had long been constructing its own railroad westward. In December, 1908, the Western Pacific, this sister line, reached Elko, Nevada, to great rejoicing. By August 1910, after much grief at Harriman's instigation, it reached Oakland, California.[35] The Utah coal fields now had a direct, locally-connected route to the Pacific coast.

The nation as a whole was turning toward the Pacific. The clearest manifestation of this urge was the Panama Canal, completed in 1914. A year before it opened, a former US Senator predicted new benefits would flow to Utah's coal fields. He stated, "When the Panama Canal is opened, ships will stop at San Pedro harbor .... From Utah the coal supply ... will come ... [and the] chief market for this [coal] will be in Los Angeles."[36] Ongoing events, however, dimmed this rosy prediction.

The carefully-constructed western coal market network did not long thrive unmolested. The first major disruption began with the anti-trust actions of newly inaugurated Democratic President Woodrow Wilson in 1913. Wilson's views marked the culmination of the anti-trust movement which characterized the so-called Progressive Era, defined by historians as the period from 1900 to World

War I. According to historian Samuel Hays, the anti-monopoly impulse, like most other aspects of American public life, came as a reaction to the burgeoning power of Big Business in the late nineteenth century.[37] Beginning with Progressive Era President Theodore Roosevelt, and continuing with his successor, William Howard Taft, American government sought to control the capitalists who had previously had a virtually free rein in the economic arena. The growth of the intermountain copper, sugar, and coal industries during this same period exemplified this business trend, and were consequently as vulnerable to federal policies as less isolated parts of the nation. Thus, in April 1913, when the President took the extraordinary step of addressing a message to Congress in person – the first such appearance since 1796 – Utahns listened closely to his call for tariff reform. Wilson noted, "For a long time … we have sought in our tariff schedules to give each group of manufacturers or producers what they themselves thought they needed in order to maintain a practically exclusive market as against the rest of the world." Utah capitalists must have nodded in complacent agreement. Then came the bombshell. The result, Wilson claimed, had been "monopoly … [which] only new principles of action will save us from a final hard crystallization … and a complete loss of the influences that quicken enterprise and keep independent energy alive."[38] The resultant measure, the Underwood–Simmons Tariff, Wilson signed into law on October 3, 1913.[39]

This tariff had a direct impact on Utah coal. Production slumped by up to 20 per cent as of May 1914, resulting from British Columbian coal pouring into former Utah markets on the Pacific coast, a total of 38,000 tons so far that year. An article in the local paper excoriated the presidential program, claiming, "It is the application of the New Freedom to this state [Utah] with a disturbing commercial result similar to that occasioned by the removal of 'artificial stimulation' from the sugar industry"[40] – which had also adversely affected Utah coal production. The tariff also affected related industries, with reductions placed on 985 articles, while increases affected 86 items, mostly chemicals. Wool went on the free list immediately, and sugar was scheduled to do so in 1916.[41] This latter provision portended doom for the Utah-Idaho Sugar Company, then in strong competition with Philippine sugar, and concurrent destruction of a major market for Utah coal. In fact, the leading Utah sugar historian predicted the evisceration of the intermountain beet sugar industry had the Underwood Tariff "not been nullified in effect by the coming of World War I in August of 1914."[42]

All the strands binding Utah coal into its regional market network received a sharp tug when World War I began. By November 1914, the Utah State Mine Inspector reported, "Reduction of traffic on railroads, inactivity of mines, resulting in dwindling ore transportation and attendant shutdown of smelters, has resulted in a big reduction in the demand for coal. Also the removal of the tariff on coal from Canada has taken from Utah the northwestern coal market."[43] Already spurred to action, Utah's senior Senator in Washington had submitted to Congress a petition from Utah's coal operators requesting the establishment of a naval coaling station at San Francisco, to be connected to the Utah railroad network. (At that time the Navy was being supplied by eastern coal transported through the newly-opened Panama Canal, while Utah coal was cut off from government purchase for lack of a railroad connection to the Navy yard.)[44] The Panama Canal, rather than expanding Utah's coal market, had introduced new competitors.

The Great War also disrupted the world copper market, further impacting Utah coal. For three months after the assassination of Archduke Franz Ferdinand, the price of copper was not even quoted on the market.[45] Next, on November 17, 1914, the British parliament declared copper an absolute contraband of war, effectively hamstringing world trade throughout the Commonwealth. Daniel Jackling, western copper magnate and a developer of Bingham Canyon's porphyry deposits, calculated the resultant loss to United States copper producers at $144,000,000. His own numerous plants, then working at only half capacity, produced one-third of the national output.[46] Again, as copper was destabilized, Utah coal was hit hard.

Numerous examples illustrate the extent of wartime dislocation and reformation. For one, the smelting industry offered new, longer-term demands. In the scramble to replace lost European production, United States copper output, protected by wartime neutrality, soon boomed dramatically. By April 1915, copper mines were again operating to their fullest capacity, thus doubling the preceding quarter's demand for coal. A month later, the eastern Utah press predicted that future copper contracts would keep area coal mines running full time until June of 1916.[47] These rosy predictions matured as the Utah output of copper – smelted with coke, a coal derivative – rose from 109 million pounds in 1909 to 246 million pounds in 1917.[48]

By the time the 1917 statistics had been compiled, the United States had entered the Great War. Even prior to its entry, the entire global market picture had completely altered. All sorts of regional networks had shattered at the war's inception due to world-wide disruptions. When the pieces reassembled under wartime exigencies, Utah coal was cemented into the much larger sphere of Pacific trade where it had previously made only tentative connections. This economic lesson was not lost on the coal operators of geographically isolated eastern Utah.

Federal intervention occasioned by the war was a major boon to Utah coal operators. The benefits of rationalizing coal and its related industries had become blatantly obvious. In the scramble just preceding America's entry, problems had seemed to intensify. A railroad car shortage early in 1916 had prevented coal delivery between Utah points and Los Angeles and San Francisco.[49] When the Panama Canal closed in 1916, naval coal for the Pacific fleet, previously supplied from the eastern United States, was effectively cut off. Fifty tons of Utah coal was transported to San Diego for the warship *Farragut*, although this isolated incident did not result in continuing sales.[50] Ineffective delivery systems hamstrung Utah coal operators in their search for additional government contracts. In fact, late in 1916 they had refused to bid on a US Army contract for western forts because of ironclad delivery rules.[51]

In the face of these and related problems nationwide, the federal government had already begun a deliberate alteration of the economy. In preparation for the conflict, Congress had passed the National Defense Act of June 3, 1916, empowering the President to order necessary wartime supplies and prioritize orders. If cooperative measures failed, the Secretary of War could command production. A supplementary act of August 29, 1916 provided for the creation of a council to implement "the immediate concentration and utilization of the resources of the Nation."[52] A naval appropriation act of March 4, 1917 gave the Secretary of the Navy purchasing power comparable to that of the Secretary of War. The official declaration of war the following April 6 led to further bureaucratization: a urgent deficiency act of June 15, 1917 and, most important for this study, the food and fuel control act of August 10, 1917, giving the President the power over basic necessities, including coal and coke.[53]

The control of coke was crucial to the success of the war effort. Not only had demand for coke increased, but, as a mining historian noted, "War conditions had made the price of Alabama, Virginia, and Pennsylvania coke prohibitive. No Mexican coke was being produced" due to the ongoing revolution there.[54] Yet the demand for coke soared. As a government report on the iron and steel industry of September 1917, noted, "The total production of coke in 1916 was approximately 54,000,000 tons .... Owing to the insufficient [railroad] car supply and shortage of labor, the production of ... coke has fallen off in a very serious way during the past five or six months .... Coke will be, I think, the limiting factor in our iron and steel production ... ."[55] Consequently, eastern Utah coals, especially the fine local coking coal, enjoyed a remarkable boom.

Not just the war effort, but the growth of the sugar industry boosted demands for coal. Alone among World War I's disrupted industries, sugar had experienced an immediate upsurge in demand, with unpredictably disastrous results. While America's wartime economy cried out for more materiel and factories worked full time, the fall 1917 bumper crop of sugar beets demanded all the available railroad cars in the West. These same cars and their locomotives normally transported metals to factories for heavy industry. Concurrently, with the same cool fall weather that marked the harvest, the demand for coal as a heating fuel increased. A scramble for railroad cars, for coal, and for motive power led to a widespread "fuel famine" throughout the West. In a 1917 mining review article, an eastern Utah coal operator made the following observations:

> The demand for coal has largely increased as the railroad companies are using every locomotive it is possible for them to secure; factories have multiplied,

> particularly sugar factories -five new factories having been built during 1916 and four under construction for 1917. Each of these will require in the neighborhood of 10,000 tons of coal annually.
>
> There has been practically no coal received on the Pacific coast from Australia, New Zealand, China or Japan for over a year. The amount of coal from British Columbia has been greatly reduced by an act of the British government and the high price of coal on the Atlantic seaboard has prevented any coal moving through the canal to the Pacific coast.[56]

Obviously, coal from Commonwealth nations had gone to supply England's war effort; disrupted shipping in the Pacific, as well as their own wartime demands, resulted in the end of the Chinese and Japanese coal trade.

When America officially entered the war, the federal government initially relied on the goodwill of competing industrialists to put national goals ahead of corporate gain. When this strategy failed to bring results, regulations tightened up. The national Council of Defense called a Utah coal operator to Denver in May 1917 to participate in the newly-forming coal regulatory agency.[57] An ongoing coal shortage intensified, however, leading the Federal Trade Commission to call for an investigation of the national anthracite coal industry, shortly expanded to include bituminous coal, which included Utah.

A joint committee of the Utah Legislature participated in these hearings, full-day affairs which dragged on for over a week in late January and early February 1917. There, the legislators heard of the collapse of the existing network. No coal was coming in from Wyoming; the flow to Durango had been cut off by competing needs; the Anaconda smelters demanded a full complement of cars, and the beet harvest was competing with other uses.[58] The scope of the debacle was summarized in the words of one Utah coal operator:

> We talk about a coal famine here this year. There has been a coal shortage nearly every year since I have been in the coal business. It is not only this year … . The Salt Lake people say this year, because the Salt Lake people have felt it this year. Now last year the Idaho people, the Nevada people, the Washington and Oregon and Montana people felt it. It did not quite get home over here, but this year we not only had to close down on our customers there entirely, [meaning to] the north and northwest, … we had to shut down on them so hard in Utah they commence to feel it at home … .[59]

A similar pattern of need emerged on the national level. The federal report revealed a nine-fold demand for coal over that for iron ore; a demand exceeding the available coal supply – for the first time ever – in the winter of 1916–17; a consequent fourfold increase in coal prices, and the acute, continuing need for coal to power all sorts of domestic industries.[60] While coal operators scrambled to find railroad cars and fill orders, the demand doubled and redoubled.

Despite its importance, coal had not been the first focus of America's war effort. Food had. Because of the need to transport food by rail and the dependence of railroads on coal, national regulation of the coal industry began first under the Food Administration. The unwieldiness of this giant agency led, in short order, to the creation of a Fuel Administration. Its regional divisions regulated production, prices, labor, wages, and other attendant requirements of the nation's coal industry. Directly affecting the market network, on April 1, 1918, the United States Fuel Administration, in conjunction with the Director General of Railroads, created a zone system for hauling bituminous coal. Utah, along with most Rocky Mountain states, was grouped with the Pacific Coast in a single zone, while Wyoming coal was sent east, eliminating it from the Utah market for the first time in history. Both of these provisions created a major local coal boom.[61] The system was working at full tilt when peace came unexpectedly on November 11, 1918. The Fuel Administration stopped regulating the price of coal and its allocation on January 31, 1919.[62]

Coal, which had been patriotically stockpiled, went into a precipitous economic decline. Utah's output, which reached 6 million tons in 1920, dropped below 4 million tons annually until 1929.[63] It followed the national trend, as noted by economic historian Alfred Dupont Chandler, "The sudden and continuing drop in demand from the summer of 1920 until the spring of 1922 was … the first period of hard times that the modern business enterprise had to face … . This slow-down in demand caught both mass marketers and large integrated industries by surprise … ."[64] Part of the coal slump resulted from depression in related industries, especially sugar, which had prospered so dramatically during the war years. In 1920, it commanded a price of $25 to $27 a bag, which plummeted to $5 a bag in 1921. Although Congress passed the Lever Act to protect the public against high prices, including that of beet sugar, its provisions were never extended to cane sugar. In the words of one Utah producer, this competing sweetener came "pouring in from all parts of the world – from Japan, from China, from Java, Formosa, Czechoslovakia and South American countries … ." He continued that while "the Wilson Administration was active in trying to keep the price of beet sugar at about ten cents a pound, … it was allowing cane sugar from every part of the world to be sold in our market freely at from twenty to twenty-five cents a pound."[65] When the Utah-Idaho Sugar Company announced it would sell its product at market rates, its officers were indicted by federal grand jury. They were only rescued when, a few months later, the Supreme Court declared the Lever Act unconstitutional.[66] Nonetheless, this disruption had a deleterious effect on sugar production and its attendant coal demands.

In these unsettled economic times, Utah coal operatives relied on the lessons of the recent past and looked to the Pacific. Just before the end of the Great War, the head of the local Fuel Administration noted that area coal might soon go to

Chile.[67] Immediately after the Armistice, another news article reported: "Arrangements have been perfected by the United States fuel administration to handle orders for coal sent by South America to Utah at the ports of San Pedro, San Francisco, and San Diego, Cala .... It is estimated that South American ports could use as much as two thousand tons of coal each week from North America."[68] An accompanying article noted that Pacific Coast states would also be increasing their demands in the so-called reconstruction period following the war.[69] By 1920, the *Salt Lake Mining Review* reported that "The return trips of the majority of Japanese steamships are made with the use of Utah coal, according to ... a Japanese mining engineer, representing the Mitsubiski [sic Mitsubishi] Mining Company of Tokio [sic] ... ."[70] Two years later, at the depths of this early depression, a promotional local news article predicted that Utah coal would "soon be supplying the western [i.e., Pacific Coast] half of the world."[71] Regrettably, as the twenties depression wore on, the coal market constricted to the intermountain and Pacific Coast regions. A 1927 publication noted the Utah coal markets as encompassing "California, Idaho, Montana, Nevada, Oregon, Utah, Washington, and Alaska," a list that dwindled by 1935 – in the heart of the Great Depression – to "California, Oregon, Washington, Idaho, Montana, Nevada, and Utah."[72] Despite the diminution, however, Utah coal never lost its Pacific connections.

During the same period, coal was replaced as a fuel for a variety of uses. For example, in 1931 Anaconda turned to natural gas for smelting, eliminating one of the main markets for Utah coke.[73] In 1940, the Denver and Rio Grande system, the grandfather of Utah coal mining, shifted to an all-diesel powered operation, a trend that had begun with other railroads in the 1920s.[74] Electricity began replacing coal for home heating and cooking, as well as for electric lights. Coal failed to reach its 1920 high again until 1943, when the demands of World War II again caused skyrocketing production.[75]

The economic boom of World War II replicated the westward tilt of Utah's coal market that had been secured by World War I. Two huge new central Utah mines which opened in the early forties were directly tied to the World War II munitions effort, specifically to the Geneva Steel Plant at Provo, Utah and to Henry Kaiser's Fontana Steel Plant in California.[76] In this manner the Utah coal district and its market network arrived at the point postulated by Gibney as the beginning of American awareness of the importance of Pacific trade, cited at the start of this paper.

Although the Pacific orientation of the intermountain market network had begun decades earlier, in the post-World War II era it has maintained a westward outlook. Fontana still runs on Utah coal, and exemplifies the post-war "captive" (as opposed to a "competitive") mine, wherein a mine produces for a single buyer or purchasing group. (A competitive mine sells on the open market, securing contracts of from five to 20 years.) Not surprisingly, mines are increasingly captive, and most are directly tied to Pacific Coast interests. For example, in 1974, California-Portland Cement acquired its own, captive, eastern Utah mine.[77] That same year, Utah Power and Light (or UP&L), the local electric company, began the first unit of its initial coal-fired electricity-generating plant. This trend of using coal to generate electricity continued with the addition of three other plants by the early 1980s. In 1987, UP&L posted notice for a merger with Portland-based Pacifi-Corp, consummating its Pacific orientation.[78]

The ties to Pacific markets continue. A 1985 article noted that, after the oil shock of 1979 (following on the heels of the OPEC embargo of 1973–74), Japan bought a large portion of its steam coal from the United States. But in the early eighties, Japan purchased most of its steam coal from "Australia, South Africa, and Canada."[79] Consequently, in 1996 the local press celebrated the involvement of the Japanese Itochu Corporation in the purchase of three eastern Utah coal mines, whose production, shipped from the new Los Angeles Export Terminal, would go "to power plants and industrial users in the US, Japan, and other Asian countries."[80] Utah residents continue to be well aware of the importance of Pacific trade.

This market orientation for Utah coal fits right in with current analyses of the economic importance of the Pacific Basin and Gibney's view of the years after 2000 as "the Pacific Century." Yet this is not a recent phenomenon, nor did it proceed from West Coast awareness which gradually filtered back into the hinterlands. As this regional study of the Utah coal market network indicates, feelers reached the coast by the early twentieth century, and World War I cemented these expanded market connections. Since then, coal from the intermountain heartland has flowed unstintingly westward. These findings only enhance the importance of Pacific connections, not only to coastal or to national development, but to the economic progress of a huge landlocked region as well.

Beginning with a mere 400 tons of Utah coal to San Francisco in 1907, Utah's commercial interaction with the Pacific has grown to a permanent relationship. A combination of local initiative and national policy expanded the network: the tour of the Great White Fleet in 1908; the interweaving of Philippine and Canadian commerce with Utah coal thanks to the Underwood-Simmons Tariff of 1913; the effects of World War I on the entire Pacific coal trade, including Australia, New Zealand, China and Japan, and Utah's wartime feelers toward South American markets before the wrenching constrictions of the 1920s and 1930s depressions. Then, of course, came the more obvious connections widely recognized today.

This story of Utah coal begs the question: is it unique? Studies of other locales and industries are needed to compare the depth and breadth of commercial influence tied to our western seas.

Notes

[1] Frank Gibney, *The Pacific Century: America and Asia in a changing world*, New York: Charles Scribner's Sons, 1992, p. 3.

[2] Frank B. Gibney, "The Promise of the Pacific," *Wilson Quarterly* (Winter 1992), p. 64.

[3] James E. Fell Jr, *Ores to Metals: The Rocky Mountain smelting industry*, Lincoln: University of Nebraska Press, 1979, pp. 188–89.

[4] For a complete description of this torturous process, see Nancy J. Taniguchi, *Necessary Fraud: Progressive Reform and Utah Coal*, Norman: University of Oklahoma Press, 1996.

[5] Charles S. Peterson, *Utah: A history*, New York: W.W. Norton, 1977, p. 137; Taniguchi, *Necessary Fraud*, pp. 12–13.

[6] Article in *Salt Lake Tribune*, November 24, 1883, quoted in Robert Athearn, *The Denver and Rio Grande Western Railroad: Rebel of the Rockies*, 1962, reprint; Lincoln: University of Nebraska Press, 1977, pp. 127–28.

[7] Taniguchi, *Necessary Fraud*, pp. 34–46.

[8] Fell, *Ores to Metals*, pp. 196–97. For details on the copper industry, the best summary is Gary B. Hansen, "A Business History of the Copper Industry of Utah, 1860–1910", Master's thesis, Utah State University, 1963; for more on its curtailment due to pollution and legal difficulties, see Miriam B. Murphy, "The Great 'Smoke Nuisance'," *Beehive History*, 9 (1983), pp. 18–22.

[9] Gary B. Hansen, "Industry of Destiny: Copper in Utah," *Utah Historical Quarterly*, Vol. 31, No. 3 (Summer 1963), p. 266.

[10] Isaac F. Marcosson, *Anaconda* , New York: Dodd, Mead & Co., 1957, pp. 30–46.

[11] Ibid., p. 48.

[12] Ibid., p. 52.

[13] "Carbon County Coal for Montana," [Price] *Eastern Utah Advocate* (hereafter EUA), July 14, 1904.

[14] Hansen, "Industry of Destiny," p. 268.

[15] "The Rio Grande Western Railway Company Agreement with Boston Consolidated Mining Co.;" "The Rio Grande Western Railway Company Agreement with Utah Copper Co.;" "The Rio Grande Western Railway Company Agreement with Garfield Smelting Co.," all June 22, 1906, all in MS 513, Denver and Rio Grande Papers. Box 12. Folders 4552 and 4553, Colorado Historical Society, Denver, Colorado.

[16] Hansen, "Industry of Destiny," pp. 271–78.

[17] Leonard J. Arrington and Gary B. Hansen, *"The Richest Hole on Earth": A history of the Bingham Copper Mine*, Logan: Utah State University Press, 1963, pp. 23–24.

[18] "Coal Takes Another Drop at Salt Lake," EUA, January 2, 1908.

[19] Fred G. Taylor, *A Saga of Sugar* ([Salt Lake City]: Utah-Idaho Sugar Company, 1944), pp. 63–75.

[20] Ibid., pp. 85–99.

[21] Ibid., p. 102.

[22] Sidney W. Mintz, *Sweetness and Power: The place of sugar in modern history*, New York: Penguin Books, 1985, p. 195.

23 Taylor, *A Saga of Sugar*, pp. 106–107.

24 "Carbon County Coal Mines," 15 August 1907; "Springville Man Here To Buy Some Coal," August 22, 1907; "Salt Lake Smelters Are To Get Their Supply of Coal In the East," September 12, 1907, all in EUA.

25 "News of Town and Country in Brief," EUA, August 29, 1907.

26 "Of a More or Less Personal Nature," EUA, October 3, 1907.

27 "Of a More or Less Personal Nature" and "News of Town and Country in Brief," both 21 November 1907; "Salt Lake City Banks Issue Certificates," November, 14 1907, all in EUA.

28 "Of a More or Less Personal Nature," December 19, 1907; "Price of Coal is Reduced," January 9, 1908, both in EUA.

29 J.E. Pettit to E.W. Parker, January 15, 1908, State Coal Mine Inspector's Correspondence, Special Collections, Marriott Library, University of Utah, Salt Lake City, Utah.

30 "Truth and Gossip," EUA, January 16, 1908.

31 "Outlook is Bad for Coal and Coke Industry," January 30, 1908; "Union Pacific mines," 13 February 1908; "More Mines Are Closed Monday," February, 27 1908, all in EUA.

32 "Only American Coal To Be Used By Fleet On Trip Around World," EUA, May 7, 1908.

33 "Fuel Famine is Predicted," EUA, August 13, 1908.

34 "None But Utah Coals on Western Markets," September 24, 1908; "Helps the Coal Output Locally," 24 September 1908; "Ogden Gateway Opened to Carbon County Coal," October 1, 1908, all in EUA.

35 Robert Athearn, *The Denver and Rio Grande Western Railroad: Rebel of the Rockies*, 1962, reprint, Lincoln: University of Nebraska Press, 1977, pp. 209–10.

36 "Utah Coal for Pacific Coast," EUA, June 12, 1913.

37 Samuel Hays, *Response to Industrialism, 1885–1914*, Chicago: University of Chicago Press, 1957.

38 Josephus Daniels, *The Life of Woodrow Wilson, 1856–1924*, USA: Will H. Johnston, 1924, pp. 158–60.

39 Ibid., p. 161.

40 "Twenty Per Cent Loss in Coal Output," EUA, May 21, 1914.

41 Vincent DeSantis, *The Shaping of Modern America , 1877–1920*, 2nd edn, Arlington Heights, IL: Forum Press, Inc., 1989, p. 214.

42 Taylor, *A Saga of Sugar*, p. 108.

43 "War Hits Coal Mines," EUA, November 26, 1914.

44 "Coal Operators Seek Contract," EUA, September 24, 1914.

45 Marcosson, *Anaconda*, p. 154.

46 "Jackling Talks of Copper Conditions," EUA, November 19, 1994; Richard W. Sadler, "Daniel Cowan Jackling," *Utah History Encyclopedia*, Salt Lake City: University of Utah Press, 1994, p. 281.

47 "Demand for Copper to Benefit Carbon," [Price, Utah] Carbon County News (hereafter CCN), April, 30 1915; "Mines Contract to Sell Copper," EUA, May 28, 1915.

48 Leonard J. Arrington and Tom Alexander, *A Dependent Commonwealth*, Provo: Brigham Young University Press, 1974, p. 58.

49 "Coal Market Much Better On Coast," EUA, February 18, 1916.

50 "Local Coal For Navy," EUA, November, 30 1916.

51 "Utah Mines Far Behind Orders," [Price, Utah] *News-Advocate* (hereafter N-A), 29 March 1917.

52 Bernard M. Baruch, *American Industry in the War*, New York: Prentice-Hall, Inc., 1941, pp. 49–50.

53 Ibid., p. 50.

54 Isaac Marcosson, *Metal Magic*, New York: Farrar, Strauss & Co., 1949, p. 218.

55 "Appendix XIV. Report of J.L. Replogle on the Iron and Steel Situation, September 14, 1917," in Baruch, *American Industry in the War*, p. 348.

56 C.N. Strevell, "Coal Situation for 1917," *The Salt Lake Mining Review*, 16 (April 30, 1917), p. 30.

57 "Strevell Helping," N-A, May 31, 1917.

58 ACC 479, "Verbatim Report of Testimony and Proceedings ... beginning on the 29th day of January, A.D. 1917," Special Collections, Marriott Library, University of Utah, Salt Lake City, Utah,pp. 39, 108, 396, 430. (Hereafter "Testimony.")

59 Frederick A. Sweet in "Testimony," pp. 221–22.

60 Charles R. VanHise, *Conservation and Regulation in the United States During the World War*, Washington, DC: Government Printing Office, 1917, in facsimile reprint as *The United States in World War I* (no place: Jerome S. Ozer, 1974), pp. 29–30.

61 Record Group 67, Records of the Fuel Administration, Bureau of State Organizations, Utah," Box 841, Folder 1, W.W. Armstrong to W.E. Hope, March 19 and March 29, 1918, National Archives, Washington, DC.

62 Walker D. Hines, *War History of American Railroads*, New Haven, CT: Yale University Press, 1928, p. 75.

63 Helmut Hans Doelling, *Central Utah Coal Fields*, Salt Lake City: University of Utah Press, 1972, p. 546.

64 Alfred Dupont Chandler, *The Visible Hand*, Cambridge: Belknap Press of Harvard University Press, 1977, pp. 456–57.

65 Taylor, *A Saga of Sugar*, pp. 113–14.

66 Ibid., p. 114.

67 "Carbon County Coal May Soon Go To Chile," [Price] *Sun*, September 20, 1918.

68 "Market May Come On Coal From South America," *Sun*, November 22, 1918.

69 "Carbon County Coals go Out in Many Directions," ibid.

70 "With Coal Producers," *Salt Lake Mining Review* (March 15, 1920), p. 35.

71 "Coal and Steel," *Sun*, July 28, 1922.

72 Utah Coal Producers Association, "Coal: Utah's Great Industry," c.1927, Clippings Collection, Salt Lake Public Library; *Salt Lake Tribune-Telegraph*, "Market Facts About the Intermountain Empire and the Salt Lake Market," 1935 edition, Pamphlet File, Western Americana, Special Collections, Marriott Library, University of Utah, Salt Lake City.

73 Marcosson, *Anaconda*, p. 147.

74 Athearn, *Denver and Rio Grande*, p. 312.

75 Doelling, *Central Utal Coal Fields*, p. 546.

76 *Report of the State Industrial Commission*, July 1, 1942 to June 30, 1944, Salt Lake City, 1945, p. 36.

[77] "Mining Project Approved," [Price] *Sun-Advocate*, June 25, 1980.

[78] Utah Job Service, *Utah's Coal Mining Industry*, Price: College of Eastern Utah, June 1976, p. 13; "UP&L President Sometimes Yearns for Simpler Days as Engineer," *Salt Lake Tribune*, November 1, 1987.

[79] "U.S.–Japan Coal Trade Unlikely," "Energy Edition," Sun Progress, Inc., January 1985 (published jointly by the Price *Sun Advocate* and the Emery County *Progress* in Price, Utah).

[80] "ARCO Coal Company and ITOCHU units join to purchase Coastal's Utah Coal operations," [Price] *Sun-Advocate*, October 31, 1996.

9

Race and the Right Kind of Island: Immigration Policy in Hawaii and Cuba under US Auspices, 1899–1912

Katharine Bjork

> My dear Mr. Sargent:
> We are to be congratulated upon what that shipment to Hawaii shows.
> By George; we shall succeed in turning Hawaii into the right kind of island!
> Faithfully yours,
> Theodore Roosevelt
> (November 5, 1906)

The Cuban-Spanish-American War marked both the emergence of the United States as a major Pacific power and the consolidation of American interests in the Caribbean. The United States extended sovereignty over Puerto Rico at the same time it took both Guam and the Philippines from Spain. Although nominally an independent republic, Cuba in effect became a protectorate of the US while Hawaii was annexed as a territory in 1898.

The problems involved in demobilizing the Liberation Army and restoring peace and productivity after thirty years of war in Cuba were immense. At the same time Hawaii faced different but significant challenges in adapting to its status as America's newest Pacific outpost. Dominated by plantation agriculture, Cuba and Hawaii faced similar questions relating to immigration and labor policies. Debates over where to seek immigrants to work in the cane fields were significantly discussions of different visions for island development. This paper explores the debates over immigration to Cuba and Hawaii, focusing on the issues of race and citizenship under US auspices.

In articulating plans for creating the "right kind of island" in Cuba and Hawaii, strikingly similar discussions of race, immigration, and citizenship occurred. Notably, debates over the future of these two semi-autonomous plantation societies based on sugar were polarized around two racialized alternatives for labor immigration, which can be characterized as "bracero" versus "citizen" models of immigration. In the Cuban context, advocates of "whitening" Cuba, which was pursued by a white elite as a response to their fears of being overrun by the black population, favored state-aided immigration of settlers from the Iberian peninsula and the Canary Islands. Both the state and planter interests were united in their preference for white immigrants until World War I. Thereafter, they turned to other sources of labor, notably "Antillian" contract laborers from other islands in the Caribbean, especially Jamaica and Haiti, who were Black and not Spanish-speaking. Faced with increasing sugar production and inadequate labor supplies during and following the war, as Alejandro de la Fuente puts it, "the Cuban government ... sacrifice[d] whitening in the name of sugar" (de la Fuente, 1996, p. 17). While the ideal of a "white" (or less dark) Cuba remained, de la Fuente makes clear that for the employers of labor, Antillians represented "desirable" labor because "it was easier to isolate and exploit" them.

In Hawaii a similar distinction existed between "public welfare" and "private interest" approaches to immigration. Again, these were racialized alternatives: "oriental" labor was opposed to European, especially Southern European "citizen" immigration. What is interesting about the way the two alternatives were articulated is that both shared the stated goal of securing a disciplined labor force, but they differed significantly in their proposed methods for achieving it. The "private interest" approach favored legal sanctions and isolation from family and social networks as strategies for achieving control over labor; the "public welfare" view, on the other hand, envisioned the institutions of family as well as the invisible hand of a market economy as agents of "educating" citizens for productive labor.

Aside from considering the most desirable sources and racial characteristics of immigrants, immigration and labor policy making in Cuba and Hawaii at the turn of the century was also dominated by the question of contract labor. Considered by many as the successor to slavery (Tinker, 1974; Coman, 1903), labor migration under contract served as the primary mechanism for assuring sufficient tractable labor for the plantations of Hawaii and Cuba from the end of slavery until the dawn of the American era at the end of the century.

Formal incorporation into the US empire entailed a number of legal and institutional changes for the new possessions. Perhaps none was as important in shaping the early labor situation as the extension of the American prohibition on the immigration of laborers under contract, which had become law in the US when Congress passed the Alien Contract Labor Act in 1885. Annexation to the United States brought about the end of the penal enforcement of Hawaii's labor code, including its contract labor laws. Immigration into Cuba under contract was also prohibited early in the US Military Government in Cuba. In the next two sections I briefly outline the history of contract labor migration in Cuba and Hawaii up to their incorporation into the US sphere. Besides shedding light on colonial population strategies, I trace the development of immigration devised for the dependencies that differed from those followed in the US proper. The rest of the paper explores the politics of race and citizenship in debates over immigration.

Contract labor in Hawaii

In Hawaii two factors provided the basis for expansion of the sugar economy in the latter half of the nineteenth century: contract labor and duty free access for Hawaiian sugar to the United States market as a result of the reciprocity treaty between the Kingdom of Hawaii and the United States. The Republic of Hawaii (1894–98) was a form of government whose chief objectives were to keep a minority oligarchy in power and to obtain annexation to the United States, which was accomplished in 1898.

Turning Hawaii into "the right kind of island" as advocated by Teddy Roosevelt in the memorandum quoted at the beginning of the paper meant peopling it with southern European immigrants who would provide labor and citizens for America's newest territory in the Pacific. There is ample evidence that Roosevelt was very interested in immigration to Hawaii and that he intervened personally to encourage European immigration to the islands. For example, a memo jotted down by Secretary of Commerce and Labor Straus in a Cabinet meeting on March 8, 1907 indicates that Roosevelt had asked Straus to "order the landing of all immigrants en route to Hawaii" (Department of the Treasury, 1907: file 51389/14A). This is notable because such a landing of immigrants would be contrary to the provisions of the Alien contract labor law, as Secretary Straus would have been well aware. The President also gave his support to a project to recruit immigrants from Spain for Hawaii. Several days after his congratulatory note to Sargent, Roosevelt wrote to the Commissioner of Immigration again to ask him to oversee the landing of the immigrants from Portugal. "To my mind this is one of the most important matters that has ever come up in connection with the Islands since they became part of the United States, and I would like to have your personal supervision over it," he wrote (Department of the Treasury. 1906: file 51389). The preference for laborers from Europe held by federal officials and some advocates of "citizen labor" in Hawaii was at odds with the desire of the Hawaiian planters to continue "oriental" labor migration under contract.

In both the Kingdom of Hawaii and the short-lived Republic of Hawaii the dominant planter class obtained support from the state – both legal and financial – for supporting labor migration to the islands. Obtaining a supply of cheap servile labor for the sugar plantations was a perennial preoccupation for the Hawaiian Sugar Planters' Association, an organization of the major sugar growers in the islands established in 1895 (Taylor, 1935, p. 39). In addition to dealing with the question of labor supply, the HSPA provided an organization in which planters could plan and execute coordinated strategies; it made and enforced policies on wages and working conditions throughout the islands.

The HSPA sought "people as laborers, who [were] accustomed to subordination, to permanency of abode, and who [had] modest expectations in regard to a livelihood" (Beechert, 1985, p. 183). As its own Board of Immigration declared, "in dealing with the history of immigration to Hawaii, it would be difficult to conceive of a country that the government and the plantation interests have not considered as a source of supply of settlers and laborers" (Territory of Hawaii, 1907). According to an American Federation of Labor pamphlet, up to the time of annexation, successive sessions of the Hawaiian legislature (which the AFL delicately described as having been "under the benign influence of the planters at all times") appropriated more than $1,500,000 for "the encouragement of immigration" (Scharrenberg, 1921, pp. 4–5). Like planters in other sugar producing areas that experienced expansion in the late nineteenth century – Natal, Queensland, and Fiji – Hawaii sought the answer to its labor problem in a contract labor system based on a penal code, the Masters and Servants Act of 1850, which remained in force until 1897. The judicial system enforced labor contracts up until annexation, when this aspect of Hawaiian law and social relations was rejected as incompatible with American labor relations.

Of all the territories incorporated into the US empire in the late 1890s, the issue of contract labor was most prominent in the annexation of Hawaii. In his study of the responses of American organized labor to imperial expansion, John C. Appel notes that the existence of contract labor in Hawaii was one of the main arguments of anti-imperialists against annexing the islands. Labor unions warned that contract labor in Hawaii threatened US labor in both symbolic and practical ways. Contract labor would mean unfair competition for US workers. Labor leaders also expressed the fear that the practice would spread to the US (Appel, 1950, p. 107).

With the loss of penal sanctions to enforce them, Hawaiian planters complained of the unwillingness of many laborers to work out their contracts. A report of the Hawaiian Sugar Planters' Association's labor committee recommended in 1900 (as so many similar organizations had done throughout the history of sugar in the islands) that more workers be imported as a solution to anticipated labor problems. As in the past, the Planters' Association called for immigrants who would work on the plantations. Closer ties to the United States suggested new sources of immigration (former slaves from the South, and Puerto Ricans, to give two examples), while the extension of US immigration laws excluded others; the immigration of Chinese was ended as was the immigration of laborers under formal contract from all origins. While the HSPA was interested in cheap easily-controlled labor, other considerations began to influence the discussion of desirable sources of immigrants for the new Hawaii, too. I will discuss these other ramifications of immigration policy below in the section on race and citizenship. In the next section I will briefly outline the history of contract labor up to and during the US military government in Cuba.

Contract labor in Cuba

When the US extended its immigration laws to Cuba in 1898, contract labor had a 50-year history in the island. The first Chinese workers arrived in 1847. About 125,000 Chinese were brought to Cuba under contract between 1847 and 1874 (Scott, 1985, p. 29–31). The total number of bound laborers who entered during the 26 years of contract labor was "probably less than 150,000" according to a Bureau of Labor estimate in 1902 (Clark, 1902, p. 667). China contributed the largest group of contract labor immigrants to Cuba, but immigrants from Southern Europe and the Canary Islands constituted an even more important precedent for the kind of labor migration that continued after the war. Beginning in the 1860s tens of thousands of Spanish immigrants were encouraged to migrate to Cuba each year. The Spanish colonial government subsidized this immigration in the interest of increasing the labor supply in the islands as well as "whitening" the population (Scott, 1985, p. 217). As mentioned earlier, after independence, Cuban and US administrations continued to advocate white settler immigration. However, the labor demands created by an expanding sugar sector proved an increasing challenge to this kind of immigration. Short-term contract labor offered an alternative.

Early US efforts to prevent contract labor immigration into Cuba were justified by the argument that adequate labor already existed in Cuba and that contract laborers would deprive Cubans of work (Meiklejohn, 1899: file 727). In other words, the view of the military government on labor conditions in Cuba seems to have been that there was an absolute surplus of labor, and that aided immigration would prejudice the chances of Cubans to get jobs in a way that was undesirable. Initially, the United States extended its immigration laws to Cuba comprehensively and unequivocally. Circular 13, Division of Customs and Immigration of the War Department, dated April 14, 1899, put US immigration laws into effect in Cuba:

> The laws and regulations governing immigration to the United States are hereby declared to be in effect in the territory under government by the military forces of the U.S. and collectors of customs are directed to enforce said laws and regulations until the establishment of immigration stations in said territory (Meiklejohn, 1899: file 934).

As early as June 3, 1899 the Military Government in Cuba was receiving and acceding to requests by the employers of industrial labor in Cuba for exceptions to be made to the contract labor provisions which had been extended to cover the island.

The extension of the US contract labor prohibition to Cuba was opposed by planters and mine owners who had previously relied on this source of labor. In September 1899, several owners and representatives of sugar estates in Cuba signed a letter to Secretary Root in which they called for the suspension or repeal of the orders contained in Circular 13. Calling Root's attention to the scarcity of labor in the principal sugar districts of the island, they argued that a prohibition on contract labor immigration was an undesirable obstacle to obtaining "a class of labor which heretofore has proved most efficient and reliable," that is, immigrants from Spain and the Canary Islands (Bureau of Insular Affairs, 1899: file 934).

The complaint of the employers of industrial labor, particularly the iron mining concerns in the eastern part of the island who were the most vociferous lobbyists for contract labor, was that Cuban labor was not suited for work in the mines and that importing labor from outside was necessary to allow the mines to continue production. As the general manager of the Spanish-American Iron Company put it:

> The Cuban laborer is not fitted for the work of the mines and will not work there if he can get anything else to do. We have consequently no alternative but to go outside of the Island for our supply. It was hoped to secure men from Spain, as the Spaniard is the most desirable laborer, being accustomed to work in the mines, as well as a sober and quiet citizen (Bureau of Insular Affairs, 1899: file 727).

The management of this mining company sought a work force that was disciplined and reliable for industrial labor. The attributes of the Spaniard as "sober and quiet" while they are expressed in terms of their value for "citizenship" should really be understood as the necessary and desirable characteristics of an industrial labor force. Whatever inherent "sober and quiet" characteristics the laborers possessed were reinforced by the structure of contract labor.

The aftermath of the war and the demobilization of the Liberation Army created dislocations among the working population that made it difficult for employers to command their accustomed control over working conditions and wages. De la Fuente notes that:

> Sugar interests voiced their concern that, should the situation persist, the crops of 1900 and 1901 would be seriously compromised, not the least because workers were "conscious of the advantages of their position" and determined to obtain higher salaries. Operating in a market with limited labor supply, employers were unable to impose their own conditions and were forced to bargain with labor. They referred to the "demoralized" condition of workers, to their "exaggerated pretensions" concerning payment and, in the best slavery tradition, suggested that the re-establishment of forced labor was the only viable solution (de la Fuente, 1997, pp. 30–31).

Like Hawaiian sugar planters, Cuban employers sought immigration not only to lower wages but to increase their control over a workforce by reinforcing divisions among groups of workers. According to de la Fuente:

> Employers promoted open hostility through a policy of ethnically based distribution of employment, promotion and compensation, as well as by using foreign labor to break native workers' resistance – or vice versa (ibid).

Employers' strategies for fragmenting plantation labor forces along ethnic lines are remarkably similar to those followed in Hawaii. A superintendent of a sugar mill commented on the utility of employing Chinese in preventing strikes:

> Owing to the trouble last year with the centrifugal force, we have decided to contract this work with Chinese, and at the same time to house them in the batey separate from all other labor. Chinese ... would put an end to strikes in this department ... (ibid., 40).

However, the military leadership in Cuba was opposed to bringing in contract laborers. In commenting on the Spanish-American Iron Company's request, Major General John R. Brooke, the commanding officer of the Division of Cuba, said:

> One of the greatest difficulties now being encountered in the Province of Santiago is to find work for the idle, and large sums are being paid monthly from insular funds to keep them employed. I do not know that any of these men are competent to do the work mentioned, but I would consider it inadvisable to transport any of the laboring classes to Cuba at this time (Brooke, 1899: file 727).

The following day, the Secretary of the Treasury condemned such importation of laborers to Cuba as being "in direct violation of United States immigration laws" (Gage, 1899: file 727/3). Gradually, however, the Americans did come around to the view of labor conditions articulated by the employers of industrial labor on the island. An early expression of the need for accommodation was made by the Collector of Customs for Cuba, Tasker Bliss, who wrote the Assistant Secretary of War:

> From the information which has gradually come to me since public knowledge of the extension of the immigration laws of the United States to Cuba, I am satisfied that the application of these laws will, in the near future, prove a matter of very great difficulty. A large amount of labor, even in times more favorable than the present, was temporarily imported for plantations at the proper season of the year, the labor returning to the country from which it came, at the end of the season (Bliss, 1899: file 727).

By the end of 1899 the Treasury department had adopted the view that conditions, at least in the mining industry, warranted allowing a limited number of contract laborers, under the close supervision of the War Department (Bureau of Insular Affairs, 1899: file 727). A year later, on October 30, 1900 the War Department lifted restrictions on the immigration of contract laborers entirely (ibid.). What are we to make of this change in policy? Does it reflect the triumph of the interests of industrialists in the island over some more disinterested bureaucratic goals for labor and immigration in the island? Is it just the re-establishment of practices and trends operating in Cuba before the US occupation? While there is some merit to both these propositions, I would also suggest that it represents an accommodation of American principle and practice to the colonial industrial conditions, which were distinct from the home US economy and were an important aspect of defining colonial difference and determining trade relations, immigration, and labor policy between metropolitan and peripheral economies. Finally, it indicated an identification with and accommodation to the interests of employers of industrial labor in the island.

Race and citizenship in Hawaii

As changing policies on contract labor make clear, the incorporation of Hawaii and Cuba more closely into the US economic and political sphere did not mark a clear break from the past. However it ushered in a period of adjustment in the industrial relations of the islands and the regulation of immigration and labor policy. American social and especially racial attitudes added another element to the re-examination and reformulation of pre-existing practices.

Two distinct visions of Hawaiian development are encapsulated in appeals to the supposedly distinct attributes of different national and ethnic groups who were considered as prospective workers and citizens for Hawaii. Consider the following passage from the *Bureau of Labor Bulletin*:

> [The] Portuguese that one meets in Honolulu or Hilo differ in no essential respect from intelligent foreign-born citizens of the United States. Their education has been acquired in the public schools, if they are of the younger generation, under a system identical with that of the mainland, and they have acquired the habits of thought and action that distinguish an American from a European. They take an active part in politics and are prominent in both commercial and public life. The country people become homesteaders, cultivate small crops and fruits or coffee, and raise enormous families of bright, sturdy children – the most desirable crop of all in a country like Hawaii. It is rather significant, however, that they are not classed with white men on the plantations. They form a class apart, somewhere between Asiatics and the other Caucasians. This is probably because the "white man" has always been a sort of aristocrat in the islands, and a large body of immigrants who lived in ordinary plantation quarters and worked with hoes could hardly aspire to that rank in popular estimation ... The Portuguese is more individualistic – he has less of the communal instinct than either the Chinese or the Japanese ... He is

> not inclined to strike, and is quite as apt to disagree with his fellow workmen as with his employer. But he can not be counted upon to remain upon a plantation after he has saved enough to become his own master. The ambition of most of the Portuguese laborers interviewed was to get a little homestead back in the mountains and to come down to the plantation occasionally to work at odd jobs for ready money (Department of Commerce and Labor, 1903, p. 700).

Several aspects of this description of Portuguese in Hawaii point to the characteristics valued by advocates of citizen labor immigration to Hawaii. These include experience of public education and participation in politics as well as "commercial and public life." The emphasis on the supposed similarity of Portuguese in Hawaii to foreign-born citizens in the United States is particularly interesting. It suggests at once a kind of "melting-pot" trajectory for Hawaiian society while at the same time clearly implying the survival of a racial hierarchy as immigrants to Hawaii "acquire the habits of thought and action that distinguish an American" but are nonetheless not "classed with 'white men' on the plantations" and "form a class apart." Family life is also considered an important aspect of developing the "right kind of island." Children are described as "the most desirable crop of all in a country like Hawaii," for example.

In Hawaii, the encouragement of immigration of various ethnic groups under contract, which Commissioner Clark referred to as the "private interest" approach to immigration, had a long history. For half a century maintaining distinct ethnic divisions among immigrant laborers had been an important part of a planter strategy for controlling the plantation labor force and keeping wages low. One of the conscious and explicit policies that the HSPA followed to control its labor force was to import laborers of different nationalities in order to offset the possibility that they would organize for better wages and improved living and working conditions (Takaki, 1983). With the abolition of penal contract labor, the planters became even more dependent on other forms of labor control. Racial division was one of the means they employed to prevent workers from organizing.

The HSPA did not merely rely on the natural barriers that language and culture posed to workers' organization; the Association encouraged the fragmentation of the work force along ethnic lines by imposing wage scales and job allocations based on race. In his discussion of the stratification of plantation employment according to race, Ronald Takaki notes:

> On 18 November 1904 the HSPA trustees adopted a resolution that in effect made racial discrimination a formal policy. While the resolution itself did not specify race or racial groups, it did state that all skilled positions should be filled by "American citizens, or those eligible for citizenship." The restriction had a racial function for it excluded from skilled occupations Asians or

> immigrants regarded as not "white" according to federal law and hence ineligible to become naturalized citizens ... Seven years later the association made its discriminatory policy more explicit and direct by approving another resolution, which instructed plantation managers to reserve skilled and semiskilled positions for Hawaiians and whites (Takaki, 1983, pp. 75–76).

When workers of different nationalities were employed to do the same task, they were paid different wages. The wages set by the HSPA differentiated between "Orientals and Filipinos" who were paid $18.00 per month cash and allowances, and "White" laborers, who were paid $20.00 to $24.00 per month cash and allowances (Hatch, 1911, p. 6). From listings of occupations by racial and national characteristics it is clear that the Portuguese and other European laborers both received more money for performing the same job as Japanese, Chinese, and Filipino workers and they held more positions on plantations as "lunas" or overseers; they were also more likely to accomplish the transition to non-plantation labor. These distinctions, Takaki says, "reinforced divisions within the work force and also maintained the racial and social hierarchy of the plantation." Ethnic divisions prevented successful multiethnic labor organizing until the 1920s, as a woman who grew up on a plantation recalled:

> In those back years, we use to have the Puerto Rican one place; the Portuguese, Chinese, Filipino, Japanese, all each had their own camp because they did not want to mingle with one another. The Portuguese people do not want to mingle with Puerto Rican or the Spanish, you know. Or the Spanish did not want to mingle with the Puerto Ricans or Portuguese (Center for Ethnic Studies, 1976, p. 82).

The stratification of the labor force along racial lines was justified and reinforced by a hierarchical social ideology. The continuing importance of a racial hierarchy to the territorial state is underscored by the amount of space that the classification of the various racial and national groups in the plantation labor force of the islands occupies in the report of the Commissioner of Labor. Most intriguingly, the historian's attention is drawn to some anomalies in the categorization and especially the combination of "racial" groups in the compiled statistics on the labor force in Hawaii. The "nationality or race" category "Iberian" includes not only Spanish and Portuguese but also "Porto Ricans" (Bureau of Labor, 1911, pp. 724–25). This is notable because US census takers in other contexts were extremely sensitive to "Black" or "Negro" as determining and exclusive categories, and we know that Puerto Ricans were later categorized in Hawaii as Black, without specific reference to Afro-Puerto Rican identity, but merely by virtue of their Puerto Rican origin (Adams, 1945; Mintz, 1959).

More surprising than the classification of Puerto Ricans with other Iberians, however, is the inclusion of native Hawaiians in the category "White" (Bureau of

Labor, 1911, p. 676). This category clearly does not reflect either national, phenotypic or even linguistic similarities. Instead, an explanation of the meaning of the category must be sought in the social relations in the islands in the nineteenth century when, as the Commission of Labor report explained it:

> The color line is very loosely drawn between the Hawaiians and Caucasians. The former have hitherto included the rulers, the nobility, and many of the largest landowners of the country. Schools, churches and society are opened to them, and they have intermarried with leading American and European residents" (Department of Commerce and Labor, 1903, p. 701).

In this case a "race or color" category that results in combining Hawaiians and other South Sea Islanders with Caucasians clearly has more to do with class relations in nineteenth-century Hawaiian society than it has to do with definitions of race or color likely to be imposed by a late twentieth-century historian.

The elaborate effort to construct meaning out of race evident in the compilation of labor statistics also points to the paramount importance of race in planning for the development of Hawaii as a plantation society within the American sphere. For example, racial categories played an important part in calculating scope for "Americanization." As the US Commissioner of Labor put it in 1911:

> I think the Americanization of the Islands is the principle that should underlie and control every enterprise which affects either directly or indirectly the matter of bringing settlers and laborers into the Territory. It can readily be seen by reference to my table segregating the population into its component races that the populace hardly can be described now as of an American character (US Department of the Treasury, 1911).

The idea that immigration is the key to Americanization, and that such Americanization depends on white or European immigrants is very clear in this excerpt.

In Cuba, too, American regimes embraced the official Cuban preference for white immigration. In September of 1900 the Secretary of Agriculture, Commerce, and Industry, Perfecto Lacoste, proposed a scheme for encouraging immigration from Spain that created debate and led to changes in US policies on contract labor. In a published letter to the Military Governor, Lacoste argued that further development of Cuba's agricultural potential depended on increasing the available labor supply. He called for the establishment of an "immigration service" under state supervision. Lacoste further asserted that public opinion was unanimous in the belief that "the only immigration desirable is white immigration," and proposed that $400,000 be allocated to bring people from the Canary Islands, Balearic Islands, and the northern provinces of Spain (Lacoste, 1900: file 5304).

In Cuba as in Hawaii, ethnic division was pursued as a means of labor control. The encouragement of white immigration was a state policy that preceded US intervention in the island. After the Cuban-Spanish-American War, as Alejandro de la Fuente argues, white immigration was considered a solution to two "intimately linked dangers," the black and labor dangers: "Both employers and the Cuban state worked to deepen and reinforce the barriers that separated native and foreign workers, as well as those separating foreign workers of different origin among themselves" (de la Fuente, 1997, pp. 32–33). De la Fuente also argues that there was "nothing natural" about racial categories in Cuba and that "race" was constructed as a line separating native and foreign workers, rather than native workers of different racial backgrounds among themselves" (ibid, p. 31).

Conclusion

The labor and immigration policies followed in Cuba and Hawaii under American auspices differed both from those that preceded the war and formal incorporation into the US empire; they also departed significantly from American domestic practices. In particular, the departure from domestic precedent with regard to continuing contract labor migration in both Cuba and Hawaii highlights two points that were central in articulating and defining the supposed differences between the colonial and domestic spheres. The first was the lack of "disciplined" labor to participate in those sectors of the economy (plantations, mining, and other industrialized enterprises) that were increasingly integrated into the US economic sphere by closer political and economic relations with the US; the second was the lack of "citizen" laborers. Both problems were conceived and addressed in racial terms. Not surprisingly, the solutions proposed to deal with them also privileged race.

One of the most pervasive ways of signaling the difference of the colonial realm was race. Racial difference functioned in various ways to symbolize, rationalize, and sometimes to disguise other more germane differences between the mainland United States and its new insular possessions. Among other things, appeals to racial vocabulary and stereotypes provided powerful and accessible metaphors not only for the political status of the islands vis à vis the United States, but also for their respective levels of civilization and their presumed potential for development. Race provided colonizers with a convenient language for categorizing and managing colonial projects, from organizing labor migration to dealing psychologically with the novel challenges of colonial administration.

In both Hawaii and Cuba, incorporation into the US empire was accompanied by disruptions in labor supply and discipline. In both places the extension of US immigration laws necessitated new strategies for meeting the "labor problem." The colonial state acted to support the interests of elites in recruiting, transporting, and even reinforcing divisions among different ethnic groups imported to answer the demands of planters and other employers of industrial labor. The American preoccupations with race in Cuba and Hawaii and the use of the concepts and categories of race as a means of articulating and structuring discussions of labor and immigration policy both drew upon notions of race operative on the "mainland" but also significantly altered their meanings to suit the "difference" of colonial situations. In turn, contract labor policy was both based upon and at the same time reinforced a set of differences between the domestic and colonial sphere that justified the application of different measures in the realm of labor and immigration policy. Contract labor practice in the periphery violated US domestic policy. This contradiction was resolved by a rationale that appealed to supposedly self-evident distinctions between the US domestic sphere and the "peculiar conditions" existing in American dependencies, thereby naturalizing and reinfocing these same colonial distinctions.

Note

The author wishes to thank Alejandro de la Fuente, for sending a chapter of his dissertation, as well as Arjun Guneratne, for all his help.

References

Archival sources

References are to materials held in the National Archives of the United States, Washington, DC, unless otherwise noted.

Bliss, T.H., letter to the Assistant Secretary of War, Bureau of Insular Affairs (Record Group 350), file 727, June 12, 1899.

Brooke, Maj. Gen. J.R., 2nd endorsement on letter from the General Manager of the Spanish-American Iron Company to the Assistant Secretary of War, Bureau of Insular Affairs (Record Group 350), file 727, June 7, 1899.

Bureau of Insular Affairs, letter from the General Manager of the Spanish-American Iron Company to the Assistant Secretary of War, Record Group 350, file 727, June 7, 1899.

——, Letter to Elihu Root, Secretary of War, signed by the president of Constancia Sugar Co. (name illegible), Cienfuegos, *et al.*, file 934, September 20, 1899.

Center for Ethnic Studies, oral history interview with Trinidad Marcella (tape No. 1–10–1–76), by Norma Carr, Oral History Project, University of Hawaii, transcript, June 18, 1976.

Gage (Secretary of the Treasury), Endorsement on communication from the Spanish-American Mining Company, including a copy of a labor contract between the company and laborers of the Bahama Islands, Bureau of Insular Affairs (Record Group 350), file 727/3, June 16, 1899.

Hatch, F.M., to Charles Nagel, Secretary of the Department of Commerce and Labor, in response to a report on the labor situation in Hawaii made by Daniel J. Keefe, Commissioner General of Immigration and Naturalization, January 25, 1911, Department of the Treasury (Record Group 85): 6, May 23, 1911.

Lacoste, P., recommendation to the Military Governor on state support for immigration, Ministry of Agriculture, Commerce and Industry, Military Government of Cuba (Record Group 140), September 24, 1900.

Meiklejohn, G.D., Acting Secretary of War, "Circular 13," Bureau of Insular Affairs (Record Group 350), file 934, April 14, 1899.

——, Telegram to the Spanish American Iron Company and to Collector Davis, port of Santiago; and (June 1899), letter to Colonel T.H. Bliss, Collector of Customs, Havana, Cuba, Bureau of Insular Affairs (Record Group 350), file 727, June 3, 1899.

US Department of Commerce and Labor, "Report of the Commissioner of Labor on Hawaii," No. 47 (July 1903).

——, "Statistics of immigration, Honolulu, 1905 to 1909 and First six months of 1910," Bulletin of the Bureau of Labor 22(May, 1911).

US Department of the Treasury, memo from Secretary of the Treasury Straus, Record Group 85, file 51389/14–A (1907).

——, letter from President Theodore Roosevelt to Hon. F.P. Sargent, Commissioner General of Immigration and Naturalization, file 51389/14–A, Record Group 85 (November 5, 1906).

——, response of Commissioner of Immigration and Naturalization General Daniel J. Keefe to F.M. Hatch, attorney for the Hawaiian Sugar Planters Association (1911).

Secondary sources

Adams, R., "Census Notes on the Negroes in Hawaii prior to the War," *Social Process in Hawaii*, 9–10 (1945), pp. 25–27.

Appel, J.C., "The Relationship of American Labor to United States Imperialism 1895–1905," unpublished PhD Dissertation, University of Wisconsin, Madison, 1950.

Beechert, E.D., *Working in Hawaii: A labor history*, Honolulu: University of Hawaii Press, 1985.

Clark, V.S., "Labor Conditions in Cuba," *Bulletin of the Department of Labor*, 41 Washington, DC, July 1902.

Coman, K., "History of Contract Labor in the Hawaiian Islands," *American Economic Association Reports*, 3rd series, Vol. 4 (1903).

de la Fuente, A., "Two Dangers, One Solution: Immigration, race, and labor in Cuba, 1900–1930," *International Labor and Working-Class History*, 51 (Spring 1997).

—, "Immigration," second chapter of unpublished PhD Dissertation, "'With All and For All': Race, inequality and politics in Cuba, 1900–1930," University of Pittsburgh, 1996.

Mintz, S.W., "Puerto Rican Migration: A threefold comparison," *Social and Economic Studies*, 4 (1959).

Scharrenberg, P., "Labor Problems in Hawaii," *American Federationist*, San Francisco (1921), pp. 4–5.

Scott, R., *Slave Emancipation in Cuba: The transition to free labor, 1865–1899*, Princeton: Princeton University Press, 1985.

Takaki, R., *Pau Hana: Plantation life and labor in Hawaii, 1835–1920*, Honolulu: University of Hawaii Press, 1983.

Taylor, W.H., "The Hawaiian Sugar Industry," unpublished PhD Dissertation, University of California, Berkeley, 1935.

Territory of Hawaii, "Introduction to the First Report of the Board of Immigration to the Governor of the Territory of Hawaii for the period begin April 29, 1905 and ending Jan 31, 1907" (1907).

Tinker, H., *A New System of Slavery: The export of Indian labour overseas, 1830–1920*, London: Oxford University Press, 1974.

US Department of Commerce and Labor, "Report of the Commissioner of Labor on Hawaii," *Bulletin of the Department of Labor*, 42 (July 1903), p. 701.

10

The 1934 Tydings–McDuffie Act and Filipino Exclusion: Social, Political and Economic Context Revisited

James Sobredo

When the first large group of Filipinos came to the United States, they came as government-sponsored scholars. The *Pensionado Act* of 1903 allocated funds for Filipino scholars to attend American universities. The goal was for these scholars to obtain an education in preparation for becoming "successful and powerful leaders" of the Philippines and also to act as goodwill ambassadors.[1] These *pensionados*, as the student scholars came to be known, were chosen through a competitive national examination process: 100 students out of a field of 20,000 candidates would be chosen each year for the scholarship program.[2] Not surprisingly, many of the *pensionados* were "characteristically of the elite class."[3] The *pensionado* program paid for the students' tuition, room, board, books, medical insurance, and provided the scholars with a stipend of $40 per month.[4] After the completion of their scholarship programs, the *pensionados* were required by their contract to serve one-and-a-half years in government service. The majority finished their education and returned to the Philippines, although some did stay and settled in the United States.

The first large group of Filipino labor migrants, however, came to the United States under the auspices of the Hawaiian Sugar Planters' Association (HSPA). Like the *pensionados*, they also came as *sojourners*; unlike the *pensionados*, for the vast majority of subsequent Filipino labor migrants, their sojourns became extended stays and eventually changed to permanent residency in the United States. This is not to imply that all subsequent Filipino immigrants were "sojourners." What exactly distinguishes a "sojourner" from an "immigrant" can only be gleaned upon examining their life history, that is, whether they settled in America or not.[5] It is safe to say that the *pensionados* and first labor "recruits" by the HSPA were "sojourners" – the vast majority returned to the Philippines and very few stayed permanently in America. The *second* group of HSPA recruits, however, did remain in Hawaii, and it would be safe to consider their migration as an "immigration."

On the afternoon of December 20, 1906, the *SS Doric* landed in Hawaii with 15 Filipinos from Manila.[6] They were recruited by Albert J. Judd, an attorney sent to Manila on behalf on the HSPA to negotiate a labor recruitment deal with the Philippine Commission, the American governing body in the Philippines.[7] This first group of Filipino labor recruits came from the province of Ilocos Sur in Northern Luzon. The names and ages of these immigrants were:

Simplicio Gironella	56	Prudencio Sagun	28
Mariano Gironella	23	Cecilio Sagun	27
Vincente Gironella	19		
Francisco Gironella	18	Filomeno Rebollido	30
Antonio Gironella	14	Marciano Bello	28
		Emiliano Dasulla	26
Mauricio Cortez	21	Apolonio Ramos	26
Celestino Cortez	19	Martin de Jesus	22
		Julian Galmen	20

Simplicio Gironella, 56, the oldest of the labor recruits, brought along his four sons, and his 14-year-old son Antonio was the youngest of the labor recruits. The Cortezes and the Saguns immigrated as pairs of brothers. Four of the labor recruits were married – their wives remained in the Philippines – and the rest were single. This first group of Filipino laborers was an experimental group that the HSPA hoped would return to the Philippines and provide propaganda for their future recruitment efforts.[8]

The "First Fifteen" Filipinos, as Fred Cordova refers to them, were sent to Olaa Plantation in the Big Island of Hawaii. However, they were an experimental group who were recruited for the purpose of spreading the good news to Filipinos about the better working conditions and life in the sugar plantations, especially as compared to life in the Philippines, and hopefully encourage other Filipinos to work in Hawaii.[9] The next group of Filipinos, 30 recruits, arrived in Hawaii on February 25, 1907 and were also sent to Olaa Plantation. This group of Filipinos was larger and included families – two women and two children – and they were staying for the entire three-year duration of their HSPA contract. A few months later on July 29, they were followed by a third group of 43 Filipinos, which included eight women and eight children. These labor recruits were also sent to the Big Island but at the Hawaiian Agricultural Company Plantation at Pahala.[10]

But this initial recruitment phase was not successful. Most of the Filipinos recruited had little or no agricultural experience, and as soon as their contracts expired, they left for the City of Honolulu. By 1907, only 188 Filipino workers were recruited to Hawaii, and the prospects of more laborers coming in the future looked dim. E. Faxon Bishop, President of the HSPA, concluded that the first recruitment drive was "all but a failure" and no recruitment occurred in 1908.[11]

By 1909, however, the policies of the 1908 Gentlemen's Agreement was fully in effect: the Japanese government had stopped issuing visas to labor migrants, and the supply of labor from Japan was no longer available. To make matters even worse, in May 1909, Japanese workers went on strike in all the major sugar plantations of Oahu. The Great Strike, as it came to be known, involved thousands of Japanese workers striking for higher wages, lasted for four months, and was "one of the most massive and sustained strikes in the history of Hawaii."[12] With their source of labor recruitment gone and now having a labor force that was no longer reliable and controllable, the HSPA desperately needed an alternative labor source.

Thus, in 1909 the HSPA embarked on a full-scale recruitment drive in the Philippines, which was now seen as the next source of cheap, reliable, and, most important of all, non-striking plantation workers. Furthermore, unlike Japan, the HSPA did not have to worry about immigration restrictions in the Philippines. This time, instead of recruiting workers only in the Manila area, HSPA recruitment expanded out to the provinces: recruitment offices were set up in the Visayan region, particularly in the islands of Cebu, Bohol, Panay, and Negros, and in the Ilocos region, particularly in the provinces of Ilocos Norte and Ilocos Sur.

New recruitment tactics designed to entice more labor recruits were also utilized. HSPA recruiters passed out pamphlets describing how the trans-Pacific voyages on Dollar Line steamships were "healthy, happy, and comfortable," showed films extolling the good life in Hawaii and America, and gave a 10-peso bonus for signing a contract and a 20-pesos bonus for persons bringing along their families.[13] The bonus offered for bringing family members was part of a strategy to encourage married men and their families to immigrate. Married men with families were seen as being less likely to leave the plantations and less likely to agitate for strikes.

Ruben Alcantara called these labor recruits who immigrated to Hawaii *sakadas*, a term used in the Philippines to refer to migrant labor workers in the sugar plantations of Negros and Luzon.[14] The subsequent Filipinos who stayed and worked in the plantations had labor contracts of three years, and, after completion of their contract, they hoped to make enough money to return to a better life in the Philippines. Among the terms of the contract, which the HSPA called a "labor agreement," were "free transportation and subsistence" for the worker "*and* his family" (emphasis mine) from Manila to plantations in Hawaii, "wages at the rate of $20 (equal to P40 pesos) per month" for "labor performed per month of 26 days," 10 hours in the fields or 12 hours in the "sugar factory," and "work all days except Sundays and legal holidays."[15] The HSPA would also provide "free of charge" housing, fuel for cooking and heat, and medical coverage.

California and the Pacific West Coast

After finishing their contracts in the plantations, many Filipinos left Hawaii for agricultural work in California and also in the West Coast states of Oregon and Washington. During their summers, they worked in the fishing canneries of Alaska. Filipinos heard that wages and working conditions were better in California. At "a dollar-day," the wages in California – six day-weeks multiplied four times totals

$24 per month – were only slightly better than the HSPA's $18–20 per month. Unlike working in the sugar plantations, however, where their mobility was limited, the vastness of California offered Filipinos the freedom to leave if the working conditions in a particular farm were not bearable. Another reason for Filipino emigration from Hawaii is that *labor recruiters* from California came to Hawaii and recruited Filipinos to work in California's farms. Still another reason, however, is that after the 1924 Strike organized by Filipino labor union leader Pablo Malapit, many Filipinos were blacklisted and had to leave Hawaii.[16] The 1924 Strike was a very bloody strike in which five police men and 16 strikers were killed. All of these factors contributed to a second migration of Filipinos.

Taking a steamship to San Francisco via the Matson Line or to Los Angeles via the Los Angeles Steamship Company, Filipinos would then head out to the farm fields of the San Joaquin Valley.[17] The Port of San Francisco, however, was where the majority of Filipinos arrived. Upon arriving in San Francisco, Filipinos did one of two things: they stayed in the City or left immediately for San Joaquin Valley and the town of Stockton, which by this time had become the largest "Filipinotown" in America.

The Filipinos who stayed in San Francisco congregated around a four-block area on Kearny Street and Jackson, forming a community that became known in San Francisco as "Manilatown."[18] In the City, Filipinos lived in the various residential hotels in the Manilatown area and found work as restaurant cooks, dishwashers, hotel workers, janitors, chauffeurs/drivers, or started their own business by opening restaurants, barbershops, and pool halls, the most commonly owned businesses of Filipinos. Manilatown was located next to San Francisco's "Chinatown," and often Filipino restaurant owners would purchase food supplies from Chinese merchants. These Filipino-owned businesses performed double-duty as Filipino employment and communication centers – places where Filipinos could find out where jobs were available, and where friends and relatives were located.

The majority of Filipinos, roughly 80 percent, ended up working in the agricultural sector.[19] Upon landing in San Francisco, they boarded a taxi and headed out to Stockton. From the beginning, Filipinos would be at an economic disadvantage: at $2 a fare, local people would take the bus or train to Stockton. On the other hand, Filipinos unwittingly paid $75 for a very expensive taxi ride to Stockton. Even though the fare was generally shared between four to five Filipinos per taxi, the cost was still around $15 per person. In Stockton, "Little Manila" was located on a two-block radius on El Dorado Street and Lafayette. Like the Filipino community in San Francisco, it was also located next to "Chinatown." Stockton's Little Manila was lined with Filipino restaurants, barber shops, pool halls, hotels, and a photography studio and clothing store. Filipino women helped run these mostly family-operated businesses. And like the Filipino-owned businesses in San

Francisco, these establishments also acted as employment and communication centers. For instance, in places like the Aklan Hotel on Lafayette Street between Center and El Dorado, Pablo Mabalon, the Filipino proprietor of the hotel, kept a "mailbox" which Filipino migrant workers used as an "address" and also picked up their mail.[20] Signs were posted on pool halls announcing which farm was hiring, whom to contact, and the wages paid.

By the 1920s asparagus became the main crop grown in Stockton and the outlying farming areas. At over 90 percent of the work force, Filipinos comprised the majority of the workers. Asparagus crown ("seeds") are planted in late autumn or early winter and harvested in late February (the "early" harvest), but the peak season is usually in March or April. In the 1920s, asparagus was also the most valuable vegetable crop harvested in San Joaquin County. Prior to World War II, nearly all the asparagus in the United States were grown and canned in Stockton, and Filipino workers planted, harvested, and packed the crops.[21] A California newspaper editor expressed a commonly held prejudiced view of white farmers when he said, "White men can't do the work as well as these short men who can get down on their hands and knees, or work all day long stooping over."[22] Filipinos were not too happy, however, with the type of labor they performed. In recalling his experience of working in the farms, Magnos Cabreros, then only 15 years old, described how difficult the "stoop labor" was: "It was hard work and at night, I'd feel all kinds of pain in my body – my back, my arm. Imagine less than 15 years old. After I got to my bed, I'd be crying."[23]

Filipinos also worked in other sectors of the agricultural industry. In Salinas and Watsonville, at 80 percent of the work force, Filipinos comprised the majority of the farm workers in the lettuce fields.[24] Other agricultural areas in California in which Filipinos worked were strawberries (Central Coast), sugar beets (Tracy), grapes (Delano, Cochella, and Lodi), and cotton (Central Valley).[25] In Washington State's Yakima Valley, Filipinos also picked apples, pears, hops, and sugar beets.[26] During the summers, many Filipinos migrated to Seattle to catch the ferry up to Alaska, where they spent the summer working in the fish canneries. After their summer in Alaska, they would return to Seattle to begin their migration back to Stockton and other agricultural centers in the Pacific West Coast states to begin their work cycle again. This was the life of Filipino migrant workers in the 1920s and 1930s.

Congress, the Depression, and Filipino exclusion

The first Filipino exclusion laws proposed to Congress were from California, the state with the largest Filipino population. Responding to the anti-Filipino movement in his home state, California Representative Richard Welch (Republican-California) proposed two bills that were designed to exclude Filipino immigration. House Resolution 13900, introduced on May 19, 1928, and H.R. 8707, introduced in 1930, proposed to exclude Filipinos by including them under the classification of "alien" in the 1924 Immigration Act, which would in effect exclude them. The first bill died in committee without much attention, but H.R. 8707 gained national headlines. By early 1930 the United States was facing a severe depression. The stock market crashed just a few months before, on October 24, 1929 ("Black Thursday"), and, by the end of the month, stockholders had lost $15 billion, which resulted in millions of investors losing their entire life savings. Filipinos were being blamed and scapegoated for the economic downturn and massive unemployment. Comparing them to Chinese and Japanese, Congressman Welch called Filipinos "the Third Asiatic invasion" and called for their outright immigration exclusion.

A major problem, however, was that a provision in the 1924 Act specifically states that Filipinos were excluded from this definition: "this definition shall not be held to include Indians of the Unites States not taxed, *nor citizens of the islands under the jurisdiction of the United States*" (emphasis mine) (Sec.28(b)). The Welch bills proposed to remove Filipinos from being excluded in the category of "alien." The American Federation of Labor and nativists organizations such as the National Grange and the Native Sons of the Golden West testified in favor of the Welch bills, whereas American business companies, such as the HSPA and the Pacific American Steamship, testified in opposition to exclusion.

Worried that even if the Welch bills were to pass, they might be ruled unconstitutional, Senator Samuel Morgan Shortridge, also of California, introduced a new Filipino immigration bill (S.8183) that attempted to circumvent the 1904 Supreme Court decision. The Shortridge bill proposed to "restrict" immigration for the next five years to "students, visitors for business or pleasure, merchants, government officials, their families, attendants, servants and employees."[27] In effect the bill proposed to stop all Filipino labor from immigrating to the United States by using a tactic similar to the 1882 Chinese Exclusion Act which excluded labor but allowed the entry of "teachers, students, and merchants."[28]

Congress learned from these previous failed attempts at exclusion that, as American nationals, Filipinos were not classified as aliens, and consequently could not be excluded from immigration. With the legal precedent set by the Supreme Court in *Gonzales* v. *Williams* (1904), any attempts at adding an amendment to the 1924 Immigration Act for the purpose of excluding Filipinos, would be ruled unconstitutional by the Supreme Court. Therefore, the only way in which Filipinos could be excluded from further immigration was by *changing their legal status* from that of an American *national* to that of an *alien*. The only way to accomplish this was by granting the Philippines independence and then stipulating in the law that along with independence came a change in the political and legal status of Filipinos from *nationals* to *aliens*. And if Filipinos were aliens, then they were not eligible for citizenship, since they were not "white" or "of African descent." Hence, Filipinos would be excluded from entering the United States by the 1924 Immigration Act. This is, in effect, what the Tydings–McDuffie Act of 1934 accomplished. After 1934, Filipino immigration came to a virtual halt.

The established migration route through which Filipinos entered the mainland United States was through Hawaii, but in 1935 immigration figures revealed that only two Filipinos left Hawaii for California, an indication that the exclusion goals of the Tydings–McDuffie Act were fulfilled.[29] Immediately after the passage of the Tydings–McDuffie Act, the exclusion effects of the new law were already being felt. On April 26, 1934, the *San Francisco Chronicle* reported that the San Francisco-bound steamship *S.S. President Grant* sailed from Manila *without a single Filipino passenger on board.*[30] The Dollar Line steamship company had instituted a policy of virtual exclusion by refusing to accept any Filipino passengers.

The door to Filipino immigration was effectively closed shut, but this did not satisfy the anti-Filipino forces, for there still remained thousands of Filipinos in the country. Several "repatriation" bills were introduced to deport Filipinos from the United States. As early as 1933, Congress attempted to pass H.J.R. 549, which stated that "there are large numbers of *natives* [emphasis mine] from the Philippines residing in the Continental United States who have fallen into financial distress, are not employed, have been and are beneficiaries of public and private charity."[31] The bill advocated "for the removal from the United States" of these "unemployed and financially distressed Filipinos to return to the Philippine Islands."[32] The construction of the phraseology is interesting for it still refers to Filipinos as "natives from the Philippines" and elevates the geography of the United States to a "Continent." The bill called for the "removal of these Filipino *wards* [emphasis mine] of public and private charitable organizations and these unemployed Filipinos to relieve the burdens now borne by the cities and communities in which they live." Still assuming a patriarchal stance towards Filipinos by referring to them as "wards," the claim goes against the commonly held belief among Filipinos that, in spite of the severe hardships they faced during the depression, Filipinos depended upon themselves and their community for assistance and survival. "When the Depression came, they stuck together," wrote N.V.M. Gonzalez. "Years later, they could boast: 'We never joined the breadlines!'"[33]

Although Congress' initial attempt at "repatriating" Filipinos failed, the desire to deport Filipinos remained, which was led by strong anti-immigration lobby from the Pacific West Coast states. For instance, on April 16, 1934, the *Los Angeles Herald* reported that LA County Supervisor Roger W. Jessup advocated the "Deportation of approximately 7,000 indigent Filipinos on the County Welfare rolls."[34]

Even after the passage of the Tydings–McDuffie Act, Filipinos remained, in the imaginations of politicians in Congress, "burdens" to "public and private charitable organizations," which implied they were a financial drain that exacerbated the depression. Although they were effectively excluded from entering the United States, these "natives" remained in the country in "large numbers." To address this issue, Congressman Richard J. Welch introduced a "Filipino repatriation" bill (H.R. 6464), which was a veiled attempt to deport Filipinos from the United States. Approved by Congress and signed by President Roosevelt on 10 July 1935, the "Repatriation Act of 1935" would empower the Secretary of Labor to secure transportation for "any native Filipino residing in any State … who desires to return to the Philippine Islands" to have a free return passage on any US Navy, Army or any US-registered commercial ship. Upon accepting these "benefits," "No Filipino who received the benefits of this act shall be entitled to return to the Continental United States" [Sec. 4]. Finally, Welch got an anti-Filipino legislation approved.

Race and the political and economic context

A careful analysis of the Tydings–McDuffie Act indicates that there is very little difference in the political status of the Philippines prior to and after the passage of the Act. The first key statement in the 1934 Act is in the phrase: "All citizens of the Philippine Islands shall owe allegiance to the United States" (Sec. 2(a) (1)). This was precisely the legal and political category of Philippine citizens prior to the Tydings–McDuffie Act. A second key statement reinforces the point of American sovereignty: "Every officer of the government of the Commonwealth of the Philippine Islands shall, before entering upon the discharge of his duties, take and subscribe an oath of office, declaring, among other things, that he recognizes and accepts the supreme authority of and will maintain true faith and allegiance to the United States" (Sec. 2(a)(2)). Thus, from a strictly legal perspective as written in the Tydings–McDuffie Act, the Philippines remained a colony of the United States. As written in the law, the Philippines was still politically and economically dependent upon the United States and, according to Sec. 2(a)(10), had no legal rights to establish diplomatic relations with foreign countries. Prima facie, it should be very clear that the Philippines remained a colony and that the United States maintained complete sovereignty over the country.

Alfred McCoy has argued that, during his term, Commonwealth President Manuel Quezon ran the Philippines as if it were an independent country.[35] Quezon was in a constant power struggle with the US High Commissioner, and he would circumvent the authority of the Commissioner whenever possible. For instance, he was able to extend his presidential term from six years to an eight-year term, and, at another time, he was also able to secure rifles to arm the Philippine Army – much to the objection of the High Commissioners.[36] McCoy argues that Quezon was a "dictator" in his form of government. In a word, Quezon was the precursor to the infamous dictator Ferdinand Marcos, whose martial law government was financed and fully supported by the United States.

I am in agreement with McCoy, whose arguments make sense when examined within the context of the development of the British Commonwealth of nations and the growing assertion of independence of these Commonwealth nations. During the 1930s, economic considerations weighed heavily in favor of granting certain dependent nations autonomy and independence rather than keep them within the British Empire. They were an economic burden on the Empire. Those nations that had a long and developed history of greater autonomy and self-rule were granted Commonwealth status. The Philippines was in a similar situation in its relation with the United States. America's vision of the Philippines as a major economic asset did not come to fruition. Prior to the Great Depression, imperialistic and business interests would prevail, and the country could afford to keep the Philippines as a colony. But with the United States in economic crisis, the Philippines was too expensive a country to keep and maintain.

Race

A crucial analysis that is missing in all the scholarship written about Philippine independence and the 1934 Tydings–McDuffie Act is the importance of race in the negotiations and eventual passage of the 1934 Act. Bernardita Reyes Churchill, one of the leading authorities on the Philippine Independence Bill, dismisses the importance of race and the contributions of the anti-Filipino immigration groups who were pushing for Filipino exclusion.[37] The numerous remarks and discussions about race which are mentioned throughout the Filipino immigration exclusion and Philippine independence debates are conspicuously omitted in her interpretation. Churchill's analysis focused primarily on the importance Filipinos, particularly Manuel Quezon, who were involved in the independence "Missions" and who negotiated the terms of the independence bill. For instance, in the concluding chapter ("Summing Up"), the reader learns that the book is really about Manuel Quezon's role in negotiating Philippine independence. Although there is ample evidence which showed the crucial role of the exclusionists in supporting the passage of the independence bill, Churchill's work, nevertheless, neglects this important feature. This omission is indeed puzzling in the light of the fact that some of the most prominent independence advocates, like, for example, Camilio Osias in the United States and Mauro Baradi in the Philippines, acknowledged as early as 1933 their "indebtedness" to nationally recognized groups like the American Federation of Labor and the National Grange and the Railroad Brotherhoods for supporting Philippine independence.[38] Churchill's analysis interprets the Tydings–McDuffie Act as a bill concerned primarily with the independence of the Philippines, and leaves out the crucial political alliances made between the exclusionists and pro-independence groups.

On the other hand, an analysis, such as the one given by Grayson Kirk in his book *Philippine independence*, that relies wholly on economics as the main driving force behind the Tydings–McDuffie Act also misses the point, because it fails to show how racial ideologies provide a justification for the need to preserve the privileged economic position of white Americans. Kirk cites the economic protestations of farm groups as being instrumental in the passage of the Tydings–McDuffie Act. The main economic arguments propounded by farm groups were that Philippine sugar and oil imports were providing unfair competition to American farmers and agricultural companies. The problem with these arguments is that the American sugar industry had been advocating tariffs against Philippine products and supporting independence since the 1920s, and their efforts were never successful until the exclusionists joined the independence campaign. Their arguments are also groundless because the success of the American sugar and dairy markets had very little or nothing to do with the importation of Philippine products.

For example, through the National Diary Union and the National Cooperative Milk Producers Association, dairy farmers argued that the importation of coconut oil threatened the survival of the dairy industry, especially the butter industry. During the Depression, people preferred to buy margarine mainly out of economic necessity: a pound of butter cost nearly 17.8 cents more than margarine, and this price has remained stable since the early 1920s.[39] Even if the free trade terms between the Philippine and the US were abolished, the increase of the cost of margarine would only be 2 cents more, which would still make margarine roughly 15 cents *cheaper* than butter, and hardly a good economic reason for consumers to switch to butter.

There were racial overtones in the dairy farmers' arguments to exclude coconut oil from the Philippines. For example, in an August 7, 1929 edition of the *Butter and Cheese Journal*, an article appeared arguing that margarine is an inferior product and possibly unhealthy for American consumers because of the preparation process used in making the "impossibly filthy" copra: "When dry, copra looks and smells something like stable manure or worse. When the stuff is ready for shipment, *swarms of half-naked Malays* load it on ships, *Malays sweating under the tropical heat, tramping copra* that is going to be made into the poor man's butter. Think of it!" (emphasis mine).[40]

Even in the economic arguments used by pro-Philippine independence forces, there are very heavy racist overtones, which made it easy for dairy farmers to understand the arguments of Californians pushing for Filipino immigration exclusion.

American sugar companies, on the other hand, present a much more complicated group, because they comprised a number of companies dealing with different "sugars," not all of which were threatened by the imporation of Philippine sugar.

In 1933 a breakdown of the 6,316,004 tons of sugar consumed in the United States yielded these percentages:[41]

American beet sugar	21.63
American cane sugar	4.98
Hawaii (cane sugar)	15.67
Puerto Rico (cane sugar)	12.52
Virgin Islands (cane sugar)	.08
Philippines	19.65
Cuba	25.34

The cause of farmers' alarm was the fact that since the early 1920s, Philippine sugar imports increased by 450 per cent while the American farmers' share decreased by 50 percent from 1920 to 1929.[42] Alarmed at their loss of profits and share of the market, American farmers, who grew mostly beet sugar, blamed the importation of Philippine sugar as the source of their economic problems. But as Grayson Kirk pointed out, the only market affected by the importation of Philippine sugar was American sugar companies in Cuba: 90 per cent of all Philippine sugar competed directly with Cuban sugar. Beet sugar companies did not compete directly with Philippine sugar, and a tariff against Philippine sugar would not affect their beet sugar prices. The only sugar companies that would have benefitted from taxing Philippine sugar were American sugar companies in Cuba, so although it was the American Farm Bureau, the National Grange, and the National Beet Growers' Association that publicly called on Congress for taxing of Philippine sugar imports, American sugar companies in Cuba were actually the main agents advocating quietly behind the scenes to stop the flow of Philippine sugar.

The crucial point of my analysis is that, although these were the necessary political alliances that had to be forged in order to pass the 1933 Hare–Hawes–Cutting Bill and eventually the identical 1934 Tydings–McDuffie Act, the fact remains that when Filipinos were excluded from the United States, their social construction as a race changed from being "Indians," on the legal terms stipulated by the 1904 *Gonzalez* v. *Williams* Supreme Court decision, to "Asiatics," who were then excluded by the 1934 Tydings–McDuffie Act.

My argument is *not* that race was the most crucial factor in getting the Philippine independence bills passed; rather, race considerations were the missing crucial ingredient to make the formula work. Economic considerations have always been presented to grant the Philippines independence, but until the introduction of the idea of Filipinos as a racial threat to American labor and social-moral standards, no such bill would have passed. When both sides realized that in order for their goals to succeed, they must form a political alliance for accomplishing a compromise bill, then such a bill could finally pass. The Tydings–McDuffie Act finally gave the Philippines independence, but it also set a quota of 50 Filipino immigrants per year, which, in effect, functioned as an outright Filipino exclusion legislation.

Notes

1 Aquilino B. Obando, *A Study of the Problems of Filipino Students in the United States*, Los Angeles: University of Southern California, 1936, p. 6, originally written for Obando's master thesis in USC's School of Education.

2 From H. Brett Melendy's *Asians in America: Filipinos, Koreans, and East Indians*, New York: Hippocrene Books, 1981, p. 32. I use the term "*pensionados*" inclusively, since Filipino women (*pensionadas*) also participated as government-sponsored scholars.

3 Emily Porcincula Lawsin, "Pensionados, Paisanos, & Pinoys: An analysis of the *Filipino Student Bulletin*, 1922–1939," *Filipino American National Historical Society Journal*, Vol. 4 (1996), p. 33C. Lawsin points out that initially some scholars circumvented the examination programs: some were "appointed by Philippine governors and American superintendents," while other scholars who had wealthy parents were fully funded by their families (ibid.). N.B. Many writers refer to these family-funded scholars as *pensionados* – although if "*pensionados*" were to refer only to government-funded scholars through the Pensionado Act of 1903, then technically they were not *pensionados*.

4 Obando, op. cit., p. 16. Students attending universities in New York City received a higher stipend of $80 per month.

5 Suchang Chan gives an insightful discussion of the distinction between "sojourn" and "immigration" that sheds light on this issue (see *This Bitter-sweet Soil: The Chinese in California agriculture, 1860–1910*, Berkeley and Los Angeles: University of California Press, 1986, p. xv).

6 Fred Cordova, *Filipinos: Forgotten Asian Americans*, Dubuque, Iowa: Kendall/ Hall, 1983, p. 26; Sister Mary Dorita Clifford, "The Hawaiian Sugar Planter Association and Filipino Exclusion," in Josefa M. Saniel (ed.), *The Filipino Exclusion Movement, 1927–1935*, UP-Diliman: Institute of Asian Studies, Occasional Papers, No. 1, 1967; Jonathan Okamura, *Immigrant Filipino Ethnicity in Honolulu, Hawaii*, London: University of London, 1982, p. 71; Ronald Takaki, *Pau Hana: Plantation Life and Labor in Hawaii*, Honolulu, HI: University of Hawaii Press, 1983, p. 27.

7 Initially, Puerto Ricans, who like Filipinos resided in a US territory, were also recruited as a HSPA labor, but by 1909, Filipinos became the dominant labor source (Ruben Alcantara, *Sakadas: Filipino Adaptation in Hawaii*, Washington, DC: University Press of America, 1981, p. 3). It was cheaper to ship labor from the Philippines than from Puerto Rico.

8 Robert Anderson, Richard Coller, and Rebecca F. Pestano, *Filipinos in Rural Hawaii*, Honolulu: University of Hawaii Press, 1984, p. 2.

9 Ibid., pp. 2–3.

10 Cordova, op.cit., p. 28.

11 Quoted in Clifford, op. cit., p. 14 – original citation is *Planter's Monthly* (November 1907), p. 383.

12 Takaki, op. cit., p. 153.

[13] The quote from the Dollar Line is in Bruno Lasker's *Filipino Immigration*, Chicago: University of Chicago, 1931, p. 215; Andersonl, op. cit., p. 5.

[14] Alcantara, op. cit.

[15] Hawaiian Sugar Planters' Association "Labor Agreement" in *Exclusion of Immigration from the Philippine Islands* (*Hearings before the Committee on Immigration and Naturalization*), Hearings on H.R. 8708, a Filipino exclusion bill proposed by Congressman Richard J. Welch, Republican-San Francisco, CA, 71st Congress, Second Session, House of Representatives, 1930. In 1909, the wage paid was $16 a month, which increased by $1 each year until the end of the three-year contract (Alcantara, op. cit., p. 4). By their use of the term "labor agreement" and the fact that Filipinos were legally bound to stay in the plantation for only three years, the HSPA was able to circumvent the 1883 Foran Act, which prohibited bringing contract labor to the U.S. (cf. Alcantara, op. cit., p. 3).

[16] Carey McWilliams, *Brothers Under the Skin*, Boston: Little, Brown, and Company, 1944, p. 231.

[17] Ibid. Unless otherwise noted, the information provided on Filipino communities in San Francisco and Stockton was gathered through oral history interviews I conducted. I wish to thank Jovy Angat, Fred Basconcillo, Cecil Bonzo, M.C. Canlas, Felipe Daguro, Perfecto delos Santos (1904–95), Emile De Guzman, Rudy Delphino (1933–96), Jean Ishibashi, Orvy Jundis, Violeta "Bullet X" Marasigan (1940–2000), Ernesto Mabalon, Pacifico Mortel, Al Robles, Lucia T. Silverio, Bill Sorro, Luis Syquia and Lourdes Tumbokon Sobredo for their oral history participation in this section.

[18] James Sobredo, "Filipinos in San Francisco," in James Brook, Chris Carlsson, and Nancy Peters (eds), *Built on Shifting Sands: Histories on San Francisco*, San Franciso: City Lights Books, 1998. The book is accompanied by a CD-ROM disk entitled "Shaping San Francisco" (Chris Carlsson, project director), which contains five segments on the Filipino community – funded by the California Council for the Humanities, a state branch of the National Endowment for the Humanities.

[19] Benicio T. Catapusan, "The Social Adjustment of Filipinos in the United States,"PhD dissertation, Los Angeles: University of Southern California, 1940, p. 26.

[20] Oral interview with Lourdes Tumbokon Sobredo and Lucia T. Silverio conducted by the author in Stockton, California, October, 1993. Sobredo's great-uncle, Pablo Mabalon, was the proprietor of the Aklan Hotel. Mabalon also ran the Lafayette Lunch Counter, which was across the street from the Aklan Hotel. Today, California's Highway 4 slices through the former location of Stockton's Filipinotown, and in the former site of the Aklan Hotel sits a barbed-wire parking lot for the Stockton Police Department. Each morning, migrant workers – these days mostly Mexican immigrants – still congregate along El Dorado Street, waiting for daily, temporary employment. Nevertheless, signs of the Filipino community still remain. On Center Street and Market, next to the Stockton Police Department, stands the eight-story brick building of the Filipino Plaza, a retirement center for Filipino and Mexican farm workers, which is surrounded by several Filipino businesses: two restaurants, a grocery store, bookstore, video-rental store, and publishing company. And on 443 East Sonora sits a newly constructed Filipino Community Center and residential building.

[21] Lourdes Tumbokon Sobredo's grandfather (Perfecto de los Santos), mother (Patria de los Santos) and stepfather (Pacifico Macahilas), all worked in the asparagus industry. Lourdes's 74-year-old uncle, Ernesto Mabalon, still works as a labor contractor for the Yamada Brothers Growers and Packers, which today remains the only all packing company

that employs an all-Filipino crew, but unlike the 1920s and 30s, women now comprise half the workers – see James Sobredo, "Stockton: The Capitol of Filipino America in the 1920s and 30s," *Manila Mail*, February 25, 1997.

22 Ronald Takaki, *Strangers From a Different Shore: A History of Asians in America*, New York: Penguin, 1989, p. 320.

23 Cordova, op. cit., p. 42.

24 See Howard DeWitt's *Violence in the Fields: Filipino Farm Labor Unionization During the Great Depression*, Saratoga, CA: Century Twenty One Publishing, 1980 and his essay "The Filipino Labor Union: The Salinas Lettuce Strike of 1934," *Amerasia Journal*, 5:2 (1978).

25 Lillia Villanueva and Craig Sharlin, *Philip Vera Cruz: A personal history of Filipino immigrants and the farmworkers' movement*, Los Angeles: UCLA Labor Center (Institute of Industrial Relations) and Asian American Studies Center, 1992; Kevin Starr, *Endangered Dreams: the Great Depression in California*, New York: Oxford University Press, 1996, p. 75; and Miriam J. Wells, *Strawberry Fields: Politics, class and work in California agriculture*, Ithaca, NY: Cornell University Press, 1996.

26 Gail Nomura, "Within the Law: The establishment of Filipino leasing rights on the Yakima Indian Reservation," *Amerasia Journal*, Vol. 13, No. 1 (1986–87).

27 *Congressional Record*, April 16, 1930, p. 7104.

28 Bill Ong Hing, *Making and Remaking Asian America Through Immigration Policy, 1850–1990*, Stanford: Stanford University Press, 1996, p. 24. See also the collection of essays in Sucheng Chan's *Entry Denied: Exclusion and the Chinese community in America, 1882–1943*, Philadelphia: Temple University Press, 1991.

29 Benjamin B. Domingo, *The Philippines and Hawaii*, Manila: Foreign Service Institute, 1983, foreword by Senator Daniel Inouye, p. 282.

30 H. Brett Melendy, *Asians in America: Filipinos, Koreans, and East Indians*, New York: Hippocrene Books, 1977, p. 43.

31 Quoted from Casiano Pagdilao Coloma, *A Study of the Filipino Repatriation Movement*, San Francisco, CA: R and E Research Associates, 1974, p. 29 – originally Coloma's thesis from the University of Southern California.

32 Quoted in Coloma, ibid.

33 In N.V.M. Gonzalez's forward to Fred Cordova's *Filipinos: Forgotten Asian Americans*, Dubuque, Iowa: Kendall/Hunt, 1983, p. xi.

34 "Urge Filipinos on Relief be Deported," *Los Angeles Herald*, April, 16 1934, cited in Coloma, op. cit., p. 26.

35 Alfred McCoy, "Quezon's Commonwealth: The emergence of Philippine authoritarianism," in Ruby Paredes (ed.), *Philippine Colonial Democracy*, New Haven: Yale University Southeast Asian Studies, 1988.

36 McCoy, op. cit., pp. 144–47.

37 Bernadita Reyes, Churchill, *The Philippine Independence Missions to the United States, 1919–1934*, Manila: National Historical Institute, 1983.

38 In their book *The Philippine Charter of Liberty*, Baltimore, MD: The French-Bray Printing Company, 1933, p. 90. This point is also acknowledged by Grayson Kirk in his classic book on Philippine independence entitled *Philippine Independence: Motives, Problems, and Prospects*, New York: Farrar and Rhinehart, Inc., 1936, p. 102. Kirk cites p.

8 of Osias and Baradi, however, instead of p. 90, which would have made a much stronger case for his point.

[39] Kirk, op. cit., pp. 87–88; and Theodore Friend, "American Interests and Philippine Independence, 1929–1930," *Philippine Studies,* Vol.11:4 October (1963), p. 513.

[40] Quoted in Kirk, op. cit., p. 88.

[41] Ibid., p. 90.

[42] Friend, op. cit., p. 510.

11

Communists, Christians, and Japanese Imperial Subjects: Okinawan Immigrants within the Japanese Diaspora, 1899 to 1941

Edith M. Kaneshiro

In recent years, Okinawan studies has received renewed scholarly attention. Okinawa Prefecture's problematic relationship with Japan, the Okinawan people's ambivalent responses to Japanese nationalism, and the memorialization of the Battle of Okinawa have recently been examined by East Asian specialists (Christy, 1993; Morris-Suzuki, 1996; Figal, 1997). Asian American historians and economists, many of whom are community-based, and Okinawan geographers have also contributed to this growing field of Okinawan studies. Fascinated by the persistence of ethnicity among Okinawan immigrants and their descendants, these scholars have examined the phenomenon of migration among Okinawans, and have argued that internal and international migration played a significant role in the shaping of modern Okinawan identities within Japan and within the larger Japanese diaspora which extends from Asia to the Americas (Ishikawa and Taira, 1991; Kobashigawa 1998; Nakasone, 1996). Research in this area has been made possible because scholars on both sides of the Pacific have collaborated in collecting primary materials such as newspaper articles, oral histories, immigration records, and photographs related to the Okinawan immigrant experience.

Although a variety of documentary material has been collected, the western literature on Okinawan migration has focused largely on the migrations to South America and Hawaii, neglecting the migrations to Southeast Asia and North America (Tigner, 1956; ESOHP, 1981). The experiences of Okinawans in North America and Southeast Asia were probably overlooked for two reasons: the Okinawan immigrant population in the continental United States was significantly smaller than other Okinawan immigrant communities, and the Okinawan immigrant community in the Philippines ceased to exist after 1945.

The purpose of this paper is to re-examine the experiences of Okinawan immigrants beyond Hawaii and South America; it examines the migration and settlement patterns of Okinawan immigrants in southern California and in Davao, Mindanao, the Philippines before the outbreak of war between Japan and the United States in 1941. Placing the international migration of Okinawan peasants in a global context, this paper further recognizes that the economic transformation of the Pacific region during the first half of the twentieth century affected not only major centers of power and authority, but also small, underdeveloped and supposedly isolated rural and remote areas, such as the Ryukyu Islands. Moreover, this paper traces the development of Okinawan immigrant settlements in two areas of the American Pacific empire and shows how these communities responded to nativism, racism, imperialism, and economic change in their broader environment. Separated by an ocean but linked by a common heritage, the Okinawan immigrant communities in California and in Mindanao developed dramatically different adaptive strategies and identities in response to their changing economic, social, and legal status as Japanese immigrants in foreign lands.

Background to Okinawan migration

Since the 1850s, western observers had written that Okinawa, then known as the Great Loo Choo, was quickly heading toward a severe economic and demographic crisis. In 1853, Dr. James Morrow, a member of Commodore Perry's expedition to Japan, wrote, "At present the indications are that the population is increasing, which is a great evil when the soil has already attained its maximum, and where there is no outlet for the population by emigration" (Cole, 1947, p. 110). Many scholars of Okinawan history have also argued that thousands of Okinawans chose to leave the Japanese island prefecture because of the Ryukyu Islands' deteriorating conditions. Historian George Kerr wrote that natural disasters, disease, rapid population growth, and an underdeveloped economy made turn-of-the-century Okinawa an increasingly less desirable place in which to live. Consequently, "the government," wrote Kerr, "experienced no difficulty in promoting emigration to foreign lands and to Japanese colonies in the Pacific" (Kerr, 1954, p. 439). In a study about the population of the Ryukyu Islands, demographer Irene Taeuber also concluded that population growth and limited industrialization was a major cause of the mass exodus from Okinawa. "The emigration from the Ryukyus," writes Taeuber, "was the expected reaction of an economically poor and culturally retarded people who had come within the orbit of an industrializing power" (Taeuber, 1955, p. 240). Historian Mitsugu Sakihara has argued that two centuries of colonization by Satsuma domain and the eventual lack of self-rule on Okinawa after its formal incorporation into the Japanese empire in 1879 created an environment of oppression, despair, and social unrest on the main island of the prefecture. Okinawan emigration, suggests Sakihara, was an expression of peasant discontent with their new political, social, and economic circumstances (Sakihara, 1981, pp. 1–16).

Although Okinawa was one of Japan's poorest prefectures, recent research by Tomonori Ishikawa and Koji Taira has shown that emigration from Okinawa occurred in the wealthier regions of the island prefecture. As they discovered, extreme poverty was not universal throughout the islands. Ishikawa and Taira (1991, p. 111) write:

> [D]isaggregated data seem to suggest something entirely different. In Okinawa, it is the better-off areas which show higher rates of emigration. This calls for a reconsideration of the sources, types and qualities of emigrants in comparison to general characteristics of the population of an emigrant-sending country.

Recent case studies of international migration to the United States also confirm that free immigrants tended to come from the middle-level and landed segments of their native communities. Sucheta Mazumdar, for example, has argued that the vast majority of immigrants from northern India to North America at the beginning of the twentieth century were small landowners (Mazumdar, 1984). Writing on Italian migration to California, Dino Cinel demonstrated that emigration from Italy varied from region to region, and that there was "no direct correlation" between poverty and the intensity of emigration (Cinel, 1982, p. 45). In a study of Norwegian migration to the United States, Jon Gjerde has shown that strategies of migration varied according to circumstance and that "[i]solated instances of economic failure … were not the underlying cause of the widespread emigration" (Gjerde, 1985, p. 83). As Ishikawa and Taira have concluded regarding emigration from Okinawa, "People in poorer areas simply lacked the initial resource endowments to generate enough cash for international travels" (Ishikawa and Taira, 1991, p. 124).

Contrary to twentieth-century views of Okinawan poverty and backwardness, eighteenth- and nineteenth-century observers indicated that the Okinawan economy was commercially viable and actively producing goods and cash crops. In 1757, a Chinese visitor noted that many goods were being produced and circulated on the islands. Cotton, salt, tea, alcohol, and paper were merely some of the items that he had seen (The Chinese Repository 1837, p. 118). In 1850, a British missionary wrote:

> The country is exceedingly well cultivated, producing sugar, rice, grain and tobacco, and a great variety of vegetables; it is intersected by numerous good paved roads; the streams are crossed by good bridges; the houses and the walls around the enclosures are exceedingly well built; and the place is evidently in an advanced state of semi-civilization (Smith, 1853, pp. 88–89).

In the 1850s, American explorers estimated that Ryukyuans produced 200,000 bushels of rice and 50,000 bushels of wheat. Sweet potatoes were reportedly planted over 35,000 acres and sugarcane was planted over 2,000 acres (Hawks, 1856, p. 363). Needless to say, during the pre-modern era, the island kingdom did not suffer widespread economic malaise.

Although Okinawan peasants were strongly discouraged from leaving their villages because inter-village migration interfered with agricultural production and tax collection, within this semi-feudal system, Okinawan peasants like other Japanese peasants exerted a fair amount of independence. Okinawan villagers were organized into peasant work groups known as *kumiai*, and within these work groups, peasants worked the feudal lords' land. Peasants were also allotted their own lands known as *hyakusho chi*. Producing both a subsistence crop of sweet potatoes and commercial crops of rice and sugarcane, individual peasant families worked these small and scattered plots of land (Tamura, 1955).

The form of agricultural production, however, was not uniform throughout the topographically diverse island kingdom. The social and economic organization of villages varied according to environmental conditions and the size of the population. Consequently, although the entire Ryukyu Kingdom paid tribute to Satsuma, a powerful domain in what is now known as Kagoshima Prefecture, the existence of wealth and poverty varied from village to village. American explorers in the 1850s confirmed these views of significant variations in village economies as they explored Okinawa, the main island of the kingdom (Hawks, 1856). To supplement their incomes, Ryukyuan peasants engaged in part-time agricultural work and engaged in other income-producing activities such as weaving, brewing alcohol, and producing lacquerware (Chamberlain, 1895, p. 461). Ryukyuan peasant women played a significant role in buying, selling, and trading goods on the islands. "We observed numbers of women of all ages engaged in all manners of occupations," commented a western visitor, "going about and conversing with as much freedom and self-assurance as is customary in any part of the world, and it is only reasonable to suppose that some of these must have been married" (Brunton, 1876, p. 70).

However, after Japan had formally incorporated the island kingdom into the Japanese nation in 1879, significant changes in the social structure of the island prefecture led to the redistribution of the population and the reorganization of Okinawan society. As stipends for samurai and the literati of the Ryukyuan court were abolished, the former ruling elite were forced to seek new forms of income. Some fled to China, others migrated to Tokyo and Osaka and became merchants, while many remained on Okinawa and were forced to become farmers. As Tokushin Nakamoto recalled, his grandfather, who was once a teacher of Chinese, had no choice but to become a farmer during the late Meiji period: "In the Meiji period there were many changes. My grandfather was a teacher of Chinese in a town in Naha. He couldn't continue teaching and decided to go to the country to farm" (ESOHP, 1981, p. 391).

With a new population suddenly forced to turn to agriculture, the resources of numerous villages became limited as commoners and former samurai competed for land and labor. Therefore, in the 1880s, the people of Okinawa began demanding a solution to their economic and social problems. For example, between 1882 and 1889, there were numerous civil disturbances on Okinawa. Anticipating widespread economic and social problems on Okinawa, a group of commoners and intellectuals mobilized and participated in a mass movement known in Japan as the *Jiyu Minken Undo*, or the People's Rights Movement. Two individuals, Jahana Noboru and Toyama Kyuzo, became famous for their involvement in this movement in Okinawa.

When the movement failed, Toyama became an emigration agent and reportedly conceived of a program of mass emigration as a peaceful solution to Okinawa's deteriorating conditions (Sakihara, 1981, pp. 1–16).

When Toyama began to promote emigration as a solution to Okinawa's problems, the Okinawa Prefectural Government introduced a series of land reform laws in 1899, hoping to encourage enterprise among Okinawans. As land became available for purchase, commoners and former samurai eagerly purchased land and turned to sugarcane production as their major source of income. Producing sugarcane in greater quantities than before, Okinawans were forced to import rice and other staples. Competing with modern Japanese sugar plantations on newly colonized Taiwan, Okinawan farmers continued to produced sugarcane on a small-scale as they had done in the pre-modern era. But in order to compete with other sugar economies, Okinawan farmers began investing much of their resources in sugarcane production, often financing their investments by borrowing from money lenders and by mortgaging their farms. Consequently, by the 1900s, Okinawans began seeking other sources of income to help them pay off debts that they had accumulated as a result their investments in sugarcane production (Aniya, 1974). Numerous Okinawans, thus, turned to labor recruiters and emigration agencies in order to find work overseas where wages were higher.

Middlemen such as People's Rights activist-turned-emigration agent Toyama Kyuzo played an instrumental role in introducing debt-ridden Okinawan peasants to employment opportunities overseas. As an agent for the *Tairiku Shokumin Goshigaisha* and *Teikoku Shokumin Goshigaisha*, Toyama formed the Toyama Emigration Services Office in 1904, and had three satellite offices in northern, central, and southern Okinawa. And by 1908, there were as many as 20 emigration companies on Okinawa with 16 representatives. At this time, there were reportedly 507 officially authorized emigration agents throughout all of Japan (*Ryukyu Shimpo*, June 9, 1907). Undereducated and ill-informed about the opportunities of migration, Okinawan peasants turned to middlemen such as Toyama Kyuzo for advice and assistance in traveling and finding employment overseas.

Japanese emigration companies began recruiting on Okinawa well after they had started recruiting on the main islands of Japan. The first effort to recruit male laborers from Okinawa began in 1899 when Toyama Kyuzo organized a group of contract laborers, one of whom was his younger brother, to work on a sugarcane plantation in Hawaii. Within a few years, emigration companies were transporting Okinawan laborers to the Philippines, Brazil, Peru, Mexico, New Caledonia, and even as far away as Cuba (Ishikawa, 1980). Because international travel was expensive, numerous Okinawan migrants initially traveled as contract laborers to many tropical destinations. However, as contract labor laws were gradually abolished in the western hemisphere, only those Okinawans who could afford to travel as free migrants migrated to Hawaii and North America (*Ryukyu Shimpo*,

January 19, 1906). Some scholars estimated that it was three times as expensive for Asian immigrants to take transoceanic voyages as it was for European immigrants at this time (Galenson, 1984, p. 17). Poor female Okinawan migrants traveled to work in factories near Tokyo and Osaka, and the very poor, most likely the landless, migrated to tropical destinations within the Japanese empire such as Taiwan and Micronesia (Ishikawa and Taira, 1991).

The geographical distribution of Okinawan immigrants differed somewhat from the geographical distribution of Japanese immigrants from other prefectures. Late migration, restrictive immigration laws, and selective recruitment are some of the reasons for this difference. Occurring during an age of imperialism in Asia and the Pacific, planters, construction companies, and railroad companies turned to Japanese emigration agencies and labor recruiters for workers. With the abolition of black slavery in the Americas and with the colonization of the tropical Pacific by Japan and various western nations, including the United States, numerous plantations turned to Asia to replenish their labor supply (Curtin, 1990; Northrup, 1995). With the exclusion of Chinese immigrants in many parts of the western hemisphere, planters within the Pacific world looked to Japan for laborers to cultivate and harvest tropical commodities such as sugar, coffee, and hemp.

During the first two decades of the twentieth century, Japanese emigration agents recruited heavily in Okinawa Prefecture. For example, between 1899 and 1907, the Toyama Emigration Service Office regularly advertised in Okinawan newspapers for laborers to work in Hawaii. In addition, Toyama Kyuzo regularly made speeches to the public regarding the opportunities of migration. In 1906, a representative of the *Meiji Shokumin Goshigaisha* visited Okinawa to encourage workers to migrate to Peru. He stated that his company was prepared to process as many as 200 immigrants within a few months. And when recruiters sought laborers for the farms and plantations of Brazil in 1908, approximately 300 Okinawans were on the first boatload of Japanese immigrants to Brazil. The Philippines also became a popular destination for Okinawan emigrants, after an Okinawan labor recruiter-turned-planter actively promoted the emigration of Okinawans to Davao, Mindanao. Within four decades, Okinawan immigrants were located in numerous parts of the the Pacific world. By 1941, more than 16,000 had settled in Brazil, over 10,000 had migrated to Peru, about 13,000 lived and worked in Hawaii, and approximately 10,000 called the Philippines their home. As an offshoot of the migration to Hawaii, Canada, and Mexico, approximately 1,000 settled in the continental United States, mainly in southern California. And approximately 1,500 migrated to Borneo and Malaya. And a little over 100 traveled as far as Cuba (Ishikawa, 1980).

Whether they had migrated to a foreign country or to areas within Japan, Okinawan migrants regularly remitted vast sums of money to their communities. As historian George Kerr has written, "Obviously the Japanese government had ready at hand a remarkable instrument with which to relieve population pressure, and an extraordinary source of hidden revenue for the poverty-stricken prefecture" (Kerr, 1954, p. 438). Other scholars also noted that money from overseas sustained the Okinawan economy. Irene Taeuber observed that immigrant remittances from overseas enabled those who stayed behind to "preserve a remarkably stable life" (Taeuber, 1955, p. 255). And Ishikawa and Taira concluded that "emigration was … an investment which produced income streams over time. For the contemporary Okinawan level of living, it was a very good investment" (Ishikawa and Taira, 1991, p. 120).

Subjects of Imperial Japan

Although they were Japanese nationals, before they departed for foreign lands, many Okinawan emigrants were treated like foreigners or non-Japanese on the main islands of Japan. Before they departed for their overseas destinations, hopeful Okinawan emigrants were processed at immigration centers in Kobe and Yokohama. In these port cities, emigrants were clustered in poor and overcrowded housing, and numerous emigrants contracted various diseases. In addition to these uncomfortable conditions, Okinawan emigrants were also forewarned of potential conflicts between hopeful emigrants from other Japanese prefectures. The *Ryukyu Shimpo*, an Okinawan newspaper, stated that emigrants from Okinawa were particularly vulnerable to discriminatory treatment because of their impoverished appearance and their inability to speak standard Japanese. Fear of discrimination and poor treatment, especially for Okinawan women, was real. The *Ryukyu Shimpo* reported that the Japanese on the mainland found Okinawan peasant women to be particularly unsightly with their tattooed hands, their awkward hairstyles, and their unfashionable clothing (*Ryukyu Shimpo*, March 5 and 9, 1906). Thus, before they departed for their foreign destinations, Okinawan emigrants were made especially aware of their outsider status among other Japanese.

Because of strong Chinese, Southeast Asian, and indigenous influences on Okinawan culture, Okinawans were perceived by other Japanese to be a distinct people. Pointing to physical differences such as skin color, body hair, facial features, and body type, Japanese from the mainland regularly emphasized differences between themselves and Japanese peasants from Okinawa Prefecture. In turn, Okinawans also differentiated themselves from the Japanese by referring to the Japanese as *Yamatunchu*, people of Yamato, and referring to themselves as *Uchinanchu*, the people of Uchina, the name for Okinawa in the Okinawan dialect. These stereotypes and differences were further exaggerated in immigrant communities, particularly in Hawaii and the Philippines. Okinawans were treated as "foreigners" in Japan, and they were considered outsiders in Japanese immigrant communities (Christy, 1993; Cody, 1959; Kimura, 1981b; Kobashigawa, 1988).

Immigrant strategies

Nonetheless, like Japanese peasant-migrants from the mainland, Okinawans migrated as *dekasegi* laborers. They initially intended to travel overseas for a short period of time, hoping one day to return to Okinawa. At the turn-of-the-century, Hawaii was the primary destination of Okinawan emigrants. Between 1899 and 1907, more than 9,000 Okinawan migrants traveled to Hawaii. And by 1918, there were well over 10,000 Okinawans on the four major islands of Hawaii: 3,870 were on Hawaii, 2,897 were on Oahu, 2,547 were on Maui, and 1,379 were on Kauai. Working primiarily as laborers on sugarcane plantations, Okinawans performed labor-intensive tasks such as weeding, watering, harvesting, and loading sugarcane (Ishikawa, 1981).

Before the enforcement of the Gentlemen's Agreement of 1908, several Japanese laborers, many Okinawans included, left the plantations of Hawaii and migrated to California. Between 1902 and 1908, more than 37,000 Japanese used Hawaii as a "stepping-stone" to the continental United States (US Senate, 1911a, p. 6). Japanese inns served as informal recruitment centers, and advertisements recruiting Japanese workers to the mainland appeared regularly in Japanese-language newspapers in Hawaii. For example, in 1905, the following advertisement appeared in a local paper, "Employment offered in picking strawberries and tomatoes, planting beets, mining, and domestic service. Now is the time to go! … Apply to the Honolulu agency for further particulars, giving the name of your plantation" (US Senate, 1911a, p. 13). Consequently, many Okinawan laborers migrated to the mainland where wages were higher and where the work was supposedly less demanding than work in Hawaii. According to Baishiro Tamashiro, at this time, laborers in Hawaii, earned approximately one dollar a day (ESOHP, 1981, p. 367). In contrast, a Japanese laborer on the mainland of the United States could earn as much as $1.50 a day in wages (US Senate, 1911a, p. 13).

The Okinawan immigrant community that formed in California was essentially the product of secondary labor migrations. In other words, the Okinawan immigrants who had settled in the United States had worked elsewhere before they settled permanently in southern California. Dissatisfied with their working conditions on the plantations of Hawaii, the railroads of Canada, the mines of Mexico, several re-migrated to the continental United States before and after the enforcement of the Gentlemen's Agreement. In 1907, an American immigration official at the Mexican border stated:

> Japanese laborers in large numbers are, and have been for months, flocking to both Canada and Mexico. That in the vast majority of cases their intention … is to enter the United States. In other words, these laborers merely use foreign contiguous territory as a place of temporary sojourn while perfecting

> plans for proceeding to points in this country (US Bureau of Immigration, 1907, pp. 72–73).

Initially, the railroads in the western United States were an important source of employment for thousands of Japanese workers and for several hundred workers from Okinawa. Around 1910, as many as 316 Okinawans worked on the construction of railroads in North America, joining workers from Mexico, Greece, and Italy (Kobashigawa, 1988, pp. 320–21). Although the workforce in the railroad industry was internationally diverse, work responsibilities, wages and opportunities for promotion varied according to race and nationality. For example, Mexican and Japanese workers were usually found working in railroad construction and maintenance, and the few who entered shops were generally paid lower wages than European immigrant workers. The least desirable type of work was usually given to non-European immigrants. "The dirty and distasteful work of engine wiping, boiler washing, and car cleaning is, for the most part, done by these new immigrant races," noted an US immigration official. "The Japanese and Mexicans are very conspicuous in all of them" (US Senate, 1911c, p. 42).

Japanese laborers and hundreds of Okinawan workers also found employment in California's lucrative and rapidly expanding agricultural industry as farm laborers. Skilled farm work and "indoor" labor such as working in canneries and in packing-houses often went to white workers and women. Furthermore, white workers often refused to work alongside non-white workers in the canneries and packing-houses (US Senate, 1911b, pp. 601–603, 614–16, 623–24). Thus, shut out of indoor farm work, Japanese immigrants found work as field laborers. Known as "blanket boys," Okinawan laborers followed the harvest season and moved from region to region (Kobashigawa, 1988). After these laborers accumulated some savings, they invested in businesses such as boardinghouses, restaurants, and pool halls, businesses that catered to other Japanese laborers. And before the passage of California's Alien Land Laws in 1913 and 1920, a few became independent farmers. After 1913, the vast majority of Okinawans who chose to stay in the United States became tenant farmers. They grew strawberries, garden vegetables, and cantaloupe in Los Angeles County, Fresno, and the Imperial Valley (Kobashigawa, 1988).

An observer of the Japanese in American agriculture concluded that the history of Japanese farming in America proved to be "rather tragic." Like many small farmers in the United States, Japanese immigrants had to compete with large agricultural corporations. They had to deal with pests, plant diseases, and intense heat. Farming was by no means an easy task, but for Japanese immigrant farmers in California, xenophobia and racial prejudice made rural life an even greater struggle. In 1932, Yamato Ichihashi concluded that "Japanese farming would have continued to develop … had it not been artificially checked by the imposition of legal disabilities upon the Japanese (Ichihashi, 1932, p. 164).

The racialization of the Japanese in the United States as non-white immigrants and as unassimilable aliens ultimately led to their eventual exclusion in 1924. Thus, from 1924 to the outbreak of the Pacific War, hopeful Japanese emigrants were forced to look beyond the United States and Hawaii as areas of settlement. Many therefore looked to South America, Southeast Asia, and areas within the expanding Japanese empire. Ironically, although the immigration laws of the United States were enforced on the continent and in Hawaii, they were not enforced in the Philippines which was an American dependency until 1934. As economist Ryoiichi Ishii has written, "In contrast to the situation that prevails in other Pacific possessions of the United States, there are no restrictions against Japanese emigration to the Philippines" (Ishii, 1937, p. 201). Consequently, many Japanese immigrants looked to the Philippines as a place of settlement.

The first Okinawans who migrated to the Philippines were recruited to build the Benguet Road in the northern Philippines. Filipinos, Chinese, Americans and other Japanese also worked on this public works project (Hayase, 1984, pp. 116–32). Early in its administration the Philippine Commission reported that the infrastructure of the Philippines was in desperate need of repair:

> The condition of all forms of public works was such as to retard the public service. Unimproved harbors, primitive roads, unbridged streams, and a crying need for schoolhouses was everywhere evident (US Bureau of Insular Affairs, 1913, p. 39).

And according to Grant K. Goodman, foreign labor was imported because many Filipinos had come to associate work on public projects as "forced labor" (Goodman, 1965, p. 190). Seeking foreign labor, American engineers found Okinawa to be a reliable source of labor, and as American writer Willard Price noted, Okinawan workers were used to complete the Benguet Road in Baguio (Price, 1936, p. 15). When the road was completed in 1904, many Okinawans returned to Okinawa, or re-migrated to other areas such as Hawaii and Canada, but several also remained in the Philippines finding employment in Mindanao's abaca industry.

For Okinawans, in particular, the Philippines became an ideal area of settlement. By the 1920s, a large and economically successful Okinawan immigrant community emerged in Davao, Mindanao. After the Benguet Road was completed, Okinawan labor recruiter Oshiro Kozo formed a partnership with Ohta Kyosaburo, a Japanese entrepreneur, and led a group of Japanese workers to Davao. Together they formed the Ohta Development Company which became one of Davao's leading abaca plantations. Because Oshiro was the vice-president of the company, numerous Okinawans found employment as managers, shopkeepers, and laborers on plantations and farms owned by the Ohta Development Company (Nakama, n.d.).

Through legal and extralegal means, many Okinawan immigrants quickly acquired land and became independent as well as tenant farmers. Acquiring land was an essential strategy of Okinawan immigrants in Davao. The earliest immigrants from Japan usually leased uncultivated lands from American and Filipino owners. And after negotiating an agreement with a landowner, they cleared land and prepared it for abaca cultivation (Hayase, 1984, pp. 185–88; Higa, n.d.). Once the land was cleared, they dug holes and planted abaca plants in orderly rows. A Filipino observer of Japanese abaca growers in Davao commented on the methods of Japanese immigrant farmers in Davao, "Selection of the land for planting, the variety of hemp to be raised, the manner of planting in seedlings, and the cutting of the plants for stripping, all undergo careful scrutiny" (Alvarez, 1934, p. 6). Another observer wrote, "The Japanese ... have converted virgin forests into seas of waving, green abaca fields from which is derived enormous wealth" (Sulit, 1929, pp. 3–4). By 1928, Davao which had once been referred to as "the most thoroughly American community in the Philippines" had become a predominantly Japanese colony (Hayase, 1984; *Mindanao Herald*, November 24, 1906 and May 5, 1928). And as opportunities in the Japanese-controlled abaca industry expanded, many immigrants from Okinawa migrated to Davao, particularly during the 1930s.

Immigrant institutions and immigrant identities

As outsiders in their new communities, Okinawan immigrants in the United States and the Philippines established separate immigrant institutions to help them negotiate their way in society. First and foremost, the *sonjinkai*, the village association, was the most basic organization of these immigrant communities. This institution was at once a social organization and a mutual aid association. Second to the *sonjinkai* was the larger *kenjinkai*, the prefectural association, which sponsored cultural activities such as picnics, musical and dance performances, and sporting events (Kimura, 1981a). Okinawan immigrants also joined larger Japanese Associations such as the Japanese Agricultural Association in California. And when reporting births and deaths within their families, Okinawan immigrants regularly reported to their local Japanese Consulate so that such events would be recorded in their family registers in Okinawa (JARP).

Although they established and participated in Japanese-style organizations, the purpose of these institutions varied according to location. The greatest influence on the development of these institutions was perhaps interaction and contact with non-Okinawans and non-Japanese. Contact with peoples of different racial and ethnic backgrounds played a significant role in the construction of Okinawan immigrant identities. And the examples from the United States and the Philippines provide some of the most interesting examples in the range of identities that emerged in the Okinawan diaspora.

Influenced by their surroundings, Okinawan immigrants in California joined associations that were modeled after or were modified to resemble middle-class American institutions. For example, many Okinawans joined Japanese Protestant churches. As early as 1915, Okinawan immigrants in Los Angeles began attending services at the Hollywood Independent Church. Six years later many immigrants from Okinawa began attending Oriental Missionary Society meetings which were held at the Hollywood Trinity Church. Because of the charismatic leadership of a Reverend Kuzuhara and because of the church's emphasis on "aggressive evangelism," the Japanese Holiness Church quickly became one of the more popular churches among Okinawan immigrants. During the 1930s, the church rarely addressed political issues. Instead, it promoted cultural reform and spiritual salvation. Among many church members, the response to racial discrimination and economic struggle was prayer, cultural development, and education (Kobashigawa, 1988, pp. 408–12).

In contrast, at the same time, a few daring Okinawans in southern California joined the Communist Party, arguing that they had much in common with other immigrants and laborers, regardless of racial and ethnic background. Rather than focusing on cultural activities and religious salvation, Okinawan immigrant communists and their sympathizers criticized global capitalism, nationalism, and racism. They were also especially critical of Japanese expansion in Asia. In 1932, disillusioned with American capitalism and critical of Japanese militarism, the most radical and vocal members of the community left for the Soviet Union. Although many Okinawans may have sympathized with the *Akas*, "the Reds," the pervasive conservatism of California had a great influence on the Okinawan immigrant community (Kobashigawa, 1998).

Many Okinawan immigrants who were sympathetic toward communism became leaders of the Okinawan Prefectural Association in the 1930s. Frightened by the anti-communist mood in California and the United States in general, the leadership of the Okinawa Kenjinkai de-emphasized political activism, and by the late 1930s, the leadership and members of the Okinawa Prefectural Association began encouraging one another to develop their skills in art, music, literature, and performance. In other words, in an attempt to unify the Okinawan immigrant community which in previous years was divided by politics, the leaders of the Okinawa Prefectural Association turned its attention away from politics and toward cultural development (Kobashigawa, 1988, pp. 48–64; Kobashigawa, 1998). Needless to say, communism had divided the Okinawan immigrant community in the United States as it had similarly done to other immigrant groups.

Looking to the future, the Okinawan Prefectural Association in California remodeled itself in order to provide a solid base for Okinawan Nisei to develop into good American citizens. Rather than focusing on the politics of Okinawa and Japan, the leadership of the Okinawa Kenjinkai, many of whom had been in the United

States for at least two decades, called for Okinawan immigrants in southern California to think of themselves as Americans. The new leadership encouraged its members to think of themselves as part of a larger multiethnic and multiracial society, a community broader than the immigrant community itself. Within this context, the new leadership recognized that as Japanese immigrants, immigrants from Okinawa needed an organization which would serve to help them effectively withstand the daily pressures of racism and discrimination. Calling for an end to the older immigrant organization, the new leadership of the Okinawa Prefectural Association recognized a need to unify the community:

> At the time when the Okinawa Kaigai Kyokai first appeared, anti-Japanese feeling in the United States was not yet so disturbing. In South America, Japanese were quite welcome. Since then, however, we have had an anti-Japanese land law, followed by the Oriental Exclusion Act (which only allowed for minor exceptions). Worse yet, existing civil rights were removed on various pretexts, and it began to appear as if the immigrants were facing repatriation and deportation ... However we Okinawans come to be here, whether originally on a tour of inspection, or freely in search of work, or at great risk to their lives, we are all now in the same boat ... We should regard mutual aid as the source of our advancement as a people (Kobashigawa, 1988, pp. 50–51).

As Ben Kobashigawa has argued, before the outbreak of World War II, strong political differences divided the pre-war Okinawan immigrant community in southern California, and no one organization represented the interest of all immigrants from Okinawa (Kobashigawa, 1998).

In contrast, much larger than the Okinawan immigrant community in California, the Okinawan colony in Davao, Mindanao gave the appearance of a tightly-knit community. Furthermore, the issue of Japanese politics and Japanese expansion did not divide the community. Falling within the Japanese sphere of influence, the Japanese colony of Davao, of which one-third of the population was from Okinawa, openly expressed their ties with Japan. However, unlike their urban Japanese counterparts in the City of Davao, Okinawan immigrants lived on the edge of the Davao frontier. In these sparsely populated areas, these immigrants were able to recreate Okinawan village life in the rural districts of Davao. Because of their conspicuous presence and distinct culture, Filipinos often referred to the Okinawans as "the other Japanese." And as historian Cecil Cody has written, "One feature of the Japanese community stood out clearly to their Filipino neighbors: there were two kinds of Japanese in Davao – the non-Okinawans and the Okinawans. They dressed and spoke differently and discrimination existed between them" (Cody, 1959, p. 174).

The persons with whom Okinawan immigrants interacted were the Japanese business elite, American and Filipino plantation owners, Chinese peddlers, and the indigenous peoples of Davao. Cecil Cody has written that "it was the Okinawans who tended to live most intimately with their neighbors, especially in the areas of Bagobo settlement" (Cody, 1959, p. 184). Hiring the indigenous peoples as workers, Okinawan immigrants sometimes developed friendly relations with them, but more often than not, Okinawan immigrants believed and perpetuated stereotypes that the indigenous peoples of Mindanao were poor, uncivilized, and uncultured (Igei, n.d.).

In contrast, when Okinawan immigrants interacted with the Japanese business elite of Davao, they became terribly self-conscious of their status as laborers and farmers. Consequently, Okinawan immigrants looked to education as a means of improving their social status in Davao. The Japanese school in Davao, which at that time was staffed and financed by the Japanese Ministry of Education, became an important institution to Okinawan immigrants. In these schools, Philippine-born Okinawan children were taught to become subjects of the Japanese empire. In addition to mathematics and English, these children were schooled in Japanese ethics and Japanese history. As one former student recalled, the emphasis on a Japanese imperial education was especially great because the students in Davao were the sons and daughters of immigrants (Yonashiro, n.d.).

The schooling of Philippine-born children of Okinawan immigrants and the parents' support of the Japanese school occurred during the 1930s just as Japan invaded China and as the Philippines was establishing its own government. Needless to say, outside observers interpreted this immigrant passion for education as ultranationalism and potential espionage. Japanese immigrant laborers and the abaca farmers, many of whom were from Okinawa, quickly became objects of suspicion. As one Filipino nationalist wrote, "Japan's agricultural development of Davao may be disguised penetration that will someday result in the annexation of the Philippines to the Island Empire" (Nano, 1935, p. 23). Needless to say, by the 1940s, Japanese immigration to and settlement in the Philippines had become equated with war and imperialism. The equation led to tragic consequences for the Japanese colony in Davao. With the outbreak of war in the Philippines, Japanese farmers and laborers were conscripted into the Japanese army. Japanese troops in Davao were poorly trained and ill-equipped. When American troops landed in Davao in 1945, they relied on local Filipino troops to fight the Japanese army (Morton, 1953, p. 586). While Okinawan men served in the military, their wives and children fled to and attempted to hide in the mountains of Davao. Without adequate food and supplies several died of starvation. Several also became casualties of warfare (Nakama, n.d.; Yabiku, n.d.). By war's end, approximately 17,000 Japanese – soldiers and civilians – were killed; about 12,000 surrendered, and approximately 8,200 were declared missing (Smith, 1953, p. 647). Among the missing and the casualties were many Okinawans.

Conclusions

The Okinawan immigrant experience shows that the Japanese immigrant experience was varied and complex. Despite legal disabilities, racial discrimination, and intraethnic conflict, Okinawan immigrants were amazingly resilient and were building vibrant communities in foreign lands. Sadly, the Pacific War disrupted community growth as Japanese immigrants in the continental United States were interned and as survivors of the Japanese immigrant colony in Davao, Mindanao were repatriated to occupied Japan. They were gathered in refugee camps, separated by gender, and transported back to Japan on American military vessels (Ajifu, n.d.).

Although there was great intellectual and cultural diversity within the Japanese diaspora, by World War II, many nations – the United States and the Philippines included – viewed Japanese immigrants as enemy aliens and as unassimilable and undesirable immigrants. As the Okinawan example shows, these perceptions were false and tragically misleading. Japanese immigrant identification with Japan varied within the diaspora. Unfortunately, nationalism and nativism and ultimately war within the Pacific region undermined the potential to create a tolerant and cosmopolitan Pacific world during the early twentieth century.

Note

I would like to thank Jon Gjerde, Andrew Barshay, Michael Omi, Ben Kobashigawa, James Sobredo, and Masao Suzuki for their advice. I thank Yoshiko Yamamoto for her assistance with the Japanese sources. And I would like to thank Patricia Sakurai and Tan Lik Tong for proofreading this paper. Any errors are mine. Finally, I would especially like to thank the anonymous donors of UC Berkeley's Department of History Special Needs Funds for enabling me to attend the Pacific Centuries conference.

References

Ajifu, Tatsu, Kin Township Oral History Collection, Okinawa, Japan: Kin Township, n.d.

Alvarez, David, "Why the Davao Hemp Industry is Successful," *The Philippine Journal of Commerce and Industry*, Vol. 10, No. 11 (1934), p. 6.

Aniya, Masaaki, "Kengai Dekasegi to Kennai Ijuu," trans. Wesley Ueunten, *Okinawa Kenshi*, Vol. 7, Tokyo: Sentoraru Insatsu, 1974.

Anon., "Len Kew Kwo che leo: A Brief History of Lew Chew, containing an account of the situation and extent of that Country," The Chinese Repository, 1837.

Brunton, R.H., "Notes Taken During a Visit to Okinawashima-Loochoo Islands," *Transactions of the Asiatic Society of Japan*, Vol. IV (1876).

Chamberlain, Basil Hall, "The LuChu Islands and their Inhabitants," *The Geographical Journal*, Vol. V, No. 4 (1895), pp. 289–319, 416–545.

Christy, Alan S., "The Making of Imperial Subjects in Okinawa," *Positions: East Asia Cultures Critique*, Vol. 1, No. 3 (1993), pp. 607–39.

Cinel, Dino, *From Italy to San Francisco: The immigrant experience*, Stanford: Stanford University Press, 1982.

Cody, Cecil E., "The Japanese Way of Life in Prewar Davao," *Philippine Studies*, Vol. 7, No. 2 (1959), pp. 172–86.

Cole, Allan (ed.), *A Scientist with Perry in Japan: The journal of Dr. James Morrow*, Chapel Hill: University of North Carolina, 1947.

Curtin, Philip, "Migration in the Tropical World," in Virginia Yans-McLaughlin (ed.), *Immigration Reconsidered: History, sociology, and politics*, New York: Oxford University Press, 1990.

Ethnic Studies Oral History Project (1981), *Uchinanchu: A history of Okinawans in Hawaii.*

Figal, Gerald, "Okinawa's Cornerstone of Peace," *Positions: East Asia Cultures Critique*, Vol. 5, No. 3 (1997), pp. 744–78.

Galenson, David W., "The Rise and Fall of Indentured Servitude in the Americas," *Journal of Economic History*, Vol. XLIV, No. 1 (1984), pp. 1–26.

Gjerde, Jon, *From Peasants to Farmers: The migration from Balestrand, Norway to the Upper Middle West*, Cambridge: Cambridge University Press, 1985.

Goodman, Grant K, "A Flood of Immigration' – Patterns and Problems of Japanese Migration to the Philippines During the First Four Decades of the Twentieth-Century," *Philippine Historical Review*, Vol. 1, No. 1. (1965), pp. 170–93.

Hawks, Francis L., *Narrative of the Expedition of an American Squadron to the China Seas and Japan*, New York: Appleton and Company, 1856.

Hayase, Shinzo (1984), "Tribes, Settlers, and Administrators on a Frontier: Economic development and social change in Davao, Southeastern Mindanao, the Philippines, 1899–1941," PhD dissertation, Murdoch University, Western Australia.

Higa, Todo, Kin Township Oral History Collection, Okinawa, Japan: Kin Township, n.d.

Ichihashi, Yamato, *Japanese in the United States: A critical study of the problems of the Japanese immigrants and their children* (Stanford: Stanford University Press, 1932).

Igei, Goze, Kin Township Oral History Collection, Okinawa, Japan: Kin Township, n.d.

Ishii, Ryoichi, *Population Pressure and Economic Life in Japan*, Chicago: University of Chicago, 1937.

Ishikawa, Tomonori, "Okinawa to Imin: Okinawa-ken Imin ni kansuru Bunken Shokai" ["Okinawa and Immigration: An introduction to documents related to Okinawan immigration"], *Shin-Okinawan Bungaku* [*New Okinawan Sources*], No. 45 (1980).

——, "A Study of the Historical Geography of Early Okinawan Immigrants to the Hawaiian Islands," in *Uchinanchu: A History of Okinawans in Hawaii*, Honolulu: University of Hawaii, 1981.

Ishikawa, Tomonori and Taira, Koji, "The Geographical Distribution of Emigrants by Place of Origin: The Case of Okinawa," in James G. Scoville (ed.), *Status Influence in Third World Labor Markets: Caste, Gender, and Custom*, Berlin: Walter de Gruyter, 1991.

Japanese American Research Project (JARP), Special Collections Library, University of California at Los Angeles.

Kerr, George, *Okinawa: The History of an Island People*, Tokyo: Charles Tuttle and Company, 1954.

Kimura, Yukiko, "Locality Clubs as the Basic Unit of the Social Organization of Okinawans in Hawaii," in *Uchinanchu: A History of Okinawans in Hawaii*, Honolulu: University of Hawaii, 1981a.

——, "Social-Historical Background of the Okinawans in Hawaii," in *Uchinanchu: A History of Okinawans in Hawaii*, Honolulu: University of Hawaii, 1981b.

Kobashigawa, Ben, trans., *History of the Okinawans in North America*, Los Angeles: Asian American Studies Center, UCLA, 1988.

——, "Antinomies of Okinawan Immigrant Identity: Ethnic pride and shame within a double minority," unpublished paper (1998).

Mazumdar, Sucheta, "Colonial Impact and Punjabi Emigration to the United States," in Edna Bonacich and Lucie Cheng (eds), *Labor Immigration Under Capitalism: Asian workers in the United States before World War II*, Berkeley: University of California Press, 1984.

Morris-Suzuki, Tessa, "A Descent into the Past: The frontier in the construction of Japanese identity," in Donald Denoon, Mark Hudson, Gavan McCormack, and Tessa Morris-Suzuki (eds), *Multicultural Japan: Paleolithic to Postmodern*, Cambridge: Cambridge University Press, 1996.

Morton. Louis. *The Fall of the Philippines* (Washington, DC: Department of the Army. 1953).

Nano, Teodoro V., "To Save or not to Save Davao," *The Commonwealth Advocate*, October–November (1935), p. 23.

Nakama, Nabe, Kin Township Oral History Collection, Okinawa, Japan: Kin Township, n.d.

Nakasone, Ronald (ed.), *Reflections on the Okinawan Experience: Essays commemorating 100 Years of Okinawan immigration*, Fremont, CA: Dharma Cloud Publishers, 1996.

Northrup, David, *Indentured Labor in the Age of Imperialism, 1834–1922*, Cambridge and New York: Cambridge University Press, 1995.

Price, Willard, "Japan in the Philippines," *The Commonwealth Advocate*, July (1936), pp. 14–17, 25.

Sakihara, Mitsugu, "History of Okinawa," in *Uchinanchu: A History of Okinawans in Hawaii*, Honolulu: University of Hawaii, 1981.

Smith, George, *Lewchew and Lewchewans: Being a narrative of a visit to Lewchew, or Loo Choo in October, 1850*, London: T. Hatchard, 1853.

Smith, Robert Ross, *Triumph in the Philippines*, Washington, DC: Department of the Army, 1953.

Sulit, Pablo F., "Young and Prosperous Davao," *The Philippine Journal of Commerce and Industry*, July (1929), 3–4.

Taeuber, Irene B., "The Population of the Ryukyu Islands," *Population Index*, Vol. 21, No. 4 (1955), pp. 233–63.

Tamura, Hiroshi, *A Study of Ryukyuan Communal Villages*, originally published 1927, trans. Shogo Oiyama, Tokyo: Oka Shoin, 1955.

Tigner, James L. (1956), "The Okinawans in Latin America," unpublished PhD dissertation, Stanford University.

US Bureau of Immigration, *Annual Report of the Commissioner General of Immigration to the Secretary of Labor for the Fiscal Year ended June 30, 1907* (1907).

US Bureau of Insular Affairs, *The Philippine Islands* (1913).

US Senate, *Reports of the Immigration Commission. Immigrants in Industries ... Japanese and East Indians* (1911a).

US Senate, *Reports of the Immigration Commission. Immigrants in Industries ... Agriculture* (1911b).

US Senate, *Reports of the Immigration Commission. Immigrants in Industries ... Diversified Industries* (1911c).

Yabiku, Shuku, Kin Township Oral History Collection, Okinawa, Japan: Kin Township, n.d.

Yonashiro, Shigeru, Kin Township Oral History Collection, Okinawa, Japan: Kin Township, n.d.

12

Hong Kong: Constitutional Development and Corporate Culture

Frank H.H.King

The charge: 150 years without enfranchisement

The extraordinary complaint comes from all sides and is particularly relevant to any study of the history of the Pacific Rim. Hong Kong had been British for some 150 years and yet Hong Kong had not been granted a constitution which gave the right to vote until virtually the eve of the territory's retrocession to China. In this context we should overlook the claim, legitimate in itself, that, by coming to and remaining in Hong Kong, people had been voting with their feet.[1] This essay attempts a more traditional approach.

Many Hong Kong residents believe that if only Britain had given them the vote earlier then ... It is not clear what these naturally concerned people really have in mind. If the conclusion to the wish is "then everything would have been all right," it is surely unrealistic. But there is the feeling that if Britain had granted a fully-democratic constitution at some time in the past, exactly when is, not surprisingly, not always stated, a government based on elections would have been fully established and operating successfully, two arguable assumptions, when the question of the 1998 end of the New Territories lease became important. There are many in Britain who, in support, feel it a matter of shame that such a constitution was not given Hong Kong, and they supported ill-conceived measures to enact more liberal constitutional arrangements, making vague but unbelievable threats as to what they would do if China failed to accept every last minute enactment.[2] China, on the other hand, asked why, if Britain had not granted a liberal constitution earlier, it should do so on the eve of withdrawing, leaving China responsible for an untried system.

One approach to the controversy is to examine parallels in the history of the British Empire. But these are hard to find, especially if we select only those territories which have elements common to Hong Kong. If, for example, we divide former and present British colonies into three categories arising from their history and/or British attitudes to their status, (i) colonies of settlement, (ii) colonies in trust, and (iii) special purpose territories, Hong Kong would be classified as "special purpose," a decision to be discussed below.

In the first two categories some achieved democracy, some had democracy thrust upon them. In the third category, some are viable without external direction, some are, apparently, viable, and among the latter is Hong Kong. And yet even among category three territories, parallels are hard to find. Heligoland was so obviously an aggressive statement that it had to be retroceded. Gibraltar has a population capable of managing their affairs in a territory claimed by the proximate power, but the people are neither descendants of the original inhabitants nor are their origins in Spain. There is something of a similarity here with the Falklands, whose people are not related to those of Argentina. Singapore, in so many ways similar to Hong Kong, did not seek independence but merger with its neighbor, the then Federation of Malaya, a country which offered no basic objection to a democratic development matching theirs. The scattered islands which constituted the balance of this category have either been assigned to some other territory, as, for example, the Cocos Islands to Australia, or Ascension Island, for example, left as colonies directly subject to London.

The reason for Hong Kong

Hong Kong is *sui generis* and has to be considered as such. This much will become clear through a historical exposition during which one may reflect on the question "at what point would the grant of "democracy" have been appropriate?" Indeed there are three characteristics of this history which will be relevant, (i) the specific purpose of the territory and the nature of China's tolerance of it, (ii) the rationale of Hong Kong's constitution in the context of that purpose and tolerance, and (iii) the changing composition of Hong Kong's population.

Hong Kong was established for specific purposes, and its society and government were designed to further them. Or, put another way, the very question stated with such sincerity and concern, that is, why Hong Kong was not awarded a more democratic constitution in the some 150 years of British rule, rests on a misunderstanding. There was a colonial Hong Kong for some 150 years, but neither geographically, culturally, nor politically was it the same Hong Kong, nor did it have a single identifiable electorate with a common understanding of Hong Kong. Underlying the question are assumptions that a constitution suitable for one period must consequently have been suitable for another, that had the need for constitutional evolution been recognized the British government was free to adjust despite the objective realities of the territory in relationship to its origins, its stated purpose, and its geographical context. There is a failure to accept that votes are given to people, not to territories, and that the composition and characteristics of the people, their purposes for being in the territory, their concepts of their role in that territory change over time.

In the 1830s British merchants, using the arguments of free trade, were no longer willing to accept the role assigned them by the East India Company. Free of the Company's tutelage, the merchants still needed security in dealing with the Chinese. This they demanded through their government in London. As one consequence of the First Sino-British War, British forces occupied Chusan and Hong Kong, but it was the latter which, despite its southern location, was seen as an appropriate safe-house for the merchants, where British law would prevail and where Britain could base the forces necessary to execute its China policy. Chusan, in a sense better located near the mouth of the Yangtze River, was rejected not only because it was being held conditionally until the indemnity were paid, but significantly because there was a flourishing Chinese community there. Britain did not want a colony in trust, with responsibility for an alien people. Lord Palmerston might complain that Hong Kong was a barren island, but that is precisely what was wanted.[3] Hong Kong, with its minimal native Chinese population, would become a base for the military, depot for the merchant, residence only for those servicing a minimal government, the military, and the merchant, all under the control of a governor ruling with virtually unchecked authority, except after appeal back to London.[4] Here was also a situation where the military had their own commander and merchants had their own community; as British subjects they also had their political rights, to be exercised, however, in London where overall policy could be determined and transmitted to the governor.

The consequent constitutional structure

From the very beginning, therefore, the constitution of Hong Kong was authoritative and executive-led. The territory of Hong Kong was obtained from China for a specific purpose, indeed at first it was linked directly to that purpose by appointing one man as both Governor of Hong Kong (under the Colonial Secretary) and Minister Plenipotentiary and Superintendent of Trade (under the Foreign Secretary). The British rule of Chinese subjects was recognized as a *de facto* reality but rejected as a voluntary intention. Two statements, the first by Lord Aberdeen, the Foreign Secretary, and the second by Lord Stanley, the Colonial Secretary to the Governor in 1843 state the position unequivocally.

> HM's Govt conceive that any more popular form of government would be wholly unsuited to the existing or probable condition of the island.[5]

> Hong Kong is different from all other colonies; it was occupied not with a view to Colonization but for diplomatic commercial and military purposes.[6]

Consequently, the governor governed with the advice of an executive council and a legislative council, composed entirely of officials. He could override his councils and he could suspend senior officials, subject only to his reporting his arguments to London. And that is where, as noted above, the senior partners and/or "correspondents" of many leading British firms would reside, possibly with political influence. Arbitrary rule in Hong Kong was subject to review in London, and it was this which provided a telling argument when, during negotiations with China in the early 1980s, Hong Kong "belongers" faced the prospect of limited democracy without the safeguard of review in Britain. Certainly the Hong Kong government took into account the views of residents, but indirectly. There was no mutual understanding between merchant and governor. One governor was unfairly described in the relatively mild *China Mail* as a "humbug ... not of the vain, good-natured, addle-pated humbug, [but one] who never did or expected a disinterested action, or enforced a policy even when persuaded it was right, if he also felt persuaded it would require to be defended."[7] Governor Sir John Davis had argued successfully against any merchant representation on the Legislative Council on the grounds, not wholly accurate, that they were "all" engaged in the opium trade.

With this background it is not too difficult to understand that there was a prejudice against democratization which was fundamental to the very establishment of the colony. But further factors were at work. The potential voters of Hong Kong, with the exception of the original villagers and fishermen, were not necessarily British subjects, nor was their presence in the territory of their own volition, nor were the majority intending permanent residence, nor was the focus of their loyalty the "Colony of Hong Kong," nor did they need government for the performance of tasks which today are considered fundamental to any administration. Business conflicts, for example, could be adjudicated by chambers of commerce, schools could be provided by missionaries, religion by the groups concerned – there was no "established" church. The government for its part could not accept the proposition that its policy should be subject to direction by those outside government, in part because the government was not designed wholly for the conduct of Hong Kong affairs; the colony was part of an imperial polity, the demands of which might conflict with the narrower concerns of Hong Kong merchants and other residents.[8] As the population grew, taxation and government expenditures became an issue. The solution was to add unofficials to the councils and generally to consider advice from them, especially on fiscal matters. But the majority, the appointment of "unofficials," and any informal understandings continued *de jure* subject to the governor"s will.

Corporate culture and the potential electorate

There are thus many themes which might be considered in any analysis of Hong Kong's constitutional development. This paper is concerned, primarily, with the nature of the electorate, an examination which describes the corporate culture of the territory, of the absence of any pretence of a social contract, of any acceptance that the will of the majority should prevail.[9] Democracy was not only contrary to the formal Constitution, the Royal Instructions, it was contrary to the logic of settlement.

Furthermore, the implementation of policies designed to achieve political and social stability consistent with the purpose of the Colony was hindered by the impact of new forces, destablizing or challenging the policy goals even before they were fully achieved. For each of the several periods in Hong Kong's history and the corresponding stages of corporate culture, this essay considers the impact on relations between Hong Kong and China, between colonial and Chinese resident, and asks whether a more careful exposition of these relationships would not now be helpful. But primarily the absence of a true electorate is considered in terms of the corporate cultures of the territory.

An overview Pre-World War II, Hong Kong had been, at one and the same time, a very British colony, an international trading post, a point of contact between Chinese and Western cultures, and, contrary to expectations, a home to a Chinese population of growing stature. The business culture could be intensely inbred, suddenly and unexpectedly dynamic, although, in the interwar period, destitute of innovation. All of this had an immediate and definitive impact on what Hong Kong "was," its essence.

Despite observable lines of continuity, post-war Hong Kong had to a large extent to begin again. The same geography, in many cases the same multinationals, and the same Chinese families re-establishing themselves, but a different external context resulting in different cultures and consequences.

One may define pre-1970 Hong Kong as a collection of disparate corporate cultures leavened by the presence of outspoken, in some cases eccentric, individuals. But the whole lacked a common will, a common identity; as a potential body politic Hong Kong was flawed. In consequence there was consent, reluctant on occasion, that the management of the territory should be the responsibility of a non-elected government advised but not dictated to by the leaders of the most important cultures.

To a large degree this separateness, accompanied by an "advised" government was satisfactory, because the individuals involved did not associate themselves, as individuals, with Hong Kong as a mutually agreed, conscious social and political unit. One scholar has argued that the Hong Kong government's legitimacy arose from its success.[10] This is consistent with the British government's position, stated above, that it did not consider Hong Kong to be, nor did it suppose that Hong Kong ought to be, a body politic. Indeed, as the people of Hong Kong did not compose a society with a social contract, in what sense would majority voting prove acceptable or meaningful? If Hong Kong were to serve its purpose as a base for British activities as determined from London and in the context of the Treaty with China, there had to be a British headman administering British law under British sovereignty. The governor was to be held responsible by the British government for the success of the colony in this context; accordingly he was told that his councils were advisory and so composed as to present no "opposition" in the formal sense. The members were all officials. Thus the developing opposition of Hong Kong's first colonial Treasurer, Robert Montgomery Martin, in 1846 met with rebuke and eventual acceptance of his allegedly "conditional" resignation.[11]

Government and merchant, the rationale for authoritarian rule

This constitutional arrangement would seem at first glance to be contrary to the Colony's purpose in serving the British business community. Indeed, the exchange of insults, publicly by merchants and in correspondence from the governor, supports the thought that the arrangements could not be permanent, and yet they could, initially at least, be explained. The governor noted that the "damned" business men were "all" involved in some way with the opium trade – an exaggeration but still a relevant point – and consequently unsuited to be on his councils. But even granting that suitable merchant representation could be found, the British government's colonial policies would provide a more cogent argument for a continuation of the "garrison" approach to Hong Kong's government. As the colony grew and Chinese immigration developed, non-government representatives from the merchant class taken together with the likely increased demand for some degree of elected representation would result in a merchant advised government ruling a majority of non-British residents, including non-British merchants and Chinese. These latter were even less bonded socially to the territory and many could be regarded, at least in the early years, as transient. On the other hand, to permit some form of majority rule, that is, rule by the Chinese majority through an elected legislative council, would contradict the purpose of the Colony, which had been ceded by China with the argument that British rule was to prevail.

Therefore significant constitutional change, in the sense of democratization, could not come to Hong Kong until the colony ceased to be seen in terms of its original acquisition, that is, until it had changed from a garrison base to a colony of settlement. *Sound* constitutional development could not occur until the population were focused on Hong Kong as a separate political unit, understood the electoral system, and were able to accept majority decisions. And that would not come until the 1980s, coincident with a new context of change of sovereignty and new terms set by the new sovereign, thus disturbing the evolutionary process.

Discontinuity in the merchant community

Although one may accept the conceptual concern of the imperial authority in Britain over a government advised by only one section of the population, the British merchants; it was indeed for them – and for their military protection – that the territory was established.

In the period to say the 1880s the merchants and their houses were the creation of the breakthrough to Free Trade; they were aggressive, uninhibited, and critical of any governmental interference. There was a numerical predominance of single proprietors and partners, with juniors aspiring either to eventual business independence or to senior partnerships. The staff was drawn from the China coast. Whoever was there was hired. But who was there? It was a mixed group, and their employment was often haphazard, unsuccessful, frustrating, with a high rate of turnover. A three-tier system was nevertheless discernible at least in embryo: (i) the Western merchant was entrepreneur and proprietor; (ii) the miscellaneous peoples (other than Chinese) who found themselves in Hong Kong or a Treaty Port were destined for clerical and sub-management roles, and (iii) the Chinese were employed for contacts with China, for the handling of cash, and, at quite another level, for menial tasks. In this earlier period, the Portuguese fit uncertainly into the second category. When a more formal structure emerged, the Westerners in the second group, those, that is, hired in the East for managerial positions, virtually disappeared, being replaced by juniors who not only aspired to top management positions, but had been brought East with the intention of training them for those posts. This left the Portuguese alone in category two, not only performing the clerical tasks (this was shared with the juniors from Europe) but destined never to move beyond them.

These divisions in the community made, or appeared to make in the context of mid-nineteenth-century political thinking, a fully representative legislature based on majority rule an impossibility. On the other hand, the Colonial Office in London agreed that a governor could not rule effectively, advised only by his officials, in isolation and subject on occasion to the increasingly vitriolic criticism of his fellow-citizens. A first step was the agreement whereby the General Chamber of Commerce would *nominate* one of their members who, if found acceptable, the governor would then *appoint* to one of his councils.[12] The nominee represented not all residents in some geographical area but a functional constituency – and even then, only imperfectly. Indeed, the natural tendency for such a nominee to come from the senior ranks of the largest companies, while it appeared to overcome discontinuity within the merchant sector, in fact narrowed the field. In consequence government was advised by an elite. It was only a matter of time before the same principle, with the same elitist consequences, would be applied to other constituencies, including representatives of the Chinese community.

This left out an interesting group, the juniors. As long as all communities were agreed that their interests were separate and that there was only limited interchange, and that connected with business, the juniors could associate themselves with their own seniors, in the sense that they would delay their political role until they were in a position to exercise it with senior merchant status. Perhaps the point can be seen more clearly in the negative, in an example taken from the 1920s. There were social and athletic clubs to which Chinese were not admitted as members (as there were Chinese clubs to which Westerners were not admitted). This created little friction, say, in a rugby football club located in a territory where no Chinese played (or, one would assume, *wanted* to play) rugby. The issue of admittance did not arise. But by the 1920s Chinese returned from England, or perhaps from other Treaty Ports, could play and wanted to play. The juniors wanted them in the club. The older members of the club had turned a matter of mutually acceptable cultural choice into a permanent concept of separation; they vetoed the idea, and the juniors, who were dependent on them as superiors in the firm, were powerless.[13]

Communities and corporate culture, social discontinuities

The hardening of the categories and in the role-playing of each community was at least partly the consequence of the increasing size and formal organizational requirements of the leading firms, including the Hongkong Bank. Although there were exceptions, all recruitment and early training was accomplished in Britain (for British firms) and in other European countries or the Americas as appropriate. The consequence was not only that the Portuguese were fixed in category two, but that a British firm would hire only from Britain, the practical consequence of which was that they hired only British subjects, etc. Hong Kong became even more a place of "communities" in need of a government which accepted advice but which retained control in the interests of *all* the communities.

The social life reflected the separation, with the communities from time to time finding each other, often in small ways. In the 1920s one taipan's wife, a lady perhaps educated in the tradition fictionalized by Angela Brazil, was faced with a new problem.[14] Her husband had invited a senior Chinese businessman from outside Hong Kong to spend the afternoon with them in their house on the Peak, and the Chinese was bringing his wife! The lady had no experience in such a thing. What did you do with a Chinese wife? How did you entertain her? How would she mix with the other guests. And then the incredible relief. The lady in question played a very good game of tennis. There was nothing further to worry about. But that such attitudes, such crises could exist, suggests that the separation determined by the business organization, by, if you will, the prevailing business or corporate culture, impacted on the whole of society, reinforcing the role of government ruling in their combined interests as reflected by advisers from the top. Government faced a potential electorate between the members of which, generally speaking, there was not only no communication but also no means, no will, and no way in which there could be such communication.[15] This was not a basis for enfranchisement and "the vote." The authoritarian government had to control such a legislature and its advice had to be tempered by attention to colonial precedents and Colonial Office policy. If in such circumstances the councils were composed of a majority of elected representatives, however the electorate might be defined, despite any theoretical question relative to its legitimacy, government would eventually have to accept that its executive was responsible to those councils. This course, the possibility of which was seen from the first, was unacceptable and contradicted the very purpose of Hong Kong's treaty-based existence.

Particularism The discontinuities in society were exaggerated by the nature of corporate culture. Corporate control depended to a great extent on the bonding of an officer elite, through London training, subsequent living in a mess on the Peak, sports – all encouraging a specific loyalty and a rivalry with the juniors of other hongs, leaving little or no room for further experimentation. This particularness was modified only by membership of clubs or in "games," which brought one into contact with contemporaries from other hongs, but not with other communities.

For an understanding of Hong Kong's political history it is important to appreciate that this exclusiveness was a mutual characteristic. Much has been said on the subject of intercommunal marriages; the European employee of a major hong (company *or* corporation) was not permitted to marry a Chinese. There were several reasons for this, some related to the question of corporate culture. In a British hong the presence of a foreign wife, a white Russian, a French lady, caused difficulties; the problem was not racial. Hongkong Bank officers assigned to French territories did on occasion marry French wives, but their careers could, in consequence, be confined. The objection to marrying a Chinese was in part cultural among people who were constantly together socially and in part business, the fear of an officer being influenced by a power outside corporate control. And this must be understood in the context that the corporate culture depended on an association of officers who had bonded on the playing fields of Beckenham (in the case of the Hongkong Bank) and whose continued sole focus of loyalty remained with the corporation. There were no sophisticated methods of controlling a bank manager with the corporation's full powers of attorney operating at a distance where formal control was impractical and where the manager could not easily be visited by his superiors.

This was not a one-way barrier. In Siam, for example, where social intercourse between Westerner and Siamese was more likely, any suggestion of an affection between a junior and a Thai lady, that is a Thai of a class suitable for a British businessman to marry in the social context of the times, was discouraged by the Siamese. If the behavior continued, the young lady would disappear up-country and the British firm would be advised to remove their officer from the country. Similarly, in the case of a Chinese lady of suitable family, it is difficult to suppose that, in the unlikely event that an attachment could take place, a traditional Chinese family would welcome the potential connection.

When in the late 1880s the Hongkong Bank experimented with an office in Peking, the manager, (Sir) Charles Addis, a man who had, exceptionally, studied

Chinese, invited Chinese officials to his home to dine. These same officials, however, might cut him in the street, preferring not to publicize their familiarity with a foreign devil. An examination of Addis' guest book when he was in Shanghai, however, reveals no Chinese guests; back in England, on the other hand, Addis entertained the compradore's student son at his country home.[16] In Peking one might experiment, at least at first; in cosmopolitan Shanghai intercultural contacts might be possible, but in colonial Hong Kong there was rigidity, explained by the purpose of the Colony when founded and by the diversity of the society forced to develop side-by-side, but independently – not in the context of forming a Hong Kong consciousness, but rather independently, contacting each other of necessity in business, government or culture as required and as custom permitted.[17]

The atmosphere of Hong Kong was well understood. When the Hongkong Bank's Shanghai Manager, A.G. Stephen, was appointed in 1920 to the Hong Kong based position of Chief Manager, his Italian/Spanish, India-born wife refused to accompany him, the Bank instead permitting him a second official residence in Shanghai. Hong Kong, she felt, was too colonial. And by "colonial" she was referring not, surely, to the form of government, or that the British were the rulers; she was concerned at the inward looking nature of that portion of Hong Kong society to which she would be assigned – even if she were to be one of its leading ladies as wife of the Bank's taipan (chief executive).

Attempts at change, 1900–41

To the extent that Hong Kong's society was containerized, the corporate culture must be a significant cause. But did a British company never take on a non-British officer? First it must be appreciated that there was very little lateral transferring possible in Hong Kong in the colonial period. One entered as a junior and continued to retirement. Thus the junior was particularly dependent, and while initiative might be rewarded, the system was difficult to reform. Charles Addis, for example, argued for the recruiting of university graduates in the Hongkong Bank. Indeed, some were recruited and one, Sir Michael Turner, rose to be a post World War II chief executive. But as a major reform, the policy failed because it could be executed only within the existing system – requiring the university graduate to return to the life of a London junior, serve his apprenticeship first in London and then in the East ... his university career had apparently set him back three years. Addis argued that eventually the graduate would make it up, passing his non-university colleagues to the top, but who could be sure?

The interwar period was hardly static. There were great political developments both in China and in Japan. However their impact on Hong Kong was complex. The correspondence of Hongkong Bank managers indicated that they were familiar with officers in Chinese banks, and Sir Vandeleur M Grayburn (chief executive,

1930–43) particularly had great respect for the Bank of China management. But this was at the top. Juniors from Chinese and British banks might meet on duty from time to time and strike up a superficial acquaintance – enough to remember, perhaps when each was in a senior managerial position during the Red Guard period of the late 1960s. Meanwhile Britain in interwar Hong Kong was facing the challenge of Japan; Hong Kong as outpost, Hong Kong as military base, paradoxically in the dying days of Empire, was key to official political thinking. The communities were represented as advisers; there was no Hong Kong polity. A weak Britain, a set business culture, and discontinuities in the social structure made conceptual reform unlikely, and, to the extent it was attempted, ineffective. Furthermore there was a clash of interests between the British government and colonial governors espousing the cause of their Hong Kong constituents, especially with reference to China policy. A self-governing Hong Kong seemed a contradiction in terms.

There is evidence that young veterans of World War I, the Great War, of 1914–18, came East with expectations of encouraging change. Instead, this became the period when mutual agreement among communities to remain separate for cultural reasons degenerated into an imposed separation based on traditional behavior no longer necessary or desirable. Corporate culture changes in part because of pressures from the external culture. Interwar the pressures were growing but insufficient to force change, if only because of business uncertainty; many hongs were concerned with their own survival, they were of necessity inward looking. And to the extent that social change did occur, it occurred in Shanghai where the cosmopolitan pressures were greatest.

Chinese in the days of the Republic

Nevertheless, the basis of Hong Kong's constitutional legitimacy, the assumptions made at its foundation were being undermined. At first Hong Kong was seen as a base, managed by Britain, for free traders to operate on the China coast. Traders come and go. The immigrating Chinese came and went, supplementing the facilities of the merchants, but some stayed. As early as the 1870s there was a flourishing Chinese community which could be accommodated constitutionally by including their representatives in the governor's advisory councils. After the acquisition of additional territory which, contrary to the original intent of the Colony's founders, did include settled Chinese communities and market towns, that is the New Territories lease in 1898, there was a further category; rather than supplementing the existing Chinese urban and partly assimilated community, the rural population of this area provided further discontinuity, while at the same time adding to the contradictions and challenging the assumptions by which the Colony was governed.

Chinese nationalism, while making claim to Hong Kong, had its own problems, not the least being a disunity which included, in passing, the thought that the Treaty

Ports (and Hong Kong?) might develop in semi-independence, as with the Hanseatic League.[18] More relevant to Hong Kong was the disunity in China and the consequence of British China policy. The Foreign Office tended to favor continuity through recognition of the power dominating Peking; Hong Kong had a pragmatic need for sound relations with the authorities based in Canton. Thus if Hong Kong were to be governed for the purposes for which it was founded, even in a period of developing but uncertain Chinese nationalism, the fortress constitution had to prevail. Governors had to be brought in line by the Foreign Office in London and their inclination to local diplomacy, reflecting the interests of those they were responsible for governing, had to be curbed.

The Chinese, had they then been as powerful as in post-1949 days, might have argued that while a British governor administering whatever population existed in Hong Kong was consistent with the cession of the territory, for the British to allow the Chinese majority in Hong Kong to govern was a contradiction of the very excuse the British had advanced for the cession – yet another argument reinforcing the constitutional *status quo*.

World War II and its immediate aftermath

There were by the 1930s three distinct groups which identified with Hong Kong. The first were the Chinese, the second the Portuguese, and the third, non-comparable to the other two, were the major hongs. Generation after generation of British might serve in Hong Kong, even be born in Hong Kong, but continuity came from the major hongs they served.[19] Thus they associated with Hong Kong only indirectly, in a way significant, even beneficial for the territory but inconsistent with government by universal franchise. There continued to be mavericks, including journalists and local newspaper editors, who most certainly played a role in the territory's history, but not, perhaps, in the context of the present analysis.

World War II stressed the peculiar nature of Hong Kong; the British were interned, the Portuguese returned to a crowded Macau, and the majority of the Chinese, many recently arrived as refugees, left the territory. A rump survived during the occupation, and afterwards Hong Kong had to start again. Any continuity which might have argued for a democratic system, any long-term association of people with the territory was for the most part ended. And yet, while at one level Britain maneuvered to insure Hong Kong did not revert to China, at another level the Colonial Office had spent the war planning for colonial change in an atmosphere of unreality. The uncertainty caused in Malaya by the introduction of the Malayan Union and the separation of Singapore from the other Straits Settlements forced a rethinking, but such experimentation did not, in the end, impact Hong Kong; plans for a more democratic system were quickly shelved in the confusion of post-war reconstruction and readjustment.

The new residents and revolutionary China

Whatever excuse there might have been for providing a democratic system for the rump population and former residents – and one can wonder how they would have voted in the face of the subsequent influx of refugees from the China – the presence of a new population and the presence of a revolutionary power in China suggested a return to the *status quo* constitutionally, lest any change be considered a cause for Chinese intervention. The success of the Red Army led many to fear for Hong Kong's very existence as a British territory, and many left the territory. And then there were the refugees. By a long-standing policy, border crossings by Chinese who were from Kwangtung or Kwangsi provinces were uncontrolled. There were thousands of newcomers, squatters on the hillsides, waiting to return to their homes, to emigrate, or, perhaps the minority, to remain and participate in an industrial development which no one at that time imagined. Furthermore one can state a paradox: if there had been democracy in 1949, the parents and grandparents of those who today argue that the British should have introduced democracy earlier would not have been allowed to settle and consequently their descendants, if any, would not now be in a position to demand participation in that democracy. This may not be a sound historical approach, but it is a proposition illustrative of Hong Kong's dilemma.

China itself introduced border controls, prohibiting emigration, but periodically opening the gates to permit another mass exodus. Hong Kong in 1956 was still not a candidate for democratic reform. The refugees had not been absorbed, their focus was not Hong Kong. A dramatic illustration of this would be the riots during celebration of the Double Tenth.[20] Less dramatic but equally relevant would be conversations with administrators of the so-called "refugee colleges," for example, New Asia College, who would (i) argue that the Hong Kong government should fund them and (ii) drink to an expected early return to Canton.[21]

Discontinuities and post-war developments

Corporate culture revisited

Furthermore, the three-tier corporate personnel policy was still in place; the discontinuities in Hong Kong society which made any system of popular elections or majority rule untenable still characterized the constitutional scene. This, however, was to change in the next 20 years. First, many refugees emigrated. The Portuguese, not only in Hong Kong, but also from the Treaty Ports and from Sri Lanka along with members of other minority communities left for a more permanent home, as they saw it. From the corporation's point of view this meant the departure of their clerical staff. Something had to change. By the mid-1960s the first tentative changes had been made: local employees, including both remaining Portuguese and the Chinese could sign for the corporation, the compradore had gone, and the Chinese were direct employees of the corporation; by the end of the decade there were local officers undertaking the work formerly done by mid-level expatriate management. The internal culture of the corporation had yielded to external pressure; in return that change would be reflected in the nature of the body politic.

At first such changes were minimized. Pre-war all officers had been trained in London, now a Chinese officer candidate would be sent to London for training. But it could never be the same – although the Mercantile Bank (of India) was perhaps the most successful in retaining the old spirit in its new Asian officers, at least at first.[22]

China: revised relations and attitudes

Despite the potential for change, the revolution in China, especially its manifestation in the Red Guard movement, made all in Hong Kong very conscious of their relationship to China. The British, who had never intended to rule a colony of Chinese, found themselves doing just that, but in constitutional terms more suitable to an outpost of Empire, a trading post, a fortress concept. Led by internal pressures to perfect the consultation system, radical constitutional change appeared unacceptable, and this position was at least tentatively accepted. Thus, as in the expatriate type corporation, any adjustment was imperfect, arbitrarily checked at a particular point by external requirements, or what were seen as requirements.

Meanwhile the corporations which had appeared to be inseparable parts of Hong Kong began to diversify geographically, even to establish a head office overseas. Indeed, several, like Jardine Matheson, had always been multinational, but despite their scope, appearance had connected them with the continuity of Hong Kong. In the late 1950s the Hongkong Bank acquired the British Bank of the Middle East, absorbed the Mercantile Bank of India, and in 1980 reached out to buy Marine Midland Banks, the holding company of America's twelfth largest bank. At first the Hongkong Bank would argue that it was only following its customers, but it was actually doing much more. A new vision existed not only in this particular corporation but throughout Hong Kong. Actually, the bank needed a European base in the worldwide competition which was now accepted in the banking industry. Having failed to obtain the Royal Bank of Scotland, it turned, during the 1980s to one of the big four British clearing banks, Midland. To this point, the acquisitions had been undertaken by the Hongkong Bank itself, thus making it an untidy operating bank and financial holding company. This unsatisfactory state of affairs had to be corrected, and the Bank of England's insistence that Midland Bank could not be acquired by an overseas bank led the Hongkong Bank to engineer a take-over by one of its British subsidiaries, the tiny HSBC Holdings plc. Finally, HSBC Holdings, which was London based but managed from Hong Kong, became the true senior company, losing its overseas status, and drawing the Hongkong Bank's top management to Britain.

Internationalization and its limits

As locally headquartered companies reached out to participate globally, the Hong Kong government, under pressure to afford reciprocity, removed restrictions which had been part of its colonial heritage, and multinationals stationed themselves in the territory. Hong Kong, many publicists proclaimed, had become an "International City." Hong Kong was seen as a "free city." But the facts were otherwise. Government policy was made in a context far different. In the view of Governor David Trench,

> Every single policy, social, political, or economic, is coloured by China's nearness, China's attitudes, and the consequent difficulty of being certain of an assured future.
>
> The situation demands great realism in all our thinking ... Hong Kong cannot afford the luxury of making mistakes, and particularly of well-meant mistakes, in any of its policies.[23]

Indeed free cities, for example Danzig, Tangiers, did not have long histories as independent entities in the modern era, and Hong Kong was an admitted anomaly. That it was "tolerated" by China was obvious, but this should not have blinded observers to the fact that Hong Kong had become, in politically incorrect terms, a "third China" and that the basis of British rule, the rationale of British rule, was accordingly under question. But despite appearances and despite its industrial revolution and its increasingly Hong Kong oriented Chinese population, the British Crown Colony, a term frowned upon as politically incorrect, was still a trade and financial entrepôt, just as in the days of the Treaty Ports. Rather than classifying the territory as the first of the post-war city states it would be more accurate to call it "the last of the Treaty Ports," the last of those cities on the China coast which, independently of current Chinese political thinking, were open to trade and where, *de facto*, the foreigners were encouraged to confine themselves and where their influence in China itself could be minimized.[24]

In support of this approach, the Chinese government informed the United Nations that Hong Kong should be removed from the list of "colonies;" Hong Kong was, China asserted, Chinese territory under British administration, the provisions of the "unequal treaties" notwithstanding, and this anomaly would be corrected at the appropriate time. This the Chinese government was later to determine as June 30,

1997, the date the 99-year lease on the New Territories ended; Hong Kong without this land would in any case have ceased to be economically viable.

The development of a Hong Kong identity

These developments were in parallel with the growth of Chinese companies in Hong Kong. The result visibly lessened the exclusive role of the British or, indeed, of the expatriate. As communities of equal significance the Portuguese were gone, and the Indians, although continuing to play an important role and remain separate, could not alter the growing image of Hong Kong as a Chinese city with a potential Chinese electorate. If this were the end of Hong Kong, as one writer would suggest in the mid-1980s, it was Hong Kong as an international city administered by one particular overseas power unconnected with its neighbor.[25] With the increasing number of Chinese born or brought up in a modern Hong Kong, this was to be expected and, with the declared determination of China itself to modernize, the concern for interference by a revolutionary China had undergone a change.

In the years since the war, the success of Hong Kong had bred a kind of assurance or assertion of excellence, not only by the resident Chinese but by all those connected with the territory. In one form it was recognized by eliminating colonial titles. The term correctly describing the legal status of Hong Kong, "British Crown Colony," if used, was seen as an attempted insult. The "Colonial Secretary" became the "Chief Secretary" in a manner reminiscent of changes made in colonies moving to independence.[26] And yet at the very moment that the discontinuities in Hong Kong society were being removed, at the very moment when constitutional change began to make sense, the question of 1997 arose and took priority over purely internally motivated reform.

Corporate culture in industrial Hong Kong

Ironically, in the corporate culture, the particular became international – at least in the Hongkong Bank. At first the "purity" of the expatriate role was maintained by the differentiation of officers – the expatriates were "international," the local officers were "regional" or "local." How did these discontinuities become adjusted in parallel with the adjustments of Hong Kong's body politic? The parallels are not precise, but the pressures were similar. The international corps changed to include qualified non-British – Canadians, Australians, but also Indians and Chinese. These would carry the torch of alleged Hong Kong entrepreneurial genius and seed or inspire the officers of the various companies comprising the HSBC Group, or HSBC Holdings, plc and its subsidiaries. Management in Hong Kong would be undertaken by both international and regional officers, but in a mix which no longer had objectively defined boundaries or traditional exclusions.

The corporate culture had adjusted to the extent that the communal factor was minimized. The traditional Hong Kong, the international city, was now best represented in the culture of Hong Kong inspired multinationals. In the body politic, the discontinuities too had been minimized but with the consequence that Hong Kong was basically Chinese, requiring constitutional recognition of the fact.

But these Chinese were not the Chinese who had been in Hong Kong for 150 years. Their need for the key political power did not stem from the colony's history, nor did the recent recognition of a legitimate Hong Kong electorate suggest their neglect in the past. Rather they were the development of the 1970s arising from events in the 1950s. The different early years and the post-war change, this essay has urged, is both reflected in changes in Hong Kong's corporate cultures and the consequence of an interaction between relevant corporate decisions and major changes in the structure and composition of Hong Kong society which influenced them and were in turn influenced by them.

A disservice is done to these variations if, in considering the history of Hong Kong, the relative sameness of the territory is not seen in the context of dynamic changes in the human composition of Hong Kong and the interplay of internal and external forces on the potential for constitutional change.

Changing the colonial category: the problem

The question remains, however, that regardless of the relevance of the territory's earlier history to the question of the establishment of democracy in Hong Kong in the period after 1970, when Hong Kong was seen *de facto* as a colony of settlement, why did the issue become controversial?

The transfer of power – from an appointed executive to an executive responsible to the legislature, the transfer of sovereignty – from the United Kingdom to a newly created local sovereign, virtually followed a pattern, with more or less resistance from the British government, first in the colonies of North America and Australasia and then post-war in Africa, Ceylon, etc. There was a certain logic to the course of development: the election by limited franchise to a minimal number of seats in the governor's councils to election by universal franchise (by citizens as defined) for all the seats, accompanied or followed by the change in sovereignty. But this course was argued with and eventually forced on Britain by pressures from the future sovereign nation-in-waiting. Only in territories with separate and potentially conflicting communities, as in Ceylon/Sri Lanka, Malaya, or Fiji, was the colonial power in a position to demand a constitution which seemed to ensure participation by the several communities based on whatever compromises could be negotiated.

Despite the apparent inevitability of this development, progress could not be made without taking note of the context in which the colonial territory existed. At one extreme, a colony could be taken over by its neighbor, Goa for example, and integrated into that country's system. At another, the conflict between the demands of a neighbor and the aspirations of the colonial subjects, as in Gibraltar, has led to a stalemate short of invasion. But more relevant to Hong Kong is perhaps the story of Singapore, which in its conception and development had to take into account that it was a Chinese city in a Malay sea, that it had an important Malay minority whose interests were the subject of regional discussion. Thus whatever sovereign powers might be vested in the Republic of Singapore, their exercise had to take into account regional concerns. And the progression of Singapore through various constitutional stages in the 1950s was designed to lead not to independence but to integration, under certain modified conditions, as a state in a new Malaysian federation.

We may distinguish between those colonies whose rights to sovereign independence were unchallenged by others and those, like Goa and Gibraltar, whose integration into another country would constitute a real factor in the decision making. We may also distinguish between colonies which were claimed by others on purely territorial grounds, for example Gibraltar, Portuguese East Indies, and West Irian, and those claimed on grounds of cultural, historical, or other ties with the people, for example Goa – and indeed Singapore.

The formation of an electorate

One can also discern that the problem of moving from a special purpose territory – Gibraltar, Singapore – to recognition that the territory had become one of settlement, is not unique to Hong Kong.

In Hong Kong's context the process of eliminating the discontinuities and establishing an electorate regarding Hong Kong's interests as their own was bound to be biased in favor of a recognition of the Chinese proximity and claim to the territory and for the Chinese in Hong Kong to make their Chinese origins part of the unifying process, especially since "Chinese" could stress the cultural rather than the specific political aspects of life in revolutionary China. The recognition that Hong Kong's Chinese culture had developed along different paths and that Hong Kong's Chinese expectations were different from those in the rest of China was a key element of statesmanship, whatever ultimate motivations might exist, in China's Hong Kong policy. One might argue that the concept of "one country, two systems" was superior to the absolute military solution imposed on Goa, a judgement independent of the actual political compromises or appreciation which followed in India's administration of that territory.

Considering the factors mentioned above there is a strong argument to support the view that, even as a matter of political principle (as opposed to political reality), the terms of the move from special purpose colony to territory of settlement and its consequences could not be determined without the agreement of the ultimate sovereign. And this ultimate sovereign would not have origins within the territory, that is it would not be an internal political party or person leading the electorate to an "inevitable" independence. Even before the 1984 agreement, China's ultimate post-1997 role could not be ignored. On a more theoretical level one might reasonably argue that although China had little power to control the terms of the original treaty of cession, nevertheless there had grown an understanding relative to the nature of Hong Kong, one which argued against Chinese military intervention in times when her power made it possible, although not necessarily prudent, for her to do so.

The final solution

Preserving the Hong Kong "way of life"

Hong Kong possessed, as already noted, a constitution designed for a special purpose colony, adapted both in text and usage to the development of an open society and the rule of law, given legitimacy by success, protection by the colonial power, and participation of the people through advisory and consultative processes short of democracy – defined as the right to vote, universal suffrage, and an elected government. This system China's government saw as successful, apparently accepted by the people, and presumed unthreatening. This was surely the "way of life" China promised to preserve for 50 years.

But the special purpose constitution, already stretched beyond recognition, could not survive a Hong Kong detached from its colonial base. An assumption of the existing constitution was that one narrowly defined group of people, appointed expatriates from the United Kingdom, would rule another ill-defined group of people called "Hong Kong belongers." Take away the first part and there is a vacuum. The *de facto* colony of settlement had to have some recognition as such, consistent with China's acceptance of Hong Kong's way of life. The eventual solution to this takes us beyond the scope of this paper. The direction of this discussion, however, leads to the conclusion that in the final years of the territory, the British authorities reversed their acceptance of the evolution agreed with China and attempted, despite all the controlling factors, to interpret the new constitution or basic law as if they were preparing the territory for independence, passing through the stages which led, say, to the independence of Ghana and other former British colonies. The process of eliminating traces of this policy is now in evidence and should be completed within a year of the handover.

In consequence Hong Kong has received a bad press. But this is not the problem that confronts us in the context of the title of this essay.

The fading of the discontinuities

One well reported aspect of Hong Kong's post-war history has been the declining political and relevant economic role of leading commercial and banking "colonial" hongs, which has been especially marked since 1970, paralleling the period of general political awareness and development. Looking once more at the history of the Hongkong Bank, we observe that its role as quasi-central bank, always difficult to separate from its role as the largest and one of the two oldest banks, was ending with the increased role of supervisory and government bodies in the banking and monetary systems. Of course there remains the rivalry between the hongs and the separate corporate cultures, but this no longer contributes to the discontinuities in the body politic. The impact of these developments is strongest on the newly employed and upwardly mobile Chinese employee, thus reinforcing both the increased role of the individual Chinese and the trend to a more unified electorate, albeit a mainly Chinese one.

The privileges which the traditional British hongs probably enjoyed, especially in the interwar period, were incompatible with the concept of Hong Kong as a free economy and an international financial centre. Hence the influence they exerted on Hong Kong's way of life needed to be marginalized.

Furthermore the external impact of the traditional hong's corporate culture on Hong Kong's culture has also been marginalized. These cultures may still play an important role in the working of the corporation; indeed, in the history of the Hongkong Bank a case can be made to support the thesis that the role of the corporate cultural impact on HSBC Holdings is of vital significance in understanding its international success. However, that corporate culture has its greatest social impact on the expatriate, redefined to refer to members of the executive elite corps, including those of Hong Kong birth who are "international officers" or their equivalent. This changed situation further suggests Chinese or other local employees may be influenced by the corporate culture, but not monopolized by it. Thus they become at the same time Hong Kong oriented and, in all matters of relevance to the creation of an electorate, independent of that culture.

One may take a step further and note that the corporate culture of the historic hongs has itself responded to external business pressures and has itself evolved. There always was some uniformity in terms of service, but this was after comparison between the British hongs. Today the non-business features which marked the culture as unique, the long-term, low-level training in London, the trip East by steamship – P&O, Blue Funnel, etc. – the company hostel for juniors, the focus on sports – as well as rules on marriage, the five-year tours of service in the East – have been eliminated or put in a context which would be understood elsewhere. These are referred to as "colonial vestiges" and to be discarded as such – often with excessive sensibility. In fact, the discard has been forced by real change: the long tour of duty by the reality of air travel; the low-level training by the business school, by the cost and expectations of today's graduates – and more could be cited.

Then as the businesses merge back into the business sector, their cultures reflecting and impacting on their own internal requirements and traditions, they fade as determining factors in the interplay of forces forming Hong Kong's electorate, their relationship to the territory, and the potential effectiveness and relevance of an electorate unified in their consciousness of Hong Kong.

Conclusions

Why did the British hold Hong Kong for 150 years without granting a universal franchise? Placed in historical context, the question poses no difficulty until the mid-1970s. At this time, it may be argued, there had developed a Hong Kong electorate perfectly capable of running their own affairs and, indeed, "ready for independence," had that been an option. Instead the British were riding a tiger. They had to govern a "colony in trust," that is a territory populated by mainly non-British people (although British citizens in one category or another), until it could be determined precisely what China, the power claiming sovereignty, would tolerate. There would be negotiations leading to the 1984 declaration, but it was China which held all the cards. To argue what China might or might not have done had Britain unilaterally changed the territory's constitution is only part of the puzzle of analysis. China held all the negotiating cards; Hong Kong while capable of democracy did not have the tools for immediate exercise of the franchise. Nor, given later problems in LegCo was it obvious that any radical change would pass. Orderly management suggested strongly that the question of 1997 be resolved and the terms known so that, within those terms, a suitable constitutional arrangement could be made. That the final resolution has not proved satisfactory to all is hardly surprising. That this is so, however, is in no way a consequence of Britain's failure to enfranchise the population at some earlier date. There had been no opportunity, taken in its historical context, to do so.

Fortress Hong Kong, the dilemma of a Chinese majority in a territory seized from China for the express purpose of meeting British requirements, the changing population, the impact of refugees, the presence of revolutionary China, the spill-over of the Cultural Revolution and the Red Guards, and the upheavals of the early 1970s spoke out against constitutional reform, despite the determined voice of a few Hong Kong "reformers." In colonial Hong Kong people did vote with their feet, in colonial Hong Kong there was legitimate government, not by votes but through success.

If Confucius had asked a Hong Kong belonger why she was weeping and received the reply that neither she nor her husband were permitted to vote, he might well have asked her why then did she remain. Would she not have replied, as did the woman of the classics, "because here there is good government."

There have been policy errors in the history of Hong Kong, but, if the analysis of this essay be valid, Britain's failure to grant the vote during its 150 years of rule is not one of them.

Notes

The author is Professor Emeritus, University of Hong Kong, and is a former Director and presently Hon. Research Fellow of the university's Centre of Asian Studies. A version of this paper was presented at the International Conference on Hong Kong and modern China, December 1997, in the Centre of Asian Studies. This revised paper is based on the version presented at a Pacific Centuries conference, University of the Pacific, Stockton, CA, April 1998.

1 Those despairing of more traditional politics and who, like the people of Minnesota, want a real choice, might argue that voting with one's feet is perhaps a more effective way of expressing a political opinion. However, the choice available in the 1950s, as between life in the People's Republic and Hong Kong, while it did offer a sizeable choice, did not, it is now claimed, thereby make Hong Kong a "democracy."

2 Including those enactments passed by a Legislative Council which the new sovereign, China, declared illegal. Governor Chris Patten had "reformed" LegCo, but his ordinance passed only after arguably improper political pressure on a non-official member and through the votes of official members. But this takes us beyond the scope of the essay. Regrettably, Patten's own explanation in his *East and West: The last governor of Hong Kong on power, freedom and the future*, London, 1998 appears unhelpful and self-serving.

3 Lord Palmerston: Henry John Temple, 1784–1865, 3rd Viscount Palmerston, was Foreign Secretary, 1830–41.

4 Although a minimal presence in Hong Kong, the Chinese from the first constituted a majority of the island's population.

5 Lord Aberdeen: George Hamilton Gordon, 1784–1860, 4th Earl of Aberdeen, succeeded Palmerston as Foreign Secretary. These quotations are found in a collection of published colonial documents, Frederick Madden with David Fieldhouse (eds), *The Dependent Empire and Ireland, 1840–1900*, Vol. V of *Select Documents on the Constitutional History of the British Empire and Commonwealth*, New York, 1991.

6 Lord Stanley: Edward G. Stanley, 1799–1869, later 14th Earl of Derby, Colonial Secretary in Peel's government 1841. Note the origins of the place names of two early British settlements on Hong Kong Island.

7 The governor was Sir George Bonham, and the quote is from Frank H.H. King and Prescott Clarke, *A Research Guide to China-coast Newspapers, 1822–1911*, Cambridge, Massachusetts, 1965, p. 6.

8 Governors, however, very often fought hard for the interests of Hong Kong against imperial dictats originating in the Colonial Office in London. In the end, it is true, if their arguments failed to convince, London's order prevailed.

9 For a discussion of corporate culture with particular reference to the Hongkong and Shanghai Banking Corporation and Hong Kong, see my "Does the Corporation's History Matter? Hongkong Bank/HSBC Holdings: A case study," in Andrew Godley and Oliver M. Westall (eds), *Business History and Business Culture*, Manchester and New York, 1996, pp. 116–37.

10 See Ming Sing, "The Democracy Movement in Hong Kong, 1986–1990," an unpublished Oxford University doctoral dissertation and an extremely sound analysis of the growth and limitations of political parties in Hong Kong.

11 Martin was the only member of the Legislative Council not also a member of the Executive Council. He considered himself close to Lord Stanley because of their earlier concern with the preservation of the Irish union with Britain, but in this he was mistaken. See my *Survey our Empire! Robert Montgomeray Martin (1801?–1868), a Bio-bibliography*, Hong Kong, 1979, esp. Ch. 8.

12 The first such appointee from the Hong Kong General Chamber of Commerce was (Sir) Thomas Jackson, chief executive of the Hongkong Bank, in 1884. It should be noted that some firms, with headquarters outside Hong Kong, did not permit their local taipans to become involved in such high profile (and presumably time consuming) public positions.

13 This and similar material in this essay is based on oral history interviews with retired executives of the Hongkong and Shanghai Banking Corporation. The originals are in the Group archives of HSBC Holdings, plc, London. For a full history, see Frank H.H. King (and others), *The History of The Hongkong and Shanghai Banking Corporation*, 4 vols, Cambridge, 1989–91.

14 Angela Brazil wrote schoolgirl versions, indeed parallels, of "boy's stories" in the 1920s, for example *Schoolgirl Kitty* or *The Headgirl at the Gables*. A recent London play, *Daisy pulls it off*. was an amalgam of several of these novels. Oral history interviews. conducted by Catherine E. King, of the wives of Hongkong Bank managers found them familiar with these works.

15 In 1954 after two years in Hong Kong, I suddenly realized that I knew no Chinese – outside the few on the University of Hong Kong faculty. I knew more Chinese in distant Taiwan! In consequence I joined the Hong Kong Junior Chamber of Commerce, where friendships lasting to the present day were happily plentiful.

16 See references to Addis in King, *History*, op. cit., vols I and II.

17 For a recent survey of Chinese/foreigners relations, mainly in the Treaty Ports, see Frances Wood, *No Dogs and not many Chinese, Treaty Port life in China, 1843–1943*, London, 1998.

18 Although such thoughts were vilified, they sound extraordinarily like the advocacy of special economic zones, even of special administrative regions, but the nationalists could then go no further than "One country!"

19 One senior executive attempting to renew his British passport under new nationality regulations had problems because none of his male ancestors had been born in Britain since the middle of the seventeenth century.

20 This is October 10, the national day of the Republic of China under the Kuomintang.

21 I was there and personally experienced this. In 1953 in Taiwan it was quite usual for invitations to dinner to be qualified by "unless we are back on the Mainland by then."

New Asia College was eventually the beneficiary of government assistance and is now a constituent college of the Chinese University of Hong Kong.

[22] For a history of the Mercantile Bank, see Edwin Green and Sara Kinsey, *The Paradise Bank, the Mercantile Bank of India, 1893–1984*, Aldershot, 1999.

[23] Sir David Trench, governor of Hong Kong, 1964–71, quoted in Steve Tsang, *Democracy Shelved*, Oxford, 1988.

[24] The term "treaty port" is being used here as a "type." Hong Kong was never a "treaty port," understood legally.

[25] Robert Cottrell, *The End of Hong Kong: The secret diplomacy of imperial retreat*, London, 1993. Such phrases, including "Hong Kong is dead," etc., refer not to Hong Kong but to a particular vision or interpretation of Hong Kong, which may or may not have any relation to reality. Read: "Hong Kong as the city I think it ought to be is dead." Cottrell's study, however, is of great interest and value. We are quibbling over the title.

[26] As of the date of writing, street names, etc., have remained unchanged.

13

The Philippine Annexation: An Experiment of Profound Interest

Arthur Power Dudden

Yale University Professor Edward Gaylord Bourne's historical essay of October 1902, "Discovery, Conquest, and Early History of the Philippine Islands," concludes on a prophetic note:

> The old regime in the Philippines has disappeared forever. In hardly more than a generation the people have passed from a life which was so remote from the outside contemporary world that they might as well have been living in the middle ages in some sheltered nook, equally protected from the physical violence and the intellectual strife of the outside world, and entirely oblivious of the progress of knowledge. They find themselves suddenly plunged into a current that hurls them along resistlessly. Baptized with fire and blood, a new and strange life is thrust upon them, and they face the struggle for existence under conditions which spare no weakness and relentlessly push idleness or incapacity to the wall. What will be the outcome no man can tell. To the student of history and of social evolution, it will be an experiment of profound interest.[1]

Nothing could have been more likely. The Americans intended to stay. In February 1899, the Senate had ratified the Treaty of Paris to end the Spanish-American War. Spain yielded independence to Cuba, and for $20 million surrendered sovereignty over the entire Philippine archipelago of more than 7,000 islands, 11 of the islands accounting for most of the land mass and its population of nearly nine million inhabitants, to the United States, as well as the islands of Puerto Rico, Guam, and Wake. By July 1902, American forces crushed the Filipinos' second uprising for independence, even as Spanish authorities had, in 1897, thwarted their first attempt.

The Spanish-American War broke out over the intervention by the United States on the side of Cuban rebels struggling to end Spain's centuries-old dominion. In contrast, Spain's troubles with its Filipino insurgents on the far side of the globe were virtually unknown to Americans. Congress, in declaring war, had declared that Cuba must be made free and independent, while, by the Teller amendment to their declaration, the lawmakers disclaimed any territorial ambitions. Somehow, during and after the fighting against Spain, those limited horizons became greatly extended. President William McKinley, who once held that annexing territory by the United States would constitute "criminal aggression," changed his mind step by step, to instruct his peace negotiators that, "we must keep what we want."

Imperialists pressuring McKinley, led by Theodore Roosevelt, managed to transform the war to liberate Cuba into a Spanish-American-Cuban-Filipino War. This war ensued for three years after 1898 against the Filipinos, even for years longer in remote regions of the islands while featuring grisly atrocities and serious causualties on both sides, with scores of thousands of hapless civilians killed. The Filipino-American War of 1899-1902, like the recent Indian Wars on the Great Plains, turned into a racist slaughter of unfortunates by an invading enemy determined to destroy any resistance. Official policy to the contrary, American soldiers clung to homebred prejudices, regarding Filipinos as their inferiors, disdaining them as "gooks" or "niggers."

Heeding Kipling to "Take up the White Man's Burden," Senator Albert Beveridge of Indiana toasted the star-spangled standard of duty and destiny:

> We cannot fly from our world duties; it is ours to execute the purpose of a fate that has driven us to be greater than our small intentions. We cannot retreat from any soil where Providence has unfolded our banner; it is ours to save that soil for liberty and civilization. For liberty and civilization and God's promise fulfilled, the flag must henceforth be the symbol and the sign to all mankind – the flag!

As for a flag for the Philippines Colony, Mark Twain growled at the fury for expansion "we can have just our usual flag, with the white stripes painted black and the stars replaced by the skull and crossbones."[2]

Self-deceived, the United States imposed a protectorate over the independence-seeking Cubans, for whose freedom Americans ostensibly waged war against Spain. Next the USA surged ahead to annex and colonize the recalcitrant Filipinos, who were just as independence-minded as the Cubans, though much farther away, 7,000 miles from California across the Pacific Ocean and 10,000 miles from Washington, if not coincidentally, almost on the threshold of China. Any full account must also embody the massive building up of the United States Navy, the annexations of the Hawaiian (1898) and easternmost Samoan (1899) islands, the Open Door Policy as proclaimed for China (1900), and joining the international relief expedition against the Boxer rebels.

Filipino rebelliousness arose from the inequities of Spain's colonial control. A spirit of independence expressed itself through the secret machinations of the Katipunan society launched by Andres Bonifacio, a warehouse laborer, and by the influential writings of José Rizal, a physician turned novelist and poet. The prosperous elite, known as *ilustrados*, wanted home rule and local autonomy in place of Spanish autocracy. When coupled with demands to separate church and state by ending the historic functions of the regular clergy, or friars, as administrators of the parishes, popular emotions swelled into a patriotic anthem, to decry alien rule of any persuasion, whether Spanish or American.

Spain's rule was effectively strongest around Manila Bay, one of the world's finest natural harbors, in particular at the city of Manila on Luzon, the Philippines' largest and most populous island, and likewise over the eastern coasts of the Visayan Islands where river valleys facilitated penetration upstream from the coastline. The Moros inhabiting the southernmost islands of Mindanao and the Sultanate of Sulu descended mostly from Malayan ancestors, who had converted to Islam in the great missionary extension from India during the fifteenth and sixteenth centuries. Having resisted Spanish authority and acculturation until the latter part of the nineteenth century, the Moros would likewise remain isolated for some time to come from the spreading insurgency and even afterward from American governance.

Twice the Filipinos' revolution erupted. The first stage advanced from August 1896 to an early climax, when, on May 31, 1897, Emilio Aguinaldo, 23 years old, had proclaimed a Philippine Republic. Five months later, Aguinaldo authorized the distribution of the Republic's constitution, then was himself chosen president. Spanish forces halted this insurgency by abruptly executing Rizal and banishing the other leaders, Aguinaldo included.

Commodore George Dewey's spectacular naval victory over Spain's Asiatic flotilla, May 1, 1898, at Manila Bay, nevertheless re-ignited the Filipino rebellion. Dewey had based his Asiatic Squadron at Hong Kong under orders to strike the enemy close at hand if war broke out with Spain. When the United States declared war on April 25, 1898, purportedly to free Cuba from Spain's misrule, Dewey raced his ships down the South China Sea to the Philippines, where his gunners sank Spain's overage warships at their anchorage. Hastening home from exile, Aguinaldo, on June 12, once more proclaimed the Philippine Republic.

While their control lasted, Aguninaldo's revolutionaries introduced sweeping changes into the social order, in religion, education, and politics. To oust the friars from their lands and age-old positions of power, they launched a National Church, and determined to seek its papal validation from the Holy See. The National Church constituted a wholly Filipinized congregation of the Roman Catholic faith, from worshippers and acolytes to priests and nuns to the archbishop. Aguinaldo left the structure of primary schools largely unchanged, but dismissed the Spanish friars from their administrative and teaching posts. The first secular and state-supported institution of higher learning, a short-lived Literary University of the Philippines, was the republic's most important attempt at educational innovation. In politics, where individual rights were the major concern, the *ilustrados* claimed a fair share in governing themselves.

The Treaty of Paris transferred Spain's sovereignty to the United States of America without Filipinos themselves being seriously considered, let alone consulted, though the Teller Amendment to the Congressional declaration of war earlier disclaimed any territorial ambition. For a number of reasons, President

William McKinley's and the nation's appetite for territory grew by leaps and bounds. Dewey's spectacular victory at Manila Bay and Congress's annexation of the Hawaiian Islands by joint resolution, July 6, 1898, in order to gain Pearl Harbor for a naval base astride the oceanic highway to the Philippines, toppled all restraints. The 11,000 soldiers from the American Expeditionary Force, who landed during the summer of 1898 to take Manila, were already beginning, if only by their presence, to Americanize the Philippines. Unfazed, Aguinaldo announced the members of his first cabinet, and formally inaugurated the independent Republic of the Philippines, on January 23, 1899. When President McKinley proclaimed United States sovereignty over the entire archipelago, a bitter controversy over the annexation treaty erupted in the United States Senate. However, on Saturday night, February 4, 1899, Private William Walter Grayson fired on four native soldiers, and Filipino troops retaliated by killing or wounding several American soldiers. Two days later in Washington, February 6, United States Senators, outraged at the shedding of American blood, vengefully ratified the treaty with Spain. For the next ten months of 1899, American soldiers and marines fought one pitched battle after another against dogged Filipinos, until Aguinaldo switched tactics thereafter to wage guerilla warfare.

In the years to come, Americans would minimize the crushing of the fledgling Filipino republic as an appropriate response to a lawless insurrection against legitimate United States sovereignty. It developed, in truth, into a vicious all-out war lasting over three years until 1902, against diehard Filipino patriots. Two-thirds of the United States Army was engaged at the war's peak, around 70,000 troops. In all, 120,000 Americans served in the war in the Philippines. Sporadic fighting broke out after 1902, until resistance was crushed at last in the bloody battles of Bud Daho (1906) and Bud Dagsak (1913) on the island of Jolo in the Celebes Sea. Total casualties far exceeded those of the Spanish-American War. Nearly 4,200 Americans died, and 2,800 were wounded. Twenty thousand Filipino warriors were slain , while an estimated 600,000 noncombatant Filipino civilians, men, women, and children, perished from conflict-related causes.[3]

During the so-called "Taft Era" between 1900 and 1913, the constitutional, educational, and landed property bases for American rule in the Philippines materialized under William Howard Taft's leadership and the two presidents, William McKinley and Theodore Roosevelt, he served. Congress and the corpulent, jolly Taft, initially as president of the Second Philippine Commission, and, in turn, the first civil governor, the first governor-general, and, next, following Roosevelt's election in 1904, secretary of war in direct charge of the Bureau of Insular Affairs, and, finally, president of the United States, installed the enduring structures of America's new empire. The United States government defined a twofold responsibility toward its possessions. The first requirement was to install a properly administered colonial regime, while the second would follow to train the Filipino people themselves through their own participation in the principles and practices of self-government.

Toward the latter goal, President McKinley promptly instructed the Taft Commission to extend the secular system of primary education launched earlier by the military government under Major General Arthur MacArthur. The military transport ship *Thomas* disembarked some 600 carefully selected teachers at Manila, on August 23, 1901, as predecessors of latter-day Peace Corps volunteers. Men and women alike, these "Thomasites," as they would become recognized, began at once to teach the English language throughout the Philippines, and, as energetically as they could, to Americanize their youthful charges.

The Commission took over existing schools, and established many more, including intermediate and secondary schools, to introduce everywhere American-style public schooling. In Manila itself, a normal school for training teachers, an arts and trades school, a nautical school, and a nursing school were opened, as well as an agricultural institute on the island of Negros. The University of the Philippines opened in Manila, in 1908, patterned after the burgeoning state universities at home. Galvanized by a secularizing fervor, all of the foregoing was accomplished in less than ten years, while coincidentally reducing in everyday life the influence of the Roman Catholic Church.

Nevertheless, no other educational or religious reform perplexed Taft more than the all-pervasive issue of the friars' lands. Holdings of the religious orders totalled over 420,000 acres, the choicest arable lands in the islands, yet the 1898 Treaty with Spain required the United States to uphold existing private property rights of all kinds. "All the evidence … shows clearly," the Commission reported to Secretary of War Elihu Root, "that the feeling of hatred for the friars is wellnigh universal and permeates all classes," contending that, though the Filipino people were not anti-Catholic, the revolution against Spain had originated as an anti-friar movement. To which, Taft added his personal opinion: "If we, the Americans, could rid the islands of the friars, the gratitude of the people for our action would be so deep that the slightest fear of further insurrection would be entirely removed." Sensing trouble if this question remained unresolved, the Vatican conveyed through Archbishop John Ireland its willingness to receive the proposals of the United States from any authorized representative.

So Taft, who was at home in the United States recuperating from surgery, proceeded on President Roosevelt's instructions to Rome late in May 1902, accompanied by Bishop Thomas O'Gorman of Sioux Falls, General James F. Smith, a Catholic justice of the Philippine Supreme Court and later governor-general, with Major John Biddle Porter as secretary. Taft's mission was to purchase the friars' lands, and win a recall of their orders from the Philippines. The Vatican proved willing only to consider a sale of these lands while insisting that any such transaction must take place in Manila, and flatly rejected the American proposal to withdraw the regular orders of clergy. Taft advised Root that, "the answer of the Vatican was a great disappointment and surprise to me." Even so, practicality prevailed. By December 1903, the United States arranged to purchase the friars' estates for around $7.5 million, the proceeds being divided among the orders. In years to come, Catholic authorities would protest repeatedly against the Americanization of the Philippines on such a touchy matter as the proselytizing activities of more and more Protestant missionaries.

American policy always emphasized the political development of the Filipinos. Had not American authorities announced that their paramount goal was to prepare the Filipinos for self-government, they would have violated the nation's most cherished traditions. Yet how could the constitutional democracy of the United States, founded as it was on natural law and the rights of mankind, legitimately rule a colonized population thousands of miles away, especially if independence for its subjects could not even be seriously considered before a lengthy apprenticeship? Only, the answer lay, by devising opportunities for the Filipinos to master the methods of operating governmental institutions while preserving individual liberty for themselves. Such a process would be lengthy, one generation at least, if not longer.

On July 1, 1902, Congress passed the Philippine Organic Act to define constitutional authority. Executive power remained with the Commission. Legislative power was to be shared with an elected assembly as the lower house, the Commission serving as the upper house. Judicial independence, first instituted by the military government, would be maintained, except for the omission of trial by jury. The act also provided for a bill of rights, the conservation of natural resources, and the election of two Filipino resident commissioners to the House of Representatives in Washington. In 1904 following a census, slightly more than 100,000 men voted, out of 105,000 registered, for the 80-member assembly. Taft himself, by then secretary of war, returned to Manila, October 16, 1907, to open the first session of the Philippine Assembly. Taft's successors as governors-general to 1913, experienced Philippines administrators themselves, followed his continuing guidance from afar. A young Chinese mestizo, Sergio Osmeña, leader of the Nacionalista Party, became the Assembly's speaker, a position he would hold until 1916, and for six more years in its successor body, the House of Representatives. Manuel Quezon, a former guerrilla captain, went off to Washington as a Resident Commissioner, 1909–1916, to begin his own brilliant political career.

Meanwhile, in the so-called Insular Cases, the United States Supreme Court defined the relationship of the United States to its overseas acquisitions and their populations. After vacillating whether or not the Constitution followed the flag, the Court determined that the Philippine Islands were possessions, yet not parts of the United States of America. The Court further ruled that, though their inhabitants were citizens of the Philippines, they were only nationals of the United States, without the rights or privileges of American citizenship. Americans, who opposed the outcry favoring territorial self-government and eventual statehood for the Philippines, through the Constitutional procedures for the preparation and admission of new states to the Union (Art. IV, Sec. 3), could stop worrying.

It fell to President Woodrow Wilson, a Democrat, to terminate the Taft Era, and, incidentally, to afford historians a moment for reflection. The annexation of the Philippines scuttled the most radical hopes of the *ilustrados* and their followers, who wanted only to be left alone to consolidate their revolution against Spain, though efforts at conciliating them commenced with their subjugation by American troops. President McKinley, in 1898, had proclaimed his policy of "benevolent assimilation" to substitute, in his own words, "the mild sway of justice for arbitrary rule," while Taft as civil governor, in 1901, ventured so far as to predict home rule for the Filipino people one day, a government of their own, which drew ridicule back home from Mark Twain and William James among the still bitter opponents of the bearers of the white-man's burden.

As Professor Glenn May points out, the record for the Taft era of annexation's "profoundly interesting experiment," was uneven:

> For example, although more than a thousand U.S. teachers were hired to oversee the educational system, the schools could not overcome the problem of maintaining attendance during planting and harvest seasons. Matriculation rates were low, and most children received less than two years of schooling. There was not much progress in political education as well, partly due to the Commission's own policies. Initially limiting the franchise to adult males with education, wealth, or previous governmental experience, the Commission insured that the families that had dominated local politics in the Spanish era would also control local politics in the U.S. period.

The Commission failed to realize its economic objectives as well. Taft aimed to attract US investment in Philippine agriculture by offering huge tracts from the public domain. But the US Congress proved uncooperative, allowing the Philippine government to sell no more than 1,024 hectares (about 2,530 acres) of public land to corporations. One measure favored by the Commission did receive Congressional approval and ultimately had an impact: the granting to the Philippines of free trade with the United States. The chief beneficiaries of that legislation were the growers of cash crops – above all, owners of large sugar estates – who now had a guaranteed market for their exports. Once again, US policy had the effect of strengthening the power of indigenous elites.[4]

In August 1913, President Wilson nominated Francis Burton Harrison, a Tammany Hall politician with no experience in the islands, to become governor-general underscoring the Democratic Party's platform promise of independence for the Philippines. Wilson also appointed Filipinos to a majority of seats in the upper house of the legislature. Most important, the Jones Act, or Autonomy Act of August 29, 1916, greatly enlarged Philippine powers of home rule, and promised independence as soon as a stable government could be established.

From this time on, there arose between American authorities and the Filipinos a fascinating, yet paradoxical, system of collaborative colonialism exercised through the politics of mutual manipulation. The Americans cautiously moved ahead, unwilling too abruptly to yield the task they had begun of constructing a stable, self-governing, and comparatively self-sufficient republic. Governor-General Harrison (1913–21) proceeded to Filipinize the civil service, the cabinet, and even his own executive powers. He leniently relinquished certain prerogatives to Manuel Quezon, now president of the Senate, and he yielded other rights to Sergio Osmeña, the leader of the lower house's majority. Quezon, Osmeña, and the aristocratic Dr Trinidad H. Pardo de Travera, leader of the Federalista Party, exemplified Filipino collaboration in the highest degree. Accommodating themselves to the increasingly complex patterns of assimilation, Filipino leaders acquiesced in the promise of eventual independence, yet inside themselves grew ever more reluctant to allow the United States to withdraw altogether.

However, by 1921, after eight years of Tammany-style personal politics and the disruptions to global markets induced by the First World War, the colony was noticeably slipping. Diseases including malaria and hookworm went unchecked. The mismanaged national bank headed by Quezon's and Osmeña's friend, Venancio Concepción, was virtually bankrupt, lacking, as it did, a central accounting system to oversee the huge loans it granted without collateral or to curb currency speculating by its officers.[5]

Reaction set in under Presidents Warren G. Harding and Calvin Coolidge through Governor General Leonard Wood (1921–27). Wood himself was a lifelong comrade-in-arms of "Teddy" Roosevelt dating from the 1898 campaign of the Rough Riders in Cuba. Sent to the Philippines in 1903 as military governor of Moro Province encompassing Mindanao and Sulu, Wood crushed the lingering resistance to American rule, to earn his reputation for ruthlessness. Wood repudiated Harrison's Filipinizing policies, and reinstated measures of military control to allow but scant prerogative to the legislature. Filipino leaders sent a memorial to President Calvin Coolidge, January 8, 1924, condemning Wood's arbitrary actions and seeking his recall. Supporting Wood, Coolidge upbraided the Filipinos as if they were ill-mannered children, and warned them that further outbursts might be proof enough of their unreadiness to govern themselves. Furious, Quezon derailed the Fairfield Bill for independence then making its headway through the United States Congress. His popularity soaring, Quezon complained he would "prefer a government run like hell by Filipinos to one run like heaven by Americans." Filipinos could no longer openly display any harmony of purpose with American authorities. This fracas delayed, perhaps by a decade, the movement toward home rule for the Philippine Islands.

The fundamental problem was economic. Tyranny was not the problem, neither too much nor too little. Since 1913, United States free-trade policies had fostered dependence on American markets, which increasingly ran counter to the Filipinos' movement toward political autonomy. Domestic sugar and tobacco interests within the United States joined together to resist Filipino competition. In 1933, the Democratic Party returned to power led by Franklin D. Roosevelt, which revitalized the forces supporting independence for the Philippines. Furthermore, the New Deal's autarchic programs for economic recovery united the nation's workers and farmers against outside competitors. Tobacco planters and sugar growers, producers of animal and vegetable fats hostile to coconut oil imports, and organized labor's spokesmen opposed to admitting any more job-busting immigrants from the colonial islands joined the party's core of anti-imperialists, to press for freeing the Philippine Islands as soon as possible. Together with the foreign policy isolationists and strategists, who were worrying over Imperial Japan's rising sun, the strength added by these new protectionists soon outweighed the power of vested interests defending their long-standing privileges, to make the time suddenly ripe for independence.

With Roosevelt's blessing and Congressional approval, the Tydings–McDuffie Act of March 24, 1934, brought the promise of independence for the Philippine Islands closer to realization. Independence under the new law would be granted in ten years. Filipinos would meanwhile govern themselves within a commonwealth. American business would continue to enjoy its profitable privileges, while products of the islands could still enter the United States under existing liberal terms. In 1935, Manuel Quezon easily won election as the first president of the commonwealth. Governor General Frank Murphy (1933–35) proved to be the last American to hold that office as the result of Quezon's elevation. Vice-President John Nance Garner led the United States delegation to Manila for Quezon's inauguration bolstered by 43 members of Congress, as Murphy became the first High Commissioner (1935–36) to the commonwealth. Nearby at the ceremony, Douglas MacArthur, Arthur MacArthur's son, stood out tall and erect in his new role as President Quezon's military advisor, his profile chiseled like a statue's.

All seemed to go well enough until December 8, 1941, Manila time, the same day Pearl Harbor was bombed, when Japanese warplanes attacked the Philippines, and were followed up with overwhelming troop landings at various points throughout the archipelago. Quezon and Osmeña escaped to Australia, to be followed weeks later, on Roosevelt's orders, by General Douglas MacArthur himself promising to return.

Filipinos, who were left behind, found themselves trapped in a terrible dilemma by Japan's smashing victories. Many politicians felt betrayed or abandoned. Benigno Aquino denounced the United States's failure to defend the Philippines. José Laurel claimed that "the sovereignty of America in the Philippines has ceased, as well as that of the Commonwealth Government." Tokyo's occupying forces set up a government similar to the commonwealth promising independence, which indeed was formally granted in October 1943. Even so, Japan's occupation proved repressively harsh. In Washington, Quezon and Osmeña organized a government-in-exile. Quezon died, in October 1944, from the tuberculosis he had long endured, barely two weeks before General MacArthur's return to liberate the Philippines. Osmeña, who waded ashore with MacArthur onto the island of Leyte, was installed as president of the Commonwealth of the Philipppines. Inside Tokyo Bay, September 2, 1945, the Great Pacific War officially came to an end.[6]

Unprecedented, the final spectacle, took place in Manila, July 4, 1946, in front of the monument to José Rizal, the martyred early nationalist. Paul V. McNutt, formerly the high commissioner and now ambassador to the Republic of the Philippines, lowered the Stars and Stripes. President Manuel Roxas, who had defeated Osmeña in the election just held, raised the flag of the Philippines. Bands played the national anthems. In from occupied Japan, the Supreme Commander of the Allied Powers, General Douglas MacArthur, exulted, "America buried imperialism here today." The colonial "experiment of profound interest," originating in annexation, had yielded at last to sovereign nationhood. Yet somehow the Philippine Islands seemed fated, notwithstanding such sentiments and the uniqueness of the occasion, to remain almost as ever dependent on the United States.

The central problem rests with Americans, who exaggerate the positive effects on the Philippines of their colonial rule, while they underestimate the Filipinos' demonstrated capacity to pursue independent paths for themselves.

Notes

NB For this essay's central narrative and commentary, my own work will serve as up to date and comprehensive. Dudden, A.P., *The American Pacific from the Old China Trade to the Present* (New York and Oxford: Oxford University Press, 1992, 1993), Ch. 4.

1 E.G. Bourne, "Historical Introduction," *Discovery, Conquest, and Early History of the Philippine Islands*, Cleveland, OH: Arthur H. Clark, 1907, p. 87.

2 For Beveridge's speech, see T.G. Paterson, *Major Problems in American Foreign Policy to 1914*, 3rd edn, Lexington, MA: D.C. Heath, 1989, 391; Mark Twain, "To the Person Sitting in Darkness," *North American Review*, CLXXII, pp. 161–76 (reprinted New York: Anti Imperialist League, n.d.).

3 The Filipino fatality figures cited are available on the Internet (http://www. phil-am-war.org), yet only for the period 1899 through 1902–1913.

4 G. A. May, "Philippines," in B.W. Jentleson, and T.G. Paterson (senior eds), *Encyclopedia of U.S. Foreign Relations*, New York and Oxford: Oxford University Press, 1997, Ch. III, p. 392.

5 For the near bankruptcy of the Philippines National Bank (PNB) that plagued the administrations of Governors General Francis Burton Harrison and Leonard Wood, see

S. Karnow, *In Our Image: America's empire in the Philippines*, New York: Random House, 1989, pp. 248–49; L.E. Gleeck, Jr, *The American Governors General and High Commissioners in the Philippines: Proconsuls, nation builders and politicians*, New Day: Quezon City, Philippines, 1986, pp. 158–59, 180.

6 L.C. Dery, "Japan's New Order in the Philippines, 1942–1945: A blueprint for Asia Under Japan," *Philippines Social Sciences Review*, XLVIII (January–December 1984), pp. 291–361; A.L. Santos *et al.*, *Under Japanese Rule: Memories and Reflections*, edited with an Introduction by Renato Constantino, Foundation for Nationalist Studies: Quezon City, Philippines, n.d. (1991?).

References

Beisner, R.L., *Twelve against Empire: The anti-imperialists, 1898–1900*, New York: McGraw-Hill, 1968.

Corpuz, O.D., *The Roots of the Filipino Nation*, Vol. 2, Philippine Centennial Edition (1898–1998), Quezon City, P.I.: ALAHI Foundation, 1989.

Cotterell, A.. *East Asia from Chinese Predominance to the Pacific Rim*, New York and Oxford: Oxford University Press, 1993.

Cruz, R.V., *America's Colonial Desk and the Philippines, 1898–1934*, Quezon City, PI: University of the Philippines Press, 1974.

Dudden, A.P., *The American Pacific from the Old China Trade to the Present*, New York and Oxford: Oxford University Press, 1992, 1993.

Gianakos, P.E. (ed.), *George Ade's "Stories of 'Benevolent Assimilation'"*, Quezon City, PI: New Day, 1985.

Gleeck, Jr, L.E., *The American Governors-General and High Commissioners in the Philippines*, Quezon City, PI: New Day, 1986.

Hayden, J.R., *The Philippines: A study in national development*, New York: Macmillan, 1942.

Jenista, F. L., *The White APOs: American governors on the Cordillera Central*, Quezon City, P.I.: New Day, 1987.

Karnow, S., *In Our Image: America's empire in the Philippines*, New York: Random House, 1989.

Onorato, M.P., *Leonard Wood and the Philippine Cabinet Crisis of 1923*, Metro Manila, PI: J.E. Palabay, 1988.

Salamanca, B.S., *The Filipino Reaction to American Rule, 1901–1913*, Quezon City, PI: New Day, 1968, 1984.

Stanley, P.W. (ed.), *Reappraising an Empire: New perspectives on Philippine–American history*, Cambridge, MA: Harvard University Press, 1984.

Thomson, Jr, J.C. *et al.*, *Sentimental Imperialists: The American experience in East Asia*, New York: Harper & Row, 1981.

14

Cold War Casualties: The Impact of American Nuclear Testing Policies in the Pacific, 1954

Martha Smith-Norris

On March 1, 1954, the United States detonated a devastating, 15-megaton, thermonuclear weapon at its proving grounds on the Bikini Atoll in the Marshall Islands.[1] Code-named BRAVO, this bomb released the energy equivalent of 15 million tons of TNT. The explosion vaporized the test island, leaving a huge crater in the lagoon floor. The blast then pushed outward, stripping the nearby islands of all vegetation. After ten minutes, a cloud formed which was more than 65 miles wide.[2]

Although BRAVO has been discussed briefly in several books and articles,[3] this test warrants further historical analysis for a number of reasons. Firstly, it was the largest thermonuclear explosion ever carried out by the United States.[4] One thousand times more powerful than the atomic bomb that leveled Hiroshima, BRAVO released an unprecedented amount of radioactivity into the atmosphere.[5] Secondly, new information suggests that the immediate and long-term effects of the explosion were much more extensive than previously acknowledged by the US government. In addition to the environmental damage caused by BRAVO, 23 Japanese fishermen, and hundreds, perhaps thousands, of Marshallese were seriously harmed by the test. Thirdly, the BRAVO incident reveals much about the priorities of US foreign policy during the Cold War. In the race against the Soviet Union for nuclear supremacy, the protection of the Marshallese and Japanese was not a high priority for American decision-makers. A central assumption behind the test was that national security was more important than the health and safety of the peoples living and working near the proving grounds. Fourthly, BRAVO illustrates the importance of public relations in American Cold War policies. In order to maintain domestic and foreign support for its testing program in the Pacific, Washington downplayed the destruction caused by the explosion; it also argued that testing was necessary for the defence of the United States and the rest of the "Free World." Although these tactics helped the Eisenhower administration maintain domestic backing for the testing program, they made it more difficult for the Marshallese and Japanese affected by the March 1 explosion to gain recognition for their plight in the United States.

In addition to secondary sources and memoirs, this study is based on official documents found in the Dwight D. Eisenhower Presidential Library in Abilene,

Kansas, the National Archives in Washington, D., the National Archives II in College Park, Maryland and the Public Records Office in Kew, England. Evidence presented at a 1994 Congressional hearing was also valuable.

Of course, the BRAVO explosion must be analyzed in the context of the Cold War. Since 1946, the United States had been pursuing a policy of containment against Soviet communism.[6] Although this remained a "Europe-first" strategy, American policy makers increasingly viewed the Pacific as an important component of US security policy. As General Douglas MacArthur put it in 1949: "The Pacific has become an Anglo-Saxon lake and [our] line of defense runs through the chain of islands fringing the coast of Asia."[7]

Anti-communist policies at home reinforced the containment strategy abroad. As McCarthyism swept the United States, Americans became increasingly fearful of a nuclear attack from the USSR. According to one observer, American nuclear tests "were conducted at a time when we were teaching our school children to dive under desks to escape the effects of the [Soviet] nuclear bombs."[8] The US tested its first hydrogen bomb in 1952 but when the USSR matched this achievement the following year, there was great urgency on the part of the American government to develop more powerful thermonuclear weapons.[9]

When Dwight D. Eisenhower came to power in 1953, he remained committed to the policy of containment established under Harry Truman. However, in an attempt to cut costs and still maintain the lead in the Cold War, Eisenhower adopted a defense strategy which later became known as the "New Look." This policy comprised a number of elements including a general reduction of military costs, fewer conventional forces, and an increased reliance on nuclear weapons. Unlike his predecessor, Eisenhower attempted, as Saki Dockrill points out, "to use nuclear weapons as the main instrument of US national security policy."[10] In order to deter Soviet aggression and expansion, the United States would depend primarily upon the capacity for instant and "massive" nuclear retaliation.[11] The testing and development of a whole new "family" of thermonuclear weapons was central to this defense policy.[12] As Jane Dibblin describes it: "BRAVO was … a crucial stepping-stone in the Cold War race for nuclear superiority."[13]

In early January 1954, President Eisenhower authorized the Atomic Energy Commission (AEC)[14] to conduct a series of seven thermonuclear tests at the US proving grounds in the Pacific.[15] The previous year, the AEC had informed Congress that "tests should be held overseas until it could be established more definitely that continental detonations would not endanger the public health and safety."[16] As the United States was preparing for the "Castle" series in late January, a Japanese fishing boat, the *Fukuryu Maru No. 5*,[17] was heading south-east from Yaizu, a port situated south of Tokyo, Japan. On board the 99.9 ton vessel were 23 crewmen. About a month later, the vessel changed course and headed westward to fish in the vicinity of the Marshall Islands. On the morning of March 1, the fishermen observed a brilliant, reddish, light to the west-south-west of their vessel. The colour of this bright light gradually turned to white-yellow and back to red before fading away. Two blasts were heard before a mushroom-shaped cloud appeared on the horizon; this cloud expanded, eventually covering the sky with darkness.

On first seeing the light, the crew began hauling in the lines. About three hours later, white ash began to fall on the deck where they were working. Once the lines were secure, the vessel turned north, and the crew processed the catch (mainly tuna) on the upper deck. By noon, the decks were so covered that the fishermen were making "visible footprints" in the white dust. Within two or three days, all of them became ill, suffering from headaches and nausea. A week later, the fishermen began suffering from painful irritations, from burns to skin exposed to the ash – on the neck, the face, the ears and the area where they wore the "hachi maki" (a cotton towel wrapped around the head). On March 14, the fishermen arrived back at their homeport of Yaizu.[18]

From the beginning of the Cold War, the American government had viewed a close relationship with Japan as a critical aspect of its containment strategy.[19] After the communist victory on mainland China, followed by the outbreak of war in Korea, the United States had moved to strengthen its diplomatic, military and economic ties with Japan.[20] In 1951, Washington signed formal peace and security treaties with Tokyo.[21] Three years later, BRAVO heightened tensions in this new alliance. As Roger Dingman points out, the US government's handling of the *Fukuryu Maru* incident "imposed the most serious strain on Japanese-American relations since 1945."[22]

One of the main sources of tension between the two countries was Washington's decision to withhold information regarding the "Castle" series. About seven hours after BRAVO was detonated, the US Weather Station located nearest the test site notified the AEC's laboratory in New York that "massive" fallout was occurring in the region.[23] Then, for about 30 hours after this message, there was a mysterious "blackout" of all information coming from the Marshall Islands.[24] Four days after the test, the chairman of the Atomic Energy Commission, Lewis Strauss, advised all American personnel that "no public release will be made in regard to fallout … Washington presently plans no [report], no announcement and urgently requests that you not make anything public on these matters."[25]

Once information began to leak out from the Pacific,[26] the US government was forced to make a statement. In a brief report given on March 12, the AEC downplayed the importance of the blast, calling it a "routine" test. Although 28 Americans and 236 Marshallese had been evacuated from the area, this was merely a "precautionary measure … There were no burns and all [were] reported well."[27]

A different picture began to emerge on March 16. On that date, the Japanese press announced to the world that the fishermen aboard the *Fukuryu Maru* had been seriously affected by BRAVO. On the same day, the Japanese Foreign Office informed the American embassy in Tokyo that 23 Japanese crewmen were showing signs of radiation exposure. It also reported that, although most of the contaminated cargo from the ship was intercepted, some had been sent to markets in Tokyo, Nagoya, Kobe, Osaka, and Kyoto.[28]

Washington tried to limit the publicity damage from the incident by rushing two American experts to Tokyo. The AEC sent Dr John B. Morton, director of the Atomic Bomb Casualty Commission in Hiroshima, and Merril Eisenbud, Director of the AEC's Health and Safety Laboratory. From the beginning, it was clear that the primary responsibility of these experts was not to treat the injured crewmen, but rather, to limit public disclosure regarding the incident.[29] The two men were expected to learn as much as possible about the human effects of radiation while at the same time keeping technical information about BRAVO secret from the Japanese.[30] Once they got to Japan, the government there allowed the Americans to visit the fishermen who had been taken to Yaizu Hospital; they were also allowed to inspect the *Fukuryu Maru* itself. After these investigations, the experts informed the State Department that the crew had received a dangerous dose of radiation of between and 50 and 75 roentgens.[31] In another message, Eisenbud revised this estimate upwards, arguing that "the actual dose could have been two, ten or even one hundred times higher."[32] According to a later report prepared by the Department of Defense, the "mean gamma exposure" for the *Fukuryu Maru* crew was actually 290 roentgens.[33] At the time, the maximum permissible exposure of radiation for AEC personnel was 3.9 roentgens.[34]

The British embassy in Tokyo agreed that the fishermen had been exposed to high levels of radiation. According to the British, the Japanese crew were "showing symptoms different from the burns suffered by the people in Hiroshima and Nagasaki." The fact that they had eaten radioactive fish and smoked cigarettes on which the ash had fallen meant that fallout had been introduced into their "lungs, their digestive organs and the marrow of their bones."[35]

In order to deflect responsibility for the incident away from the US, the administration tried to make it appear that the *Fukuryu Marù* was actually a communist spy vessel. On March 25, William Leonhart, a representative for the US embassy in Tokyo, presented a long, detailed, not so subtle list of questions to the Japanese Ministry of Foreign Affairs. For example, he asked, did the *Fukuryu Maru* normally operate by itself away from all other vessels? What was known about the personal backgrounds and political activities of the crew? Did the fishermen listen to communist radio stations? Were there any known connections between crew members and the communist party? What about the fishermen's relatives? Did they have any communist affiliations?[36]

Although no evidence was ever found which linked the fishermen to the communist party, the allegations continued. On March 26, the AEC Chairman visited the Pacific Proving Grounds where he witnessed the second test of the "Castle" series. An aggressive anti-communist, Strauss raised questions about the Japanese fishermen and their boat. Even though the *Fukuryu Maru* was carrying 18,000 pounds of tuna,[37] Strauss told the US press secretary, James Hagerty, that the vessel was not really a Japanese fishing boat at all, but rather, a "Red spy outfit" commanded by a Soviet agent. Apparently, the AEC head also said that: "If I were the Reds, I would fill the oceans all over the world with radioactive fish. It would be so easy to do!"[38]

In the same vein, Sterling Cole, the Chairman of the Joint Committee on Atomic Energy, stated publicly that because the Japanese vessel might have been engaged in spying on the American test, the United States would make no commitment to pay any compensation until a full investigation had been carried out. Cole's statement was widely criticized in Japan. The people of Hokkaido, for example, found his accusations to be both "preposterous and insulting."[39]

As the United States tried to deflect responsibility for the effects of BRAVO, the Japanese press reported that new cargoes of radioactive fish were arriving from the Pacific. One scientist at Tokyo University predicted that two of the Japanese fishermen would die from radiation sickness. He described Japan as a "victimized country" and the US as an "irresponsible" nation. Sharing these views, local prefecture assemblies, youth associations and women's organizations protested against nuclear testing by sending petitions to both the Japanese and the American governments.[40]

In his analysis of the growing anti-American attitude in Japan, Robert Murphy, the Acting Secretary of State for International Political Affairs, emphasized the "emotion and ignorance" of the Japanese. In his view, they were "pathologically sensitive" about nuclear weapons.[41] Similarly, Ambassador Allison called attention to the "peculiar psychology" of the Japanese, which combined feelings of "nationalism, neutralism, utopianism" and "softness toward communism."[42] According to him, a period of "uncontrolled masochism," had followed the *Fukuryu Maru* incident as the Japanese reveled in "fancied martyrdom." In a message to the State Department, Allison suggested a quick lump-sum settlement to the injured fishermen in order to weaken the position of the "pacifists, feminists and professional anti-Americans" in Japan.[43]

As protest in Japan mounted, the government there sent an Aide Memoire to Washington listing the economic and psychological costs of BRAVO.[44] Japanese leaders demanded that the United States pay compensation to the injured *Fukuryu Maru* crew and their families and pay damages to the tuna industry.[45] In addition, Tokyo protested against Washington's decision (announced on March 24) to expand the danger zone around the US testing site in the Pacific. After BRAVO, this zone was increased from 67,000 to 570,000 square miles.[46] As the Japanese government pointed out, this enlargement would have very negative effects on the fishing industry which employed over one million people. The expansion not only made it "well nigh impossible for fishing to take place in the danger area, but also forced the Japanese fishing boats operating south of the expanded area … to make detours which involved sailing of two and a half to three days."[47] As a result of the economic and political problems caused by BRAVO, the Japanese leaders asked the United States to suspend the testing program in the Pacific, at least during the busy fishing season.[48]

The State Department was unsympathetic to the Japanese request. According to Secretary of State Dulles, the importance of the American testing program to "national and world security" outweighed the concerns of the Japanese fishermen.[49] Through Ambassador Allison, the State Department conveyed its regret for the *Fukuryu Maru* incident and its concern for the crew members. Precautions would be taken to prevent a repetition of this "accident," but the Japanese had to understand that the development of nuclear weapons was important to the "security of the free world."[50]

In Tokyo, tensions continued to increase as the US embassy received numerous reports that testing was affecting additional Japanese fishing boats and their catches. According to one account, the *Koei Maru* disposed of 7,000 tons of tuna because of its exposure to the March 1 test.[51] In order to deal with the mounting political problems caused by these reports, Allison asked the Atomic Energy Commission to send a non-technical report for public release emphasizing the "omnipresence of natural radioactivity" in the region.[52] Complying with this request, the AEC's Division of Biology and Medicine provided a statement including the assurance that "Not all of the radiation which one ordinarily observes with Geiger counters comes from atomic bombs. There is natural background radiation everywhere … on the earth's surface, in the air, and even in human and animal bodies and in plants."[53]

In another attempt to manage the domestic and foreign reactions to BRAVO, the Operations Coordinating Board (OCB), the American body responsible for disseminating public information related to nuclear weapons, recommended that the official policy should "tend to minimize the incident" in order to "under-cut Communist propaganda."[54] In keeping with this advice, Strauss presented a public statement, approved by the president, on March 31. During this speech, the AEC chairman dismissed press accounts describing the test that took place on March 1 as "devastating" and "out of control." These reports were "misapprehensions" resulting from the fact that the wind had shifted "unexpectedly" and that the yield of the explosion was "about double that of the calculated estimate."[55]

According to Strauss' version of the incident, the *Fukuryu Maru* had wandered into the danger zone established by the US at its testing site near Bikini and therefore was guilty of trespass.[56] At the time, however, Strauss and other officials knew that the fishing boat had actually been *outside* the AEC's announced danger area when it was showered with radioactive fallout. A background report prepared by the State Department circulated the day before this press conference clearly states that "Investigation showed that the *Fukuryu Maru* was 14 miles outside the … danger zone at the time of the incident."[57]

When the statement by the AEC head reached Eisenbud and Morton in Japan, they were shocked because they realized that it could not be supported by the evidence available at the American embassy in Tokyo. But, as Eisenbud pointed out, Strauss' speech was understandable from the "point of view of the liability of the US for damages sustained by the fishermen and the owner of the *Fukuryu Maru*."[58] Indeed, a memo issued the day before the press conference by the Operations Coordinating Board recommended that the administration should emphasize the "accidental" nature of the incident, "without any implication of legal responsibility on the part of the US government."[59] Perhaps still concerned about the legal implications, Strauss reiterated the inaccurate information in his autobiography. In *Men and Decisions*, he suggests that the Japanese fishing trawler "must have been well inside the danger area."[60]

During his press conference, the AEC head also minimized the environmental damage caused by BRAVO. He denied reports of widespread contamination of tuna and other fish caused by the American test. According to Strauss, at certain times of the year: "almost all fish caught [near Bikini] were normally poisonous as a result of feeding on certain seasonally prevalent micro-organisms."[61] Experts like Eisenbud were less sanguine about the environmental impact of the explosion. Even before he had left for Tokyo, Eisenbud had been informed by an AEC representative that "About one million pounds of tuna were suspected of being contaminated" by BRAVO.[62] At the time of Strauss' statement, other American scientists were not confident that the fish caught near the test site could be safely eaten. Indeed, scientists predicted that it would take at least ten years to determine the health hazards associated with the contaminated fish.[63]

Yet, in his statement, the AEC chairman downplayed the consequences of the test on human health. Although he acknowledged that fallout had rained down on 236 inhabitants of the "little islands of Rongelap, Rongerik, and Uterik," US Joint Task Force Seven had promptly evacuated all the "natives" and moved them to Kwajalein Atoll for medical observation. Strauss recounted visiting these people, explaining that he had found them all "to be well and happy." In fact, Strauss continued, "we have more natives than we started with … since one child was born while I was there and four more were expected." (This caused laughter at the press conference.) The situation regarding the 23 Japanese fishermen was "less certain due to the fact that our people have not yet been permitted by the Japanese authorities to make a proper clinical examination." Although skin lesions had been observed on the bodies of the crew, they were "already healing." According to Strauss, the injuries had been caused by the "chemical activity of the converted material in the coral rather than [by] radioactivity."[64]

Eisenbud was especially disturbed when he read these parts of the AEC chairman's statement. According to him, the argument about the cause of the burns suffered by the fishermen was "particularly painful to read since it was not so."[65] When he had inspected the crew on March 25 and 26, Eisenbud had discovered skin burns on the men, "particularly on their scalps and along the line of their trouser belts where the fallout particles had become lodged as they stood shirtless on deck when the fallout was occurring." In addition, Eisenbud found that the fishermen's thyroids contained readily measurable amounts of the radioactive isotope, Iodine 131. Curiously, US media reports stated that Eisenbud was never allowed to visit the injured crewmen.[66]

Information that was flowing into the State Department on a daily basis from the American embassy in Tokyo also contradicted the AEC chairman's soothing assurances. During the period from March 16 to 31, many telegrams arrived indicating that the health of the Japanese fishermen was deteriorating. For example, on the very morning of Strauss' press conference, the State Department received a message from Ambassador Allison warning that "Informed advice regarding patients today indicate blood counts of three [of the crew] remain dangerously low." Later that same day, the ambassador urgently cabled for "advice as to any new type of therapy to treat radiation injuries."[67]

The reports given to the public regarding the condition of the Marshallese were similarly misleading. In 1947, the United Nations had assigned the Marshall Islands as a Trust Territory of the United States. Under this accord, the American government had agreed, among other things, to "protect" the land, resources, and health of the inhabitants.[68] Shortly after BRAVO, however, the Marshallese closest to the blast began to suffer from radiation exposure.

In both his public statement and his autobiography,[69] the AEC Chairman claimed that the "natives" were evacuated "promptly." However, the evidence casts doubt on this positive spin. Although the Atomic Energy Commission recorded "massive" amounts of fallout in the region within seven hours of the blast, the Marshallese living closest to the test were not evacuated for more than two days. Uninformed about the hazards of fallout, many of the children played in the white dust and "ate it," thinking that it looked like snow.[70]

The Rongelapese probably suffered the most. After receiving about 175 roentgens of radiation, they were left on the island for approximately 50 hours before evacuation to Kwajalein Atoll.[71] In terms of blood count, they sustained the same degree of damage as did the Japanese who were about 1.5 miles from ground zero at Hiroshima and Nagasaki.[72] Prior to evacuation, about two-thirds of the people of Rongelap began to experience nausea, vomiting, diarrhea, headaches, eye pain, numbness, and burning and itching of the skin. Following their removal to Kwajalein, skin lesions and loss of hair developed in the Rongelapese, due largely to beta irradiation. When the people were examined, American medical personnel discovered that their white blood cells were "considerably depressed" and that "significant doses of radiation had probably been received." In addition to the external exposure, analyses of the urine showed that "measurable amounts of radioactive material had been absorbed internally."[73] Despite these heavy doses of radiation, the Atomic Energy Commission provided the evacuated Marshallese with only cursory medical treatment. According to Jabwl Jojur, a health aide from Rongelap: "three days [after evacuation] we had burns all over our bodies and our hair began to fall out: some people actually went bald. When we asked the AEC doctors to help us understand what had happened, they did not tell us."[74]

As a result of the health problems caused by BRAVO, representatives for the Marshallese sent a petition to the United Nations protesting against nuclear tests in the Pacific. The Marshall Islanders made it clear that they did not wish to repudiate the US as the governing agency for the islands under the UN trusteeship agreement. They hoped that the United States would stop testing, but if this was impossible, that is, if the United Nations judged that these tests were absolutely necessary, then the Marshallese asked the American government to proceed with greater regard to their safety. Next time, for example, the US should transport all inhabitants, their livestock and their possessions to safe locations prior to the explosion. In addition, it should give safety instructions to the people living near the testing sites since "the people of Rongelap would have avoided much danger if they had known not to drink the water ... after the radioactive dust had fallen on the island." Finally, the Marshallese requested that Washington provide compensation to those who were forced to evacuate their homes.[75]

Although the tone of this message was very moderate, the US embassy in Tokyo warned the State Department that the "language and form of the petition might indicate communist inspiration."[76] In its response to the Marshall Islanders, the United States issued a carefully worded statement, jointly drafted by the Atomic Energy Commission and the Department of Defense (DOD). According to this statement, it was very important for the Marshallese to understand that the United States would not be conducting nuclear tests if it had not been determined, after very careful study, that they were required in the "interests of general peace and security." The reply also reassured the Marshall Islanders that there was "no medical reason to expect any permanent after-effects on the general health [of the inhabitants] due to fallout."[77]

In his book, *Blowing on the Wind*, Robert Divine argues that although the Atomic Energy Commission tried to disguise the extent of the damage, it "did not intentionally dust the Marshall Islanders and the Japanese fishermen with fallout."[78] However, testimony and documents presented at a 1994 Congressional hearing suggest that the AEC and DOD knew at least twelve hours in advance of BRAVO that the wind direction was changing in an unfavourable easterly direction (towards Rongelap) but proceeded with the explosion anyway.[79] Additional evidence presented at the hearing indicated that the radiation fallout from the March 1 test extended over as many as 28 islands and atolls in the Marshall chain and may have affected thousands of indigenous people instead of the 236 acknowledged by the AEC.[80]

At the hearing, questions were also raised about the delay in the evacuation of the Marshallese. Importantly, 28 American servicemen were moved from Rongerik by air approximately 26 hours after BRAVO; yet the indigenous people who were closer to the blast were not removed for another one to two days.[81] The question remains: why were the Rongelapese and others not evacuated with the US servicemen? According to testimony given at the hearing, there were seven US naval vessels positioned near the test site. Indeed, the *U.S.S. Gypsy* was moored just a few miles off Rongelap as BRAVO was detonated.[82] In Eisenbud's view, the delay should have been the subject of an inquiry. Speaking before the 1994 hearing, he added, "The airmen were taken off … [by air] in 26 hours … The Rongelapese were removed by, I think, LST after 50 hours, and that was a dreadful error on somebody's part because they could have been evacuated [sooner]. There were plenty of amphibious aircraft there at the time. We used them in our work regularly."[83]

Even though Washington was aware of the destruction caused by BRAVO, it never carried out a formal investigation into the episode. Instead, the Eisenhower administration continued to use public relations strategies to gain support for the testing program. For example, the State Department recommended that all official statements emphasize the significance of BRAVO for the defense of the "Free World." Meanwhile, the Operations Coordinating Board advised that more stress be placed on the peaceful applications of nuclear energy. In keeping with this advice, the Atomic Energy Commission sent 26 government films depicting the peaceful potential of the atom to the Marshall Islands.[84]

It is doubtful that these statements and films provided much comfort to the Marshallese and Japanese affected by nuclear fallout. In late April 1954, the American embassy in Tokyo received numerous reports that more radioactive fishing vessels were entering port in Japan.[85] Over the next two months, complaints addressed to the American government continued to arrive from various prefectures in Japan; these notices detailed direct and indirect losses to fishermen from contaminated fish.[86] According to the British embassy in Tokyo, by May 10, 56 million pounds of tuna, from 61 different vessels, were found to be radioactive. Of these, at least 208,000 pounds were considered sufficiently radioactive to be dangerous, and were destroyed. Some of these fish were "caught in areas as far away from Bikini as the waters around Okinawa." Radioactivity was also detected in rainwater and vegetable gardens in various parts of Japan.[87]

Back in the US, when American citizens raised questions about these reports, Washington issued standard replies. According to a letter provided by the Chief of the State Department's Public Services Division, the information coming from the Pacific regarding extensive contamination of fish, crops, and rain was actually the result of "malicious propaganda inspired by Communist ... elements." Apparently, the reports from Japan were "entirely without foundation."[88]

At the same time, official documents showed that the US government was aware of the environmental damage caused by BRAVO. During a meeting on May 12, Eisenbud reported to the Atomic Energy Commission that "it appeared certain that some contamination [of fish] had occurred" in the Pacific.[89] The following month, Secretary Dulles notified the Tokyo embassy that an internal warning would be released to mariners to stay clear of Rongelap and Rongerik because of the dangerous levels of residual radiation there.[90] An AEC report also acknowledged that the radiation from the test had spread as far as the United States. According to this document, the radioisotope Iodine 131 had been discovered in the thyroids and urine of grazing animals in the US after BRAVO. Extremely minute quantities had also been detected in the urine of some humans.[91]

In his autobiography, the chairman of the Atomic Energy Commission recalls that the "United States Food and Drug Administration (FDA) had advised us that their inspectors found no instance of unusual radioactivity in any shipments of fish from Pacific waters."[92] But, during a meeting that Strauss himself attended in May, the AEC's Director of Biology and Medicine reported that a "contaminated tuna fish had been discovered by the personnel of the Food and Drug Administration in checking a cargo imported from Japan."[93] According to information provided by the FDA to the State Department a few months later, at least three radioactive tuna had been discovered among exports from Japan in a California cannery since March 1. The radioactive material was found largely in the skull and bones of the fish, "indicating contamination through ingestion." Upon receiving this report, the State Department decided that it would not inform the Japanese embassy of these developments "at this time."[94]

When the "Castle" series officially ended in June 1954, the AEC and DOD issued a joint announcement emphasizing the positive results of the tests. The explosions not only contributed to the development of thermonuclear weapons, but they also added to the "security of the United States and the Free World."[95] Nevertheless, in the summer and fall, more bad news arrived from Japan. In September, the *Kyodo News* reported that a 570 pound marlin caught off Kanagawa Prefecture was found to be highly radioactive.[96] On October 4, the Japanese embassy in Washington informed the State Department that a number of additional cases had been reported where "unusually high radioactivity counts" were found on the catch of Japanese fishing boats.[97]

More unsettling reports arrived a few days later when the US government learned that the *Fukuryu Maru*'s radio operator, Aikichi Kuboyama, had just died of serum hepatitis, a secondary result of his exposure to radiation.[98] The funeral ceremony took place at Kuboyama's homeport of Yaizu. Although Ambassador Allison did not attend, three of his subordinates were present; one of them read a brief note of condolence prepared by the US embassy.[99] This message emphasized the "accidental" nature of the incident. The damage could not be undone. But, in an unfortunate choice of words, the note suggested that "in these respects and in many others too, we are as the 'Haiki Monogatari' truly says, only as dust in the face of the wind."[100]

In addition to this poorly phrased message, officials from the Atomic Energy Commission and Department of Defence publicly denied that Kuboyama was a victim of American nuclear fallout. Not surprisingly, these denials touched off a flurry of renewed protest in Japan. Afterwards, the Eisenhower administration moved quickly to compensate the Japanese victims of BRAVO. The US government gave Kuboyama's wife a check for one million yen (about $2,800). Later, a $2 million settlement was reached with the Japanese government for loss of life and property caused by BRAVO and other American tests.[101] As Michael Schaller describes the situation: "Eisenhower and Dulles welcomed resolution of the dispute as an inexpensive way to curtail antinuclear and anti-alliance sentiment within Japan."[102]

Although the United States government agreed to pay compensation, Washington never carried out an official inquiry into the incident and it never accepted legal liability for the damage caused by BRAVO. Instead, the Eisenhower administration continued to use public rhetoric to minimize the consequences of the test. On February 15, 1955, for example, Chairman Strauss gave a public report entitled "The Effects of High Yield Nuclear Weapons." During this speech, which was approved by the president and the OCB, Strauss conveyed some technical information about the impact of BRAVO but implied that the blast had occurred in an uninhabited region.[103] Not surprisingly, his account was heavily criticized in the Pacific since it did not mention the environmental damage caused by the test or the health injuries suffered by the Japanese fishermen and Marshall Islanders.[104]

During his statement in February, Strauss failed to mention that the people of Rongelap were forced to live on another atoll for an extended period of time due to the dangerous contamination levels on their island.[105] Furthermore, when individual American citizens raised questions about the human and environmental damage caused by BRAVO, they received reassuring responses from the US government. According to one reply issued from the State Department's Public Service Division, rumours about severe contamination and burns in the Marshall Islands were "in error." Indeed, the "natives" from Rongelap who were exposed to fallout were "healthy and well."[106]

These comforting messages to the public contrasted with many of the private reports and statements made by officials in the Eisenhower administration. During a meeting in September 1956, the Atomic Energy Commission discussed the problems involved in resettling the Rongelapese on their home island. Commissioner Willard Libby compared this case to "a reactor accident in an inhabited area" and commented that "this was the first practical experience the AEC had in relocating inhabitants in a previously contaminated area."[107]

Despite the persistence of contamination on Rongelap, the Atomic Energy Commission announced in early 1957 that the island was now "safe" for rehabitation. In June, the AEC returned 82 of the Rongelapese who had been exposed to BRAVO to their home island. At the same time, the agency moved another group of approximately 100 Marshallese to Rongelap. The AEC considered this latter group to be an "ideal comparison population" for medical studies since it was composed of people who were genetically related to the Rongelapese but not present at the time of the explosion on March 1, 1954.[108]

Based on available data regarding food crops on Rongelap, the Atomic Energy Commission was aware that the human intake of certain radioisotopes would probably increase after resettlement on the contaminated island. Despite the obvious dangers in this plan, the resettlement program would provide an "opportunity" to investigate the relationship between the ingestion of contaminated food and human health.[109] In 1958, the Atomic Energy Commission informed the State Department that it had "found evidence of internal contamination by radioactivity in these people."[110] The agency's medical team had made this discovery using an electronic device known as a whole body counter. Not only did this device prove an "unqualified success in providing direct data on the type and degree of internal contamination of a number of islanders," but it also was "useful in establishing that there was residual radioactivity present in certain foods and other materials."[111] Based on urine analyses completed the following year, an AEC study concluded that: "the return of the people to the slightly contaminated island of Rongelap has caused some increase in the body burdens of Cesium 137, Zinc 65 and Strontium 90."[112] Significantly, the studies showed that the control group was absorbing radioactivity through locally grown food at the same rate as the population that was exposed to BRAVO. Indeed, the body levels of the comparison population had become "indistinguishable from those of the originally exposed group" by 1959.[113]

As a result of the annual medical surveys conducted by the Atomic Energy Commission, the Rongelapese became increasingly concerned about their health status. Many of them worried about the radiological safety of their food and water supplies. In response, the AEC reassured the people from Rongelap that their health was "generally good" and their food and water "safe for consumption." The agency also stressed the importance of the medical examinations "to help insure their continued good health."[114]

By the early 1960s, however, medical reports indicated that the people on Rongelap who had been exposed to BRAVO were experiencing unusually high rates of cancer and other abnormal growths of the thyroid. Although these conditions were very rare in the world population, studies showed that approximately 33 per cent of the adults on Rongelap exposed to BRAVO (and 63 per cent of children exposed when younger than 10 years of age) later developed benign and malignant neoplasms in their thyroids.[115] One of the main causes of these thyroid problems was exposure to the radioistope Iodine 131. Most of the cases on Rongelap occurred in women. Similar health conditions were discovered at Uterik and other islands located even further away from the blast, such as Ebeye.[116]

In addition, studies on height, weight and bone structure indicated a degree of retardation in the growth and development of exposed children. In one study of Rongelapese children in the 6-year chronological age group, "three boys and one girl out of five boys and two girls exposed to radiation were markedly retarded in skeletal maturation." A slightly higher incidence of the congenital anomaly known as "hypoplasia of the fifth finger" was also discovered in children exposed to fallout from the March 1 test.[117]

As a result of the human and environmental damage caused by BRAVO and other nuclear tests, the Marshallese began asking the American government for compensation in the mid-1950s. Although some small claims were settled on an ad hoc basis,[118] a comprehensive agreement was not signed until 1983. Under this accord, which is known as the Compact of Free Association, the US government provided the four Marshallese communities most severely affected by the American testing program (Bikini, Enewetak, Rongelap, and Uterik) with a lump sum of $150 million. This money was to be used to establish health programs, set up scientific radiation studies and settle individual claims.[119] Significantly, compensation was awarded for a variety of serious radiation-related illnesses, such as cancers of the thyroid, breast, ovary, colon, and pharynx.[120]

When the Compact of Free Association was negotiated, many Marshallese, especially those directly affected by nuclear tests, were unhappy with the agreement and voted against it.[121] Some Marshall Islanders were concerned that the total amount of compensation did not cover all of the atolls and islands affected by nuclear tests;[122] others worried that the $150 million would not provide sufficient funding for future medical care and cleanup costs on their islands.[123] As a result of these concerns, an article (Article IX) was added to the compact leaving open the possibility that future claims would be considered, provided that they could be substantiated by compelling new evidence.[124] As representatives for the Marshall Islanders pointed out, this clause was not completely satisfactory since the US government, particularly the Department of Energy (which had succeeded the AEC in 1977) continued to keep much of the documentation related to BRAVO and other tests classified.[125]

In addition to health problems, one of the main concerns of the Marshallese in the 1980s was the contamination of their islands. The three locations most contaminated by BRAVO and other explosions were the test sites at the Bikini and Enewetak atolls and certain portions of Rongelap.[126] In 1968, the Atomic Energy Commission determined that the level of contamination on Bikini was within "acceptable exposure limits"; the people could be returned to their homes, provided that they agreed to stay away from locally grown foods such as the coconut crab.[127] Soon after resettlement took place, the US agency discovered unacceptably high levels of radionuclides in their bodies. Despite these findings, the people were not evacuated from Bikini for another ten years.[128]

Even after extensive cleanup operations at Enewetak, 73 per cent of the land on the atoll remained too contaminated in 1993 to use for the production of crops. One island in particular, called Runit, had been used as the disposal site for plutonium-contaminated soil collected throughout the testing region. According to the policy established by the US Defence Nuclear Agency,[129] radioactive waste was supposed to be plowed into a crater (created by a nuclear explosion), mixed in a cement slurry, and then covered with a concrete dome. Unfortunately, the cleanup operation was not completed properly; instead of being plowed into the crater, chunks of deadly plutonium metal were left on the surface soil of the island. Despite the obvious hazard, there were no fences erected around the site on Runit Island and the radioactive waste was readily accessible to the residents of Enewetak Atoll.[130]

Fearful of their continued exposure to radiation, the Rongelapese decided to abandon their island in 1985. Assisted by Greenpeace, they were resettled on the tiny island of Mejetto, located on the remote northwest quadrant of Kwajalein Atoll.[131] Once there, the Rongelapese discovered that the land was so sub-fertile that they had to depend on US Direct Aid ships for food.[132] Due partly to these unsatisfactory arrangements, the Department of Energy later informed them that, if they followed certain dietary and behavioral guidelines, they could safely return to Rongelap. Without sufficient information from the US government about the contamination of their island, this was a difficult choice for the people to make. As the Mayor of Rongelap pointed out in 1994, many difficult questions remained unanswered: "How much local food can we eat? Should our children be allowed to play in the sand? How many times a day should we wash their hands? How do we keep their hands out of their mouths? Is it safe for a baby to drink its mother's milk?"[133]

As a result of their immediate and long-term experience with the effects of BRAVO, many peoples in the Pacific believe that they were the victims of human radiation experiments.[134] They cite a number of reasons to support this perspective. To begin with, Washington did not provide specific warnings regarding BRAVO to those living or working near the test site.[135] Secondly, the area was not evacuated either before or immediately after the explosion. Thirdly, the Eisenhower administration provided only cursory medical assistance to the Japanese fishermen and Marshall Islanders injured by the test. Fourthly, there was ample evidence indicating that the Atomic Energy Commission and other agencies did have research interests in the peoples exposed to BRAVO.[136] As the representative for the Marshall Islanders put it: "putting the people back on Rongelap in 1957 with a so called control group certainly smacks of an experiment to me."[137]

Based on their first-hand experience with nuclear tests, it is understandable that many Japanese and Marshallese still believe that the American government used them as "guinea pigs" during the Cold War.[138] Although the available evidence does not support this charge, the archival documents do reveal a lot about the attitudes and priorities of American decisionmakers. Even though it was aware of the extensive damage caused by BRAVO, the Eisenhower administration responded to complaints from the Pacific in a rather callous and condescending manner. When the Japanese raised concerns about the impact of the March 1 test, American representatives dismissed them as "emotional," "ignorant," and "pathologically sensitive" about nuclear weapons.[139] In most of the official correspondence regarding the Marshall Islanders, American policymakers referred to them simply as "the Natives."[140] The AEC entitled its resettlement plan for the Rongelapese, "Project Hardy (The Return of the Native)."[141] In 1956, the AEC's Advisory Committee on Biology and Medicine wrote the following memo concerning the people of Uterik:

> We think that one very intriguing study can be made and plans are on the way to implement this. Uterik is the atoll furtherest [sic] from the March 1st shot, where people [who] were exposed got initially about 15 roentgens and then they were evacuated and … returned.
>
> … now that the island is safe to live on but is by far the most contaminated place in the world … it will be very interesting to go back and get good environmental data, how many per square mile, what isotopes are involved and sample of food changes in many humans through their urines, so as to get a measure of the human uptake when people live in a contaminated environment.
>
> Now, data of this type has never been available. While it is true that these people do not live, I would say, the way Westerners do, civilized people, it is nevertheless also true that these people are more like us than the mice. So that is something which will be done this winter.[142]

Given attitudes like this, it is not surprising that the Atomic Energy Commission and related agencies provided the peoples affected by BRAVO with only cursory medical care.[143] From the perspective of the Japanese and Marshallese exposed to the test, it seemed as if the Americans were mainly interested in them as research subjects.[144] Certainly, the "resettlement" programs on the contaminated islands of Uterik, Rongelap and Bikini suggest that the health and safety of these peoples was not a high priority for the US government.

During the 1950s, one of the main objectives of the Eisenhower administration was not to protect the peoples of the Pacific but rather to strengthen the "New Look" defense policy. An important component of this containment strategy was the testing and buildup of nuclear weapons. In the interests of national security, the US government developed elaborate public relations strategies to protect and promote its nuclear testing program in the Pacific. After BRAVO, the Eisenhower administration tried to conceal information about the blast. Officials then attempted to deflect responsibility for the incident away from the United States by implying that the victims were communist sympathizers. They also made public statements minimizing the human and environmental damage caused by the explosion. In addition, the administration argued that testing was necessary for "general peace and security." Although protest against nuclear explosions began to grow in different parts of the world, these public relations ploys helped the American government maintain domestic support for its testing program in the mid-1950s.[145] Not unexpectedly, the strategies also made it more difficult for the Japanese and Marshallese affected by the test to gain adequate compensation and recognition for their plight in the United States.[146] Even in the post-Cold War era, many peoples of the Pacific (particularly women and children) continue to suffer from the health and environmental effects caused by BRAVO and other nuclear explosions.

Notes

An earlier version of this essay appeared in the *Journal of American East Asian Relations*, Vol. 6 (1997). While the earlier version included more discussion of the role of the Atomic Energy Commission and the diplomatic implications of the BRAVO test, this article places greater emphasis on the public relations strategies employed by the Eisenhower administration and the human and environmental consequences of the 1954 explosion.

1 Between 1946 and 1958, the US conducted at least 66 nuclear tests in the Marshall Islands. Of these, 23 were exploded at Bikini Atoll and 43 at Enewetak Atoll; 17 of the 66 were thermonuclear (or hydrogen) weapons. The total explosive power of these tests was equivalent to 107,000 kilotons of TNT. The Marshall Islands are comprised of 29 atolls and five separate reef islands in the Central Pacific Ocean. The total number of islands exceeds 1,200 and the total land mass is approximately 70 square miles. The islands are located 2,400 miles southwest of Hawaii. See Oversight Hearing Before the Subcommittee on Natural Resources, House of Representatives, One Hundred Third Congress, on "Radiation Exposure from Nuclear Tests in the Pacific," Serial No. 103–68, February 24, 1994, Washington, pp. 24, 217, 229, 241; US Department of Energy, *United States Nuclear Tests: July 1945 Through September 1992*, DOE/NV–209 (Rev. 14) (Dec. 1994), pp. 1–8. Of course, the United States was not the only nation that conducted nuclear explosions in the Pacific. Great Britain carried out a dozen atmospheric explosions in Australia and at least 12 on Christmas Island between 1952 and 1958. By the late 1980s, France had been responsible for an estimated 93

underground and 42 above ground tests in the South Pacific atoll of Moruroa. See Jane Dibblin, *Day of Two Suns: U.S. Nuclear Testing and the Pacific Islanders*, London, 1988, p. 202.

2 Oversight Hearing, 24; Report Prepared by the Defense Nuclear Agency for the Department of Defense, "Castle Series 1954: Nuclear Test Personnel Review," DNA 6035F, April 1, 1982, National Archives II (hereafter NA II), Maryland.

3 See, for example, Robert Divine, *Blowing on the Wind: The nuclear test ban debate, 1954–60*, New York, 1978, pp. 3–13, 27, 38, 47–8, 131–33, 185; Roger Dingman, "Alliance in Crisis: The Lucky Dragon Incident and Japanese-American Relations," in Warren Cohen and Akira Iriye (eds), *The Great Powers in East Asia, 1953–60*, New York, 1990, pp. 187–214; Richard G. Hewlett and Jack M. Holl, *Atoms for Peace and War, 1953–61*, Berkeley, 1989, pp. 174–76, 223, 271–74, 283; Michael Schaller, *Altered States: The United States and Japan Since the Occupation*, New York, 1997, pp. 72–74. 185; Dibblin, *Day of Two Suns*, pp. 3–4, 24–8, 32, 40–2, 58–63; Saki Dockrill, *Eisenhower's New Look National Security Policy, 1953–61*, London, 1996, pp. 133–4; Jonathan M. Weisgall, "The Nuclear Nomads of Bikini," *Foreign Policy*, No. 39 (Summer 1980), pp. 83–86; Barton C. Hacker, "Radiation Safety, the AEC, and Nuclear Weapons Testing," *The Public Historian*, 14 (Winter 1992), pp. 50–53.

4 Stephen Ambrose, *Eisenhower: The President*, New York, 1984, p. 169.

5 Oversight Hearing, 36, 197.

6 For a discussion of the containment strategy and the emerging Cold War tensions in the early postwar period, see, for example, John Lewis Gaddis, *Strategies of Containment: A critical appraisal of postwar national security policy*, New York, 1982; Martin McCauley, *The Origins of the Cold War, 1941–49* (London, 1995).

7 Quoted in Thomas G. Paterson, J. Garry Clifford and Kenneth J. Hagan, *American Foreign Policy: A history (since 1900)*, Toronto, 1991, p. 458.

8 Testimony by Merril Eisenbud, Oversight Hearing, p. 122.

9 Ibid. See also David Holloway, *Stalin and the Bomb*, New Haven, 1994, pp. 305–308.

10 Dockrill, *Eisenhower's New Look*, p. 47; See also Robert Bowie and Richard Immerman, *Waging Peace: Eisenhower's Strategy for National Security*, New York, 1998, pp. 197–99; H.W. Brands, "The Age of Vulnerability: Eisenhower and the national insecurity state," *American Historical Review*, 94 (October 1989), pp. 963–89.

11 As President Eisenhower himself wrote: "The basic decision was to depend primarily upon a great capacity for retaliation – instantly." Quoted in McGeorge Bundy, *Danger and Survival: Choices About the Bomb in the First Fifty Years*, New York, 1990, p. 671, fn. 39; see also Bundy, pp. 246–60; Hewlett and Holl, *Atoms for Peace and War*, p. 272; Robert Wampler, "Ambiguous Legacy: the United States, Great Britain and the Foundations of NATO Strategy, 1948–57," PT II, Dissertation, Harvard, 1991, pp. 518–20; Samuel F. Wells, "The Origins of Massive Retaliation," *Political Science Quarterly*, 96 (Spring 1981), p. 44; Dockrill, *Eisenhower's New Look*, pp. 2–3, 48–71.

12 This "family" would include hydrogen weapons in a spectrum of sizes and yields. See Hewlett and Holl, *Atoms for Peace and War*, pp. 179–180.

13 Dibblin, *Day of Two Suns*, pp. 3–4.

14 Although the development and production of nuclear weapons were the "complementary responsibilities" of the Atomic Energy Commission and the Department

of Defense, they were the "primary functions" of the AEC. See Joint Chiefs of Staff (hereafter JCS) Memo, "Control of Atomic Weapons and Tests," 1958, JCS RG218, Records of the Joint Chiefs of Staff, 471.6, National Archives (hereafter NA), Washington.

15 Two memos, January 26 and 27, 1954, Administration Series, Ann Whitman File (hereafter AWF), Dwight D. Eisenhower Library (hereafter DDEL), Abilene. For a description of the preparations for these tests, see Richard Miller, *Under the Cloud: The decades of nuclear testing* (New York 1986), pp. 188–89.

16 Quoted in Weisgall, "The Nuclear Nomads," p. 76.

17 The unfortunate English translation of the vessel's name was the "Lucky Dragon."

18 All dates are in Japanese Standard Time. This description of events is based on an investigation by the Japanese government. See the "Interim Report on the *Fukuryu Maru No. 5* Accident," March 17, 1954, and the "Aide Memoire," undated, Department of State Record Group (hereafter DSRG) 59, 711.5611/4–3054, NA. Similar information appears in an undated memo from Merril Eisenbud, Director of the Health and Safety Lab of the Atomic Energy Commission, to the State Department, DSRG 59, 711.5611/4–3054, NA, Washington.

19 In April 1947, the Joint Strategic Survey committee noted that: "Japan is the one nation which could contain large armed forces of our ideological opponents in the Far East" while the United States and its European allies were engaged in a major offensive in the West. Quoted in Akira Iriye, "U.S.–Japanese Relations," in Yonosuke Nagai and Akira Iriye (eds), *The Origins of the Cold War in Asia*, New York, 1977, p. 403. See also Burton Kaufman, "Eisenhower's Foreign Economic Policy with Respect to East Asia," in *The Great Powers in East Asia*, p. 107.

20 Dockrill, *Eisenhower's New Look*, pp. 13–14.

21 Arthur Power Dudden, *The American Pacific: From the old China trade to the present*, New York, 1992, p. 213. Schaller, *Altered States*, p. 40.

22 Dingman, "Alliance in Crisis," p. 188.

23 The Weather Station was located on Rongerik atoll, located east of the test site. According to an AEC document, the "radiation detection devices on Rongerik atoll, on which 28 sevicemen were stationed, went off the scale at 100mr/hr." See AEC Background Memo Concerning the 1954 Radiation Exposure of the Rongelapese, April 26, 1961, DSRG 59, 711.5611/4–2861, NA II, Maryland. The commander of the Joint Task Force Seven (JTF7) reported that Warrant Officer J.A. Katrol, the person in charge of the Weather Station at Rongerik, became "very frightened when he saw the high readings on his instruments" after BRAVO. See Memo for Record from P.W. Clarkson, Major General Commander, JTF7, March 6, 1954, Records of the Atomic Energy Commission (hereafter AECRG) 326, Office of the Secretary, Formerly Top Secret General Correspondence Relating to Weapons, 1951–58 (hereafter OS, FTSGCW), NA II, Maryland.

24 According to Eisenbud, who was working at the AEC's Health and Safety Laboratory in New York at the time, American personnel aboard the ship *Estes* (situated near Rongerik) were prevented from using the radio transmission for 30 hours after the notification (regarding "massive" amounts of fallout) was received in New York. They were also forbidden to carry out requested aerial surveillance flights over the affected area. See Eisenbud, *An Environmental Odyssey: People, pollution, and politics in the life of a practical scientist*, Seattle, 1990, pp. 92–93; See also Eisenbud's Testimony, Oversight Hearing, pp. 72, 119.

25 Quotation from AEC files, presented by Jonathan Weisgall, Legal Counsel to the People of Bikini, Oversight Hearing, p. 32.

[26] In August 1953, the Atomic Energy Commission sent instructions to all members of JTF7 that would be participating in the BRAVO test. Emphasizing the importance of security, these directives explained that "the details of the tests and scientific data are not made known to the general public." Any persons responsible for leaks of information to other nations, either by accident or on purpose, would be "punishable by the law of the land by severe penalties." In the interest of national security, the members of JTF7 were forbidden to take photographs or to refer to BRAVO in any personal correspondence or telephone conversations. See Joint AEC-DOD Information Plan for Operation Castle, February 16, 1954, AECRG 326, OS, FTSGCW, NA II, Maryland. Despite these instructions, some information leaked out. On March 11, a Cincinnati newspaper quoted 2 letters from a US Marine stationed in the Pacific at the time of BRAVO. The first described the test from the serviceman's perspective and the second mentioned that "two destroyers ... pulled in here today bearing natives ... They were suffering from various burns and radioactivity." See Hacker, "Radiation Safety," p. 51.

[27] This statement has been discussed in other works including Eisenbud, *An Environmental Odyssey*, 98; Divine, *Blowing on the Wind*, p. 6; Dibblin, *Day of Two Suns*, pp. 58–59; Hacker, "Radiation Safety," pp. 49–50.

[28] Background Statement Relative to the United States Action in Connection with the *Fukuryu Maru* Incident Prepared by the Department of State, March 30, 1954, OCB, 091. Japan, OCB Central Files Series, White House Office: NSC Staff Papers, DDEL, Abilene.

[29] Schaller, *Altered States*, p. 72.

[30] Dingman, "Alliance in Crisis," pp. 192–93.

[31] Telegram from the American Embassy in Tokyo to the Secretary of State, March 20, 1954, DSRG 59, 711.5611/3–2054, NA, Washington. A roentgen is equal to the amount of radiation emitted by one gram of radium at a distance of one foot. It is also known as a REM. See Miller, *Under the Cloud*, p. 399.

[32] Telegram from the American embassy in Tokyo to the Department of State, including a memo from Merril Eisenbud, written "prior to April 9," DSRG 59, 711.5611/4–3054, NA, Washington.

[33] Report Prepared by the Defense Nuclear Agency for the DOD, "Castle Series 1954," April 1, 1982, p. 242.

[34] Hewlett and Holl, *Atoms for Peace and War*, p. 174.

[35] Telegram from A.S. Halford, Counsellor, British Embassy in Tokyo, to Colin Crowe, Far Eastern Department, Foreign Office, April 7, 1954, FO371/110695, Public Records Office (hereafter PRO), Kew.

[36] Memo from William Leonhart, First Secretary of the U.S. Embassy, March 22, 1954, DSRG 59, 711.5611/4–3054, NA, Washington.

[37] Long Telegram from the American Embassy in Tokyo to the Department of State, "Chronology of the *Fukuryu Maru*," March 28, 1955, DSRG 59, 711.5611/3–2855, NA II, Maryland. According to Eisenbud, the Japanese vessel was carrying 28,000 pounds of tuna fish when it landed. See Eisenbud, *An Environmental Odyssey*, p. 95.

[38] Quoted in Divine, *Blowing on the Wind*, pp. 11–12; see also Schaller, p. 72.

[39] Telegram from Harry Pfeiffer, American Consul in Hokkaido, to State Department, March 24, 1954, DSRG 59, 711.5611/3–2454, NA, Washington.

[40] See for example, Letter from R.T.D. Ledward, British Embassy in Tokyo, to F.W. Marten, Esq., M.C., Far Eastern Department, Foreign Office, May 26, 1954, FO371/

110695, PRO, Kew; Letter from Mrs Tamaki Uemra, President of the Japanese YWCA, to Mrs Dwight D. Eisenhower, April 30, 1954, DSRG 59, 711.5611/4–3054, NA, Washington.

41 Letter from Murphy to the State Department, May 18, 1954, 711.5611/5–454, DSRG 59, NA; Memo from the State Department to the President, May 29, 1954, DSRG 59, 711.5611/5–2954, NA, Washington. Similar sentiments appeared in the Long Telegram from the American Embassy in Tokyo to the State Department, "Chronology of the *Fukuryu Maru*," March 28, 1955, 711.5611/3–2855, NA II, Maryland.

42 Telegram from the American Embassy in Tokyo to the Secretary of State, March 23, 1954, DSRG 59, 711.5611/3–2354, NA, Washington.

43 Quoted from DOE document collection in Statement of Jonathan Weisgall, Oversight Hearing, p. 31.

44 Aide Memoire, March 31, 1954, DSRG 59, 711.5611/3–3154, NA, Washington.

45 Schaller, *Altered States*, p. 74.

46 Hewlett and Holl, *Atoms for Peace and War*, p. 178.

47 Aide Memoire, March 31, 1954, DSRG 59, 711.5611/3–3154, NA, Washington.

48 Ibid.

49 Telegram from Secretary Dulles to the American Embassy in Tokyo, April 7, 1954, DSRG 59, 711.5611/3–3154, NA, Washington.

50 Telegram from Allison in Tokyo to the Department of State, April 9, 1954, DSRG 59, 711.5611/4–954, NA, Washington.

51 A list of seven other "radioactive boats" (reported between March 20 and April 5) was given to the American embassy by the Japanese Foreign Office. In addition, during the second week of April, Allison cabled Washington that reports of "new arrivals of fishing vessels with low-level radioactive readings on the hulls, crew and catch" were appearing on a daily basis. See four telegrams from the American embassy in Tokyo to the Secretary of State, April 3, 8, 9, 10, 1954, DSRG 59, 711.5611/4–954, 4–1054, 4–254, 4–3054, NA, Washington.

52 Telegram from the American Embassy in Tokyo to the AEC, April 16, 1954, DSRG 59, 711.5611/4–1654, NA, Washington.

53 Telegram from Gerard C. Smith, Acting Secretary of State, to the American Embassy in Tokyo, April 23, 1954, DSRG 59, 711.5611/4–1654, NA, Washington.

54 OCB Memo by Elmer B. Staats, March 30, 1954, OCB 091.Japan, OCB Central Files Series, White House Office: NSC Staff Papers, DDEL, Abilene. The OCB made these recommendations during a meeting on March 24.

55 Strauss' press statement, March 31, 1954, AWF, Press Conference Series, DDEL, Abilene.

56 Ibid.

57 Background Statement Relative to US Action in Connection with the *Fukuryu Maru* Incident Prepared by the Department of State, March 30, 1954, DDEL, Abilene; Hewlett and Holl, *Atoms for Peace and War*, pp. 172, 177. According to the British embassy, the *Fukuryu Maru* was "19 miles outside the notified danger zone." See 2 Telegrams from A. S. Halford, Counsellor, British Embassy in Tokyo, to Colin Crowe, Far Eastern Department, Foreign Office, March 24 and April 7, 1954, FO371/110695, PRO, Kew.

58 Eisenbud, *An Environmental Odyssey*, p. 99.

59 OCB Memo by Elmer Staats, March 30, 1954, OCB 091. Japan, OCB Central Files Series, White House Office: NSC Staff Papers, DDEL, Abilene.

60 Lewis Strauss, *Men and Decisions*, New York, 1962, p. 424.

61 Strauss' press statement, March 31, 1954.

62 Eisenbud, *An Environmental Odyssey*, p. 86.

63 Memo from Richard Hirsch to the Executive Officer of the OCB, March 17, 1954, OCB 091.Japan, OCB Central Files Series, White House Office: NSC Staff Papers, DDEL, Abilene.

64 Strauss' press statement, March 31, 1954. In this obvious attempt to deflect attention away from the US for the consequences of the BRAVO test, Strauss might have been referring to a condition known as ciguatera poisoning. This condition occurs when humans consume ciguatera toxins. These toxins are produced by a "single-celled organism called *Gambierdiscus toxicus* which inhabits coral reefs. Outbreaks of poisoning appear to be associated with the disturbance of coral reefs." See Anthony Robbins, Arjun Makhijani, and Katherine Yih, *Radioactive Heaven and Earth: The health and environmental effects of nuclear weapons testing in, on, and above the earth*, New York, 1991, p. 173.

65 Eisenbud, *An Environmental Odyssey*, p. 99.

66 Eisenbud, *An Environmental Odyssey*, p. 93. Perhaps influenced by the media reports, Hewlett and Holl state that Eisenbud was "not permitted to examine any of the fishermen." See *Atoms for Peace and War*, p. 176.

67 See Two Telegrams from the American embassy in Tokyo to the State Department, March 31, 1954, DSRG 59, 711.5611/3–3154, 4–154 NA, Washington.

68 Trusteeship for the Former Japanese Mandated Islands, Agreement Approved by the Security Council of the United Nations, April 2, 1947, Entered into Force, July 18, 1947, Department of State Publication 2992, Washington, 1948; See also Weisgall, "The Nuclear Nomads," 74; Oversight Hearing, 82. According to the United Nations Charter, the administration of each trust territory was to be carried out by a specified state with certain supervisory responsibilities performed by the General Assembly through the agency of the Trusteeship Council. Articles 87 and 88 of the charter indicated the main methods for exercising this supervisory role. These methods included the preparation of a detailed questionnaire regarding the political, economic, social, and educational advancement of the territory and periodic visits to each territory by delegates from the Trusteeship Council. By 1950, 11 territories had been put under trusteeship, with seven states acting as trustees. But, only one territory, the Trust Territory of the Pacific Islands Under United States Trusteeship, was declared a strategic area, making it theoretically subject to Security Council rather than General Assembly supervision. The purpose of this arrangement, developed in response to military pressures in the United States, was apparently to give the US a potential veto over any action considered adverse to its security interests. In practice, the Security Council never exercised its supervisory powers. Indeed, during the "Castle" test series, the Bikini and Enewetak regions were closed to visiting missions. Other members of the Trusteeship Council severely criticized the US for conducting these tests and charged that the interests and safety of the inhabitants were jeopardized. See A. Leroy Bennett, *International Organizations: Principles and issues,* New Jersey, 1991, pp. 67–68, 358.

69 Strauss, *Men and Decisions*, p. 424.

70 See statements by Eisenbud and Eni F.H. Faleomavaega, Member of Congress, Oversight Hearing, pp. 54–57, 71–72.

71 Rongelap was located approximately 100 nautical miles southeast of ground zero. See Hewlett and Holl, *Atoms for Peace and War*, p. 174.

72 The inhabitants of nearby islands also received dangerous amounts of radiation: the people of Ailinginae received 80 roentgens, Rongerik 40–98, and Uterik 17. See Hewlett and Holl, *Atoms for Peace and War*, pp. 174–75, 612 (fn. 63).

73 Report by Brookhaven National Laboratory, under contract with the AEC, by Robert Conard *et al.*, "Medical Survey of Rongelap People Five and Six Years after Exposure to Fallout," September 1960, DSRG 59, Special Assistant to the Secretary for Energy and Outer Space, Records Relating to Atomic Energy Matters, 1944–63 (hereafter SASEO, RAEM), NA II, Maryland. According to this report, the "lymphocytes (one type of white blood cells) [of the Rongelapese exposed to BRAVO] fell promptly and by the third day were about 55% of the control values in adults, and slightly lower in children." In addition, "Beta burns of the skin and epilation (loss of hair) appeared about 2 weeks after exposure, largely on parts of the body not covered by clothing ... About 90% of the people had these burns, ... Most of the lesions were superficial ... [but] ... painful ... Some lesions were deeper and more painful. A few burns became secondarily infected and had to be treated with antibiotics ... in about 15% of the people, deeper lesions, particularly noted in the dorsum (top side) of the feet, continued to show lack of repigmentation with varying degrees of scarring and atrophy ... of the skin." See also AEC Draft Background Memo to the State Department Concerning the 1954 Radiation Exposure of the Rongelapese, April 26, 1961, 711.5611/4–2861, DSRG59, NA II, Maryland.

74 Quoted in Dibblin, *Day of Two Suns*, p. 27.

75 Petition to the UN from the Marshallese People, April 20, 1954, DSRG 59, 711.5611/5–654, NA, Washington.

76 Long Telegram from US Embassy in Tokyo, "Chronology of the *Fukuryu Maru*," to Department of State, March 28, 1955, 711.5611/3–2855, DSRG 59, NA II, Maryland.

77 Telegram from the State Department to the US Delegation at the UN, May 6, 1954, DSRG 59, 711.5611/5–654, NA, Washington.

78 Divine, *Blowing on the Wind*, p. 31.

79 According to a report prepared for the Department of Defense, "At the 1800 weather briefing, the predicted winds were less favourable ... The midnight briefing indicated [even] less favourable winds ... Winds at 20,000 feet were headed for Rongelap to the east. The predicted speed of these winds was low enough to be of no concern, although it was recognized that both Bikini and Eneman Islands would probably be contaminated." See Report by the Defense Nuclear Agency for the Department of Defense, "Castle Series 1954," April 1, 1982, p. 202.

80 See statements by Jonathan Weisgall and David M. Weiman, on Behalf of the People of Rongelap, Oversight Hearing, pp. 29–30, 137–39, 145–59, 175–76. This hearing first came to my attention in "Bomb Contamination Deliberate," *Toronto Globe and Mail* (25 February, 1994): A12. Curiously, I was not able to find any reference to this hearing in the *New York Times*.

81 The peoples of Rongelap and Ailinginae were evacuated March 3; those on Uterik were left until March 4. See Hewlett and Holl, *Atoms for Peace and War*, p. 174.

82 Testimony by Thomas Hamilton, Chief, Division of Endocrinology in the Department of Medicine at the Pacific Medical Center in Seattle, Oversight Hearing, 182. Hamilton was also a clinical researcher who carried out an extensive study of the radiation damage caused by BRAVO.

83 Statement by Eisenbud, Question and Answer Period, Oversight Hearing, pp. 130–31.

84 OCB Memo for the Record, August 12, 1954, OCB 000.9 [Atomic Energy], White House Office: National Security Council Staff Papers, DDEL, Abilene.

85 See two telegrams from Allison in Tokyo to the Secretary of State, April 27 and 30, 1954, DSRG 59, 711.5611/4–2754, 4–2954, NA; Telegram from G.C. Smith, Acting Secretary of State, to the American embassy in Tokyo, April 30, 1954, DSRG 59, 711.5611/4–3054, NA, Washington.

86 In the Kagoshima prefecture alone during the months of May and June, the catches from at least 56 boats were thrown overboard due to contamination. See Letter from Katsuji Sugimoto, Chairman of the Governors Conference, Kyushu, and Governor of Fukuoka Prefecture, to James Victor Martin, Consul of the US Government, Fukuoka, Japan, June 23, 1954, DSRG 59, 711.5611/6–2354, NA, Washington.

87 Letter from R.T.D. Ledward, British embassy in Tokyo, to F.W. Marten, Esq., Far Eastern Department, Foreign Office, London, May 26, 1954, FO371/110695, PRO, Kew.

88 Letter from Howard A. Cook, (on Behalf of Secretary Dulles) to Mrs Robert H. Gallaher, August 3, 1954, DSRG 59, 711.5611/7–954, NA, Washington.

89 AEC Meeting No. 984, May 12, 1954, AECRG 326, Records of the AEC, Office of the Secretary, Minutes of the Meetings of the AEC, NA II, Maryland.

90 Telegram from Secretary Dulles to the American embassy in Tokyo, June 28, 1954, DSRG 59, 711.5611/6–2854, NA, Washington.

91 Note and Draft Report, July 7, 1954, [Atomic Energy], OCB Central Files Series, White House Office: National Security Council Staff Papers, DDEL, Abilene; See also Gordon Dunning, "Effects of Nuclear Weapons Testing," *Scientific Monthly*, 81 (December 1955), p. 266.

92 Strauss, *Men and Decisions*, p. 424.

93 AEC Meeting No. 988, May 19, 1954, AECRG 326, Office of the Secretary, Minutes of the Meetings of the AEC, NA II, Maryland.

94 State Department Memo, July 6, 1954, DSRG 59, 711.5611/7–654, NA, Washington.

95 Statement by Lewis Strauss, AEC, and Charles Wilson, DOD, May 25, 1954, AECRG 326, NA II, Maryland. The "Castle" series officially ended on June 2, 1954. In addition to BRAVO, 4 more nuclear weapons (Romeo, Koon, Union, and Yankee) were detonated at Bikini and one (Nectar) was exploded at Enewetak. See US Department of Energy, *U.S. Nuclear Tests*, p. 3.

96 Long Telegram from US embassy in Tokyo, "Chronology of the *Fukuryu Maru*," March 28, 1955, NA II, Maryland.

97 Note from the Japanese embassy in Washington to the Secretary of State, October 4, 1954, DSRG 59, 711.5611/10–454, NA, Washington.

98 Eisenbud, *An Environmental Odyssey*, p. 95. The 40 year old Kuboyama died on September 23, 1954 and the autopsy was performed the following day at the First Tokyo National Hospital. In addition to a number of Japanese doctors and experts, one American, Chief Pathologist, Lieutenant Colonel James Hansen of the 406th Corps, US Army, was in attendance. According to the conclusion of the report: "the main factor in the Kuboyama case was not so much the external radiation as the internal exposure via mouth, lungs, or skin during the 2-week period aboard the exposed ship, which resulted in degenerative

necrosis and cirrhosis, with inflammatory cell infiltration in the liver. Virus hepatitis might have occurred following the blood and plasma transfusions he received." See CIA Translation Document 507, "Information on Radiation Sickness caused by Bikini Ashes: Pathological Findings in Fatal Case of Kuboyama," January 1955, DSRG 59, SASEOS, RAEM, NA II, Maryland.

[99] Dingman, "Alliance in Crisis," p. 202.

[100] Message of Condolence from the American Ambassador in Tokyo, October 9, 1954, DSRG 59, 711.5611/10–954, NA, Washington.

[101] Divine, *Blowing on the Wind*, pp. 30–31. The compensation was paid in January, 1955.

[102] Schaller, *Altered States*, p. 74.

[103] Hewlett and Holl, *Atoms for Peace and War*, pp. 285–86; Statement by Lewis Strauss, February 15, 1955, DSRG 59, 711.5611/2–1755, NA, Washington. During this speech, Strauss allowed that "the very large thermonuclear device exploded at ground surface during the test in the Pacific on March 1, 1954, contaminated an elongated, cigar-shaped area extending approximately 220 statue miles down-wind and varying in width up to 40 miles." But then, in an obvious attempt to minimize the human impact of the test, he stated that the data derived from BRAVO permitted the AEC to make "estimates of casualities which would have been suffered within the contaminated area *if it had been populated*" (my emphasis).

[104] Department of State Instruction to All American Diplomatic Posts and Enclosure, "Summary of Reactions," March 21, 1955, DSRG 59, 711.5611/2–155, NA, Washington.

[105] The Rongelapese lived on two other islands (first Ebeye and then Ejit) for over three years.

[106] Letter from John Meagher, Chief, Public Services Division, for the Secretary of State, to Mr and Mrs Gerald Kasin, August 14, 1956, DSRG 59, 711.5611/6–1856, NA II, Maryland.

[107] AEC Meeting No. 1222, Sept. 15, 1956, AECRG 326, Records of the AEC, Office of the Secretary, Minutes of the Meetings of the AEC, NA II, Maryland.

[108] AEC Draft Background Memo Concerning the 1954 Radiation Exposure of the Rongelapese, April 26, 1961; Report by the Brookhaven National Laboratory, under contract with the AEC, "Medical Survey of the Rongelap People," September 1960.

[109] Report by the Surgeon General, US Army, in conjunction with the Division of Biology and Medicine, AEC, "The Determination of Internally Deposited Radioactive Isotopes in the Marshallese People by Excretion Analysis," March 23, 1960, SASEO, RAEM, NA II, Maryland.

[110] Letter from Charles L. Dunham, Director, Division of Biology and Medicine, AEC, to Philip Farley, Special Assistant to the Secretary, Department of State, October 31, 1958, DSRG 59, SASEOS, RAEM, NA II, Maryland.

[111] Letter from General Manager, AEC, to Admiral Arleigh A. Burke, USN, Chief of Naval Operations, Department of the Navy, October 31, 1958, DSRG 59, SASEOS, RAEM, NA II, Maryland.

[112] Report by Conard, "Medical Status of Rongelap People," June 1, 1959, DSRG 59, SASEO, RAEM, NA II, Maryland. According to another report, nine months after resettlement on Rongelap, studies showed that the urinary excretion levels of both groups had increased "140 fold for Cesium 137" and "20 fold for Strontium 90." See Report written

under of the auspices of the Surgeon General in conjunction with the AEC, "The Determination," March 23, 1960. Strontium-90 was considered to be particularly dangerous for humans. According to a 1955 article written by Gordon Dunning, a health physicist with the Division of Biology and Medicine, AEC, "if [strontium-90] is taken into the body, it is selectively deposited in the bones and continues to irradiate the surrounding cells for long periods of time, since it has a half-life of about 27.7 years. The deposition of relatively large amounts of strontium-90 in the bone would be expected eventually to produce bone tumours." See Dunning, "Effects of Nuclear Weapons Testing," p. 267.

[113] AEC Draft Background Memo Concerning the 1954 Radiation Exposure of the Rongelapese, April 26, 1961; see also Report by Conard, "Medical Status of Rongelap People," June 1, 1959; Report by the Brookhaven National Laboratory, under Contract with the AEC, "Medical Survey of Rongelap People," September 1960; Oversight Hearing, p. 333.

[114] Report by Conard, "Medical Status of the Rongelap People," June 1, 1959.

[115] According to experts, thyroid cancer is quite rare in the world, ranging from 1–10 per 100,000 people. But, in studies of the 86 Rongelapese between 1954 and 1985, 23 were found to have benign thyroid nodules and five had cancer of the thyroid. See Thomas Hamilton, "Thyroid Neoplasia in Marshall Islanders Exposed to Nuclear Fallout," 258 (August 1987), *Journal of the American Medical Association*, p. 629. See also Oversight Hearing, pp. 222, 226; Dibblin, *Day of Two Suns*, pp. 29–31, 43.

[116] Oversight Hearing, pp. 57, 138, 171, 191, 196–97, 202–203, 223, 226, 322, 332.

[117] With this condition, the middle phalanx of the fifth finger was shortened and slightly broadened. See Report by Brookhaven National Laboratory, under contract with the AEC, "Medical Survey of Rongelap People," September 1960.

[118] For example, the DOD agreed to pay $5,162.53 for each property claim submitted by the Rongelapese and $1,719.27 for each presented by the inhabitants of Uterik prior to May 1955. The Rongelapese filed 70 claims and the people of Uterik filed 37. See Memo from S.B.D. Wood, the Acting Judge Advocate General of the Navy, to the General Counsel, DOD, June 14, 1955, DSRG 59, 711.5611/6–2155, NA II; Press Release #2164, US Mission to the UN, June 5, 1955, DSRG 59, SASEOS, RAEM, NA II, Maryland.

[119] This agreement linked compensation for the tests to political sovereignty. In return for agreeing to the Comprehensive Nuclear Claims Settlement Provisions of the Treaty (Section 177), the Marshall Islanders were allowed to begin the process of self governance. By December 1993, the net amount of compensation awarded to 577 individuals was $22.8 million. See Oversight Hearing, pp. 146–47, 171, 264, 278, 301, 388.

[120] See Table, "Marshall Islands Nuclear Claims Tribunal, Admitted Claims by Condition and Amounts Awarded (As of December 31, 1993)," Oversight Hearing, p. 306.

[121] Out of the 60 per cent of the Marshall Islanders who voted, 58 per cent were in favor of the Compact. On Bikini, 90 per cent voted against the agreement, as did 85 per cent on Rongelap. See Dibblin, *Day of Two Suns*, p. 180.

[122] Only the four most severely affected areas were included even though a 1978 Department of Energy report indicated that 14 atolls and islands surveyed had received "intermediate range fallout from one or more of the megaton range tests." See Dibblin, *Day of Two Suns*, p. 62.

[123] See Statement by David Weiman and Question and Answer Period, Oversight Hearing, pp. 152–53, 252–53, 397; Dibblin, *Day of Two Suns*, p. 184.

[124] Article IX of the Compact, entitled "Changed Circumstances," provides that if personal injuries or property damage in the Marshall Islands are later discovered and could not "reasonably have been identified as of the effective date of the agreement," and if those "injuries render the provisions of the agreement manifestly inadequate," the Marshall Islands government can ask the US government to "provide for such injuries by submitting such a request" to Congress. See Oversight Hearing, p. 12.

[125] Oversight Hearing, pp. 12, 147–8.

[126] Oversight Hearing, p. 269.

[127] Because it eats its own shell after shedding it, the coconut crab was considered to be particularly dangerous. Instead of excreting radioactive materials, the crab accumulates them in higher concentrations in the body. See Dibblin, *Day of Two Suns*, p. 33.

[128] Oversight Hearing, pp. 202, 425.

[129] The Defense Nuclear Agency (DNA) was established by the Department of Defense. It was responsible for ensuring the safety and security of the US and of American military forces in the event of nuclear warfare. In addition, the agency provided assistance and advice to the chairman of the JCS and other military departments on all nuclear matters, including site security, tactics, vulnerability, and radiation effects. This information is found in the finding aid (RG 374–ANT) at the NA II, Maryland.

[130] Oversight Hearing, p. 270.

[131] Oversight Hearing, p. 323.

[132] Dibblin, *Day of Two Suns*, p. 4.

[133] Testimony by Billiet Edmond, Oversight Hearing, p. 382.

[134] See, for example, quotation by Senator Ataji Balos, representative of Kwajalein Atoll in the Marshall Islands, Nitijela, in Dibblin, *Day of Two Suns*, p. 62; Weisgall, "The Nuclear Nomads," p. 90.

[135] This was customary; Washington did not usually provide specific warnings about nuclear tests. On October 2, 1953, the Eisenhower administration had issued a general announcement regarding the upcoming "Castle" series through the world press. But, the people in the Pacific were not given any specific information about the sites, times or dates of the nuclear tests. See AEC Press Release, April 2, 1953, "Bikini Atoll Added to Atomic Proving Ground in the Pacific," AECRG 326, OS, FTSGCW, NA II, Maryland; Memo from Richard Hirsch to the Executive Officer of the Operations Coordinating Board, March 17, 1954, DDEL; Background Statement Relative to United States Action in Connection with the *Fukuryu Maru* Incident Prepared by the Department of State, March 30, 1954, DDEL, Abilene.

[136] In a letter to the Secretary of State, the General Manager of the AEC, K.D. Nichols, emphasized his agency's "research interest in the possible effects of our recent tests on the crew of the *Fukuryu Maru* and the health hazards associated with the debris which fell on the vessel." Similarly, Ambassador Allison argued that the "data possibly derived from these patients [the Japanese fishermen] and available nowhere else might have the highest importance for US science, security and planning." See Letter from K.D. Nichols to the Secretary of State, March 26, 1954, DSRG 59, 711.5611/3–2654, NA; Telegram from the American Embassy in Tokyo to the Secretary of State, March 31, 1954, DSRG 59, 711.5611/3–3154, NA, Washington. In 1961, an AEC report regarding the Rongelapese points out that: "The five-and six year post-exposure surveys were aimed primarily at evaluation of the general medical status of the people in relation to that of the exposed comparison

population, particularly in regard to any possible late developing effects of their exposure, their hematological status, and the influence of the slightly contaminated environment on the assimilation, excretion, and body burdens of radionuclides." The document also noted that AEC expenditures "have not been entirely for the relief of the inhabitants of Rongelap but have been for the acquisition of considerable radiobiological and radioecological research data." The report concluded that "study of both groups [the Japanese populations of Hiroshima and Nagasaki and the Marshallese population of Rongelap] has yielded valuable information on the acute effects in human beings of radiation from atomic bomb detonations." See AEC Draft Background Memo Concerning the 1954 Radiation Exposure of the Rongelapese, April 26, 1961. In the same year, a State Department memo stated that: "As the AEC admits a degree of negligence in this case, it was agreed by all agencies that the people of Rongelap deserve some sort of compensation. Furthermore, the AEC desires to conduct continuing medical examinations of the people of Rongelap." See memo from Mr Curtis Cutter to Mr. Gerig, March 14, 1961, DSRG 59, 711.5611/3–1461, NA II, Maryland. Years after BRAVO, abnormal thyroid glands removed from Marshall Islanders exposed to this and other tests were stored in the Brookhaven National Medical Laboratory in the United States. See Oversight Hearing, pp. 342, 387. Finally, a 1976 study prepared for DOE concluded: "Bikini atoll may be the only global source on humans where intake via ingestion is thought to contribute the major fraction of plutonium body burden … It is possibly the best available source of data for evaluating the transfer of plutonium across the gut wall after being incorporated into biological systems." Weisgall, "The Nuclear Nomads," p. 90; see also his testimony, Oversight Hearing, p. 4.

[137] Statement by Weisgall, Oversight Hearing, p. 40; see also Weisgall, "Nuclear Nomads," pp. 90–91.

[138] Oversight Hearing, pp. 40, 386; Robbins *et al.*, *Radioactive Heaven and Earth*, pp. 82–83.

[139] See, for example, Letter from Robert Murphy, Acting Secretary for International Political Affairs, to McCloy, May 18, 1954, 711.5611/5–454, DSRG 59, NA; Memo from Murphy to the President, May 29, 1954, DSRG 59, 711.5611/5–2954, NA, Washington.

[140] In Weisgall's opinion, the US officials used this term regularly because they wanted to reinforce the stereotypical Western view of "the native." "What is the image of a native?" he asked, "I don't know, some sort of peripatetic wanderer … Everyone was a native. You couldn't even be called an islander … that was just the attitude … No one really cared." Oversight Hearing, p. 51.

[141] Oversight Hearing, p. 32–33.

[142] Memo submitted by the Advisory Committee on Biology and Medicine, January 13–14, 1956, at the US Atomic Energy Commission, New York, Operations Office, Health and Safety Laboratory, presented by Hiroshi Yamamura, Senator representing Uterik Atoll, Oversight Hearing, pp. 378–79.

[143] Outside observers noted the lack of medical facilities in the Marshall Islands. In a telegram to the State Department, the US representative to the United Nations reported that: "In follow-up conversations both Andriaenssen (Belgium) and Rasgotra (India) expressed amazement over the deplorable condition of the medical dispensary on Rogelap [sic] and low level of training of medical aide assigned there. In view of the importance attached by the AEC to research possibilities and the need for careful control of the health of this group, it seemed amazing to both men that more attention had not been devoted to

medical facilities on the island." Telegram from Stevenson in New York to the Secretary of State, March 29, 1961, DSRG 59 SASEOS, RAEM, NA II, Maryland. A note attached to the telegram explains that since 1957: "The USAEC has annually sent [a] medical team to Ron. to survey the natives, both the damaged ones and an undamaged control group. Between these visits, Ron. natives [are] serviced by a clinic with one medical technician." Much later, in 1977, Dr Konrad Kotrady, a Department of Energy physician in the Marshall Islands, criticized the health care being provided to the peoples living there, especially the Rongelapese. According to him, the program set up by the US was operating in a "medical vacuum" and was primarily designed for research purposes. See Robbins et al, *Radioactive Heaven and Earth*, p. 82.

[144] See, for example, Telegram from A.S. Halford, British Embassy in Tokyo to C.T. Crowe, Esq., Far Eastern Department, Foreign Office, March 24, 1954, FO371/110695, PRO, Kew

[145] In a formal address to the Indian Parliament on April 2, 1954, Prime Minister Jawaharal Nehru proposed an immediate "Standstill Agreement" prohibiting testing by all nuclear powers. The Indian government then referred this proposal to the Disarmament Commission of the United Nations. See Memo, June 23, 1954, NSC Series, White House Office; Office of the Special Assistant for National Security Affairs, DDEL, Abilene. Later, this proposal was supported by Japan, France, and Canada. However, within the United States, a Gallup poll in April 1954 showed that 71 per cent of the American public were opposed to the US government canceling the rest of the "Castle" series in the Pacific. See Divine, *Blowing in the Wind*, 26; The college-educated in the United States (78 per cent) were even more opposed when asked whether the United States should cancel the tests. See George Gallup (ed.), *The Gallup Poll: Public Opinion, 1935–1971* (New York, 1972), II, pp. 1229–30. After BRAVO, the United States conducted 56 additional nuclear explosions in the Marshall Islands before the end of 1958. See US Department of Energy, *United States Nuclear Tests*, pp. 7–8.

[146] Oversight Hearing, pp. 359–60.

Index